£5. 50

THE SEYCHELLES AFFAIR

THE
SEYCHELLES
AFFAIR

Mike Hoare

BANTAM PRESS

NEW YORK · LONDON · TORONTO · SYDNEY · AUCKLAND

TRANSWORLD PUBLISHERS LTD
61–63 Uxbridge Road, London w5 5sa

TRANSWORLD PUBLISHERS (AUSTRALIA) PTY LTD
26 Harley Crescent, Condell Park, nsw 2200

TRANSWORLD PUBLISHERS (NZ) LTD
Cnr Moselle and Waipareira Aves, Henderson, Auckland

Published 1986 by Bantam Press,
a division of Transworld Publishers Ltd

British Library Cataloguing in Publication Data
Hoare, Mike
The Seychelles affair.
1. Mercenary troops—Seychelles
2. Seychelles—History—Coup d'etat, 1981
I. Title
969'.6   DT469.s48

ISBN 0-593-01122-8

Photoset by Rowland Phototypesetting Ltd
Bury St Edmunds, Suffolk
Printed in Great Britain by
The Bath Press, Bath

To my wife, Phyllis,
and all those loyal women
who stand by their men
when things go wrong

Contents

Map of Mahé   ix

1   Paradise Disturbed   1
2   A Visit to Mahé   16
3   A Cut-Price Coup!   36
4   The Final Plans   59
5   The Operation   71
6   The Supreme Court   101
7   Sentenced to Prison   117
8   Pretoria Central Prison   137
9   Durance Vile   160
10 Pietermaritzburg New Prison   184

Index   197

Illustration section follows   116

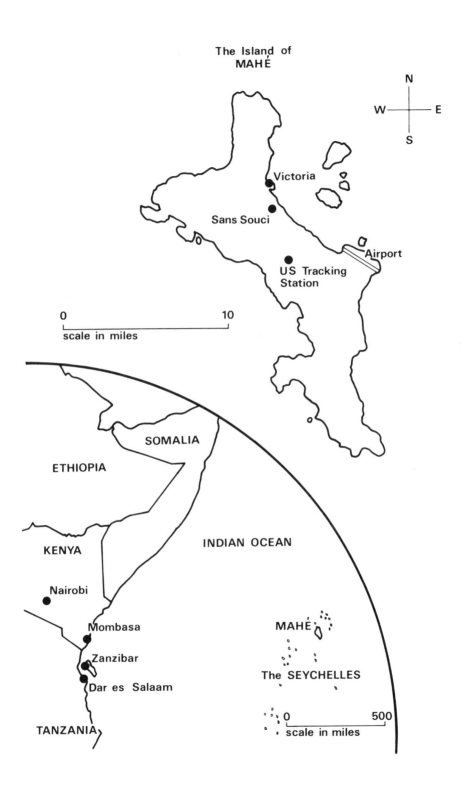

The Island of
MAHÉ

N
W E
S

Victoria

Sans Souci

Airport

US Tracking
Station

0   10
scale in miles

SOMALIA

ETHIOPIA

KENYA

INDIAN OCEAN

Nairobi

Mombasa

Zanzibar

Dar es Salaam

TANZANIA

MAHÉ

The SEYCHELLES

0   500
scale in miles

THE SEYCHELLES AFFAIR

CHAPTER 1

Paradise Disturbed

———————

IT WAS A GLITTERING OCCASION. The ladies were dressed in formal evening gowns, the gentlemen in dinner-jackets enlivened here and there by a red cummerbund. Indian waiters with puggarees and coloured sashes hovered discreetly in the background. The scene smacked a little of Britain's colonial past, but in my view was none the worse for that. The social set of Durban in 1978 maintained the highest standards of the old Empire; Natal to some extent was the last outpost.

My host, a well-known professor of anaesthetics, introduced me to a gentleman of the old school. He wore the button of a famous French order which I recognised at once. Professor Harry told me that Monsieur ———— had come specially to meet me. He led me to a quiet corner of the room behind a polished Steinway. He came straight to the point.

'You are aware of the *coup d'état* in the Seychelles last June?' he asked.

I said I was.

'Do you think anything can be done to reinstate the rightful president, Mr James Mancham?'

I replied that all things were possible given the will to succeed, the rightfulness of the cause, and men of courage. Hot air, of course. Party talk really, but to bring it down to earth I added the sordid words 'and money'. My new friend disregarded the rhetoric and came swiftly to the root of things. '*Par exemple?*' I laughed off an answer. This was neither the place nor the time for a discussion of that sort, but we parted amicably.

I

A few days later he asked me to receive a friend of his, one who had lately been a minister without portfolio in James Mancham's overthrown government. He was anxious to have a chat with me.

My first impression of the ex-minister was that he was remarkably young for such an exalted post; but, as I was to discover later, all the Seychellois leaders at this time were well under forty. He was introduced to me as Gonzague D'Offay, a descendant of one of the original French families which had colonised the Seychelles in 1789. D'Offay described the day of the coup, his arrest immediately afterwards and his deportation under armed guard. Then the seizure of his restaurant business and the confiscation of his property which had followed. He had arrived in Durban penniless and without means of support. Fortunately, other exiles had befriended him. Then he had found a job – nothing very special, he said modestly, but a job. His wife and family had joined him, and his good friend Monsieur ———— had suggested to him that a talk with me might give him some hope for the future.

Over the years since the Congo rebellion of 1964–6 I have had many such talks with exiles and the dispossessed, casualties of our modern political systems, so I was not surprised when Mr D'Offay asked me if I could suggest some means by which the usurpers of power in the Seychelles could be overthrown and the rightful president, Jimmy Mancham, reinstated. Members of his government had been forced into exile in Australia, in South Africa and in Britain, he said; they all had a burning desire to go back to the Seychelles, and were incensed at the indifference shown by Britain and France to their fate and the fate of the unfortunate people who were suffering under the new Marxist regime, and— I stopped him in full flow.

'Mr D'Offay,' I said, 'are you making this approach on your own behalf or do you represent some group of exiles?'

'I am speaking on behalf of the ex-President. He would like to meet you in Europe whenever you are available. We need somebody to help us make a plan to overthrow the illegal government of Albert René.'

I said the making of such a plan was a military exercise which could only be undertaken once all the relevant facts were known. This would probably mean a personal reconnaissance of Mahé, amongst other things, but to avoid wasting each other's time I must ask him the question on which everything turned. 'Have your people the necessary finance with which to stage a coup?' To help him to understand the purpose of this question I explained, 'You may not know about the waging of war; it can cost about one million US

2

dollars to keep one hundred mercenary soldiers in the field for one month,' adding with a smile 'if they are to be maintained in the manner to which they are accustomed'. It shook him.

'What are we looking at, then?' he asked.

'A minimum of five million dollars. Always supposing the military plan is reasonably simple.'

'Well, we should be able to raise that all right. Mr Mancham has powerful friends, and there are a number of very wealthy Seychellois landowners who might feel obliged to support the plan financially if only to safeguard themselves in the long run from sharing our fate. How long would something like this take?'

'I cannot say. Perhaps a year. Perhaps more.'

That really upset him. Plainly he was thinking in terms of weeks, not of months.

'I was hoping', he said slowly, 'that you were going to suggest an assault on the island using a C130 Hercules.'

'You mean like the raid on Entebbe? You have just seen the film?'

'Yes. Precisely. You land, the ramp goes down, your men rush out and take the airport, and the government will surrender in a state of panic.'

He developed this implausible scenario.

'Mr D'Offay,' I said wearily, 'as far as warfare and mercenary activity are concerned, Hollywood and reality are poles apart. Nothing really happens that way. Sorry, but that's a fact of life. What you need first and foremost is a sound plan. Then you must have men of integrity to back it, men with honest political convictions. If those things exist and your plan is feasible and your politicians honest and courageous, your next – and probably your steepest – hurdle is the funding of the project.'

He seemed pretty downcast, but with the resilience of his thirty-two years put a brave face on it. He said he was planning a visit to London to see the ex-President later that week and would contact me on his return. But before we parted I had a question to ask him. 'What made you choose me?' He replied that London had gone carefully into my background and found that I was a dedicated anti-Marxist, which was exactly what was required in their case. They could have found that out by simply reading my book, *Congo Mercenary*, but I said nothing. He ended with a gracious compliment or two.

The events of 5 June 1977 were already known to me in broad detail. Towards the end of May that year the sounds of rifle-fire had been heard on one of the smaller islands surrounding Mahé. In any other country this would have aroused no comment, but in the

Seychelles nobody owned a firearm, never mind fired one. There was no reason to. There was no army. Neither was there any hunting. Nothing to hunt in fact. The sounds of the firing of rifles therefore should have raised an eyebrow or two, but they didn't. The facts were reported to President Mancham in due course. He ignored them. He was too busy preparing for his attendance at the Commonwealth Prime Ministers' Conference which was to be held in London at the beginning of June.

The firing was merely the final step in a carefully laid plot to overthrow Mancham the moment he was out of the country. Albert René, his Prime Minister and political rival, with the assistance of five or six Marxist supporters who would be given Cabinet appointments later, had laid his plans carefully. With the connivance of President Nyerere of Tanzania he had smuggled in twenty or more Tanzanian soldiers in secret and hidden them on a remote island. The coup was executed on 5 June 1977. In the event a policeman was killed and two or three others wounded, but in a matter of four hours the twenty or so Tanzanian soldiers had seized the broadcasting station, the police headquarters in Victoria, and other vital centres of administration. René proclaimed himself the new head of state. The population were stunned, but with the co-operation of Rent-a-crowd a demonstration was staged that evening to rejoice at the overthrow of the tyrant Mancham. Members of his government were rounded up and deported. In most cases the deportees represented the wealthier land-owning class, and their property was forfeited to the State. René moved into Government House.

The new Cabinet was appointed the next day. Jacques Hodoul and Maxime Ferrari, both known Marxists, were given high rank and other pro-Soviet ministers appointed. But René was at pains to allay Western fears that he was a hard-line doctrinaire Marxist. Such a reputation might seriously jeopardise the liberal aid afforded by Britain and France. He declared that he was 'an Indian Ocean socialist' and a 'socialist pan-Africanist', both descriptions in keeping with his political record. It was well known that he favoured an Africanist approach to the problems of the Seychelles and had clashed with Mancham in the past on this very point. The ex-President had advocated the continuation of strong links with Britain, the former colonial power; René preferred the socialist views of President Nyerere and a closer adherence to the Organisation of African Unity. This basic difference had generated much heat among their adherents and led to some uncharacteristic violence. In the recent past bombs had exploded in Victoria – an outrage generally regarded as having been perpetrated by René's political

4

faction, the people who wished to sever all connection with Britain.

René was sincere in his socialist beliefs. He declared: 'My party wants to give a new life to the oppressed people of the Seychelles.' The declaration highlighted a quandary. Who was the oppressor and what was the nature of the oppression? These questions would have been hard to answer, particularly as the country had been self-governing for many years and freed from the colonial yoke, such as it was, in 1976. Nor could the oppressor be the charismatic Jimmy Mancham, who, single-handed, had succeeded in bringing a flourishing tourist industry to the islands in the few short years that he had been in office. Employment rather than oppression had followed, but that did not stop the new regime from unveiling a hideous statue in 5th June Avenue – where else? – depicting a native islander breaking his chains of bondage; the bondage being, presumably, colonial rule. Britain, who had brought the lamp of civilisation to this Indian Ocean backwater at considerable cost and little benefit to herself, would have been justifiably saddened at this ungracious monument. No doubt this fiction serves in some way to unify the ex-oppressed and gives expression to the success of their struggle at the same time. As symbols of liberation these chain-breaking statues seem to propagate a somewhat evanescent message. I remember admiring the famous liberation monument in downtown Jakarta some years ago, which I would describe as a genuine work of art, but I could find no local Javanese who knew what the statue was all about. They had been liberated from the Dutch colonial power some thirty years before.

Now that he was head of state, René planned to improve the living standards of the people, particularly those who were not sharing in the benefits which an improved economy had brought to the island, albeit at the instance of the much-reviled James Mancham. The gap which existed between the living standards of the landowners – *les grands blancs* as they were called – and those of the common folk disturbed his conscience. The fact that he was one of the 'grand whites' himself did not make his task any easier or enhance his credibility. His solution was nationalisation, common ownership, the panacea of all ills wherever socialists rule. Shipping, lighterage, and all transport undertakings, including taxis, were taken over by the government. Fishing and agriculture followed. Co-operatives were set up, making it an offence to sell produce privately. Free trade unions were suppressed. No doubt such systems have their uses and are successful in parts of the world where massive peasant populations render them equitable and commercially viable; but here in the Seychelles these innovative techniques, unbidden by

5

the electorate, caused nothing but hardship and misery to the very people whose lot they were intended to ameliorate.

Africa-watchers soon became aware that René was not absolute master in his own house. It was thought that he was being manipulated by hardcore Marxists in his Cabinet, not to mention friends further afield like President Didier Ratsiraka, the Marxist leader of Madagascar, and Paul Bérenger, leader of the Mauritian Marxist Movement. Pink turned to red; party membership became a condition for job-seekers; political indoctrination for party members was mandatory; then compulsory attendance at lectures, followed by examinations in political awareness for all who aspired to government appointments. A one-party state was proclaimed some months later. Elections were promised but not held. The familiar tactics of a left-wing administration afraid to face the electorate became evident.

Children were to be trained in a national youth service on a remote island. Those that did not volunteer might find it difficult to obtain a place in high school. Detachments of fourteen- and fifteen-year-olds were sent to Cuba to further their awareness of all things communist, and encouraged to emulate their Cuban comrades in the fight against Imperialism, an enemy they never knew existed. Youths were sent to Algeria and Russia for military training. The main independent newspaper, *Weekend Life*, was banned and the editor detained. Ugly rumours persisted about the strange disappearance of political opponents. Others who criticised the government or their rulers were imprisoned without trial. Curfew was introduced, the government proclaiming they had uncovered a plot by mercenaries based in Durban. Ordinary people were afraid to voice any opposition to the government for fear of reprisals. The Roman Catholic Church, which had been the mainspring of spiritual life in the Seychelles for centuries, was not excluded from oppressive treatment. Bishop Paul and the Anglican Bishop Chang-Him both accused René of seeking to eradicate Christianity from the lives of ordinary citizens. Gone were the old carefree days. This new socialist discipline was something the population did not understand or want. The quality of life deteriorated, and a common misery hung over the island like a pall.

The foreign policy of the new regime was to be one of strict neutrality as between the two Superpowers. René concurred with Mrs Gandhi in her desire to keep the Indian Ocean a zone of peace, but behind this window-dressing instigated an energetic pro-Russian campaign. The Russian embassy in Mahé was permitted to employ an abnormally large diplomatic staff, a staff whose main occupation was undoubtedly the monitoring of American warships in the Indian

6

Ocean and Persian Gulf. Visits by the new President to Russia, Algeria, Libya and Cuba followed. Their patronage was sedulously cultivated. The die was cast; the Seychelles joined the Eastern bloc. Lip service was rendered fearlessly. At the United Nations, René shook the Western world by saying he approved of the Russian invasion of Afghanistan, the Libyan invasion of Chad, and the communist puppet regime in Cambodia.

But like many an African statesman before him he found that adherence to the policies of the Eastern bloc was not necessarily good for business at home. Alarmed by this swing to the left, tourism began to drop off drastically. In place of the 12,000 tourists who visited the islands each month in Mancham's days there were now barely 4000. Loans from Libya and Algeria bolstered the economy. Faithfully, Britain and France continued to support the country despite its virulently anti-Western posture at the United Nations. Fortunately for the Seychelles, the United States tracking station on Mahé, administered by NASA, continued to pay its annual rent of millions of dollars in hard cash; but internally all was not well with the economy. The grandiose plans for a vast fishing enterprise which would follow as soon as the country declared a 200-mile international zone around its islands came to naught. The world price for tuna plummeted. The fishing industry ground to a near-halt.

The swing to the left in the Seychelles was another undoubted success for the Russian ideology. The communist incursion into Africa inched forward relentlessly. For years I had been sounding a warning, in my small way, against the dangers of apathy by the West in the face of Soviet designs to dominate the continent. Few listened. The Russians were winning by default. Over the years I had seen this juggernaut in action in various parts of Africa and had been one of the very few who had fought against it militarily. If I hold anti-Marxist views today, it is a direct result of those experiences. I have seen the struggle for the hearts and minds of African peasants taking place at grass-roots level with all the ruthlessness that Marxist doctrine enjoins on its adherents.

I can recall vividly the day I became an avowed anti-Marxist. Prior to my conversion I had gone along with the conventional view that communism could be seen as an alternative political doctrine and that it might be a solution to some of the world's problems, particularly in some of its more densely populated and underprivileged areas; it could be held that the wealth of the world was inequitably distributed and a resharing might be long overdue. These general views had to be given a hearing by intelligent people. But what I could not accept was the basic concept of communist theory. This states that, first of

7

THE SEYCHELLES AFFAIR

all, law and order must be broken down by insurrection, by total anarchy, by destruction of everything that Christian civilisation holds sacred; and that out of this condition a new and equitable order will arise. When this happened there could be fair shares for all! This seemed to me to be spurious and unworkable. But if this was the accepted theory, then the practice must entail, as a primary step, the destruction of society at its lowest level. The peasant class would be the first to suffer and the suffering would be unbearable.

At the risk of boring you, I will tell you about that day. I do not claim that it was an experience equal to that of Saul of Tarsus on the road to Damascus, but it transformed my life dramatically, nevertheless.

Let me take you back twenty years. Communist-inspired rebels had almost succeeded in overwhelming the democratic government of the Congo and had overrun two-thirds of that vast country with the speed and ferocity of a bush fire. My unit of mercenary soldiers, called in by the government of the Congo to assist the national army in a bid to stem the rebel advance, was now in the province of Orientale, the north-eastern corner of the country which borders on the Sudan and Uganda. My column had arrived at a town called Aba, an important centre for trade and communications. We had advanced too far and too fast for the safety of our lines of communication, which even now stretched over three hundred miles. It was time to consolidate. I sent for my civil liaison officer, a Belgian.

'François,' I said, 'we are going to stay here for several days. I want you to go out into the surrounding bush and bring in all the people you can find. Tell them we are here to protect them from the rebels. Then I want you to get the civil administration going as quickly as you can. In particular, I want you to reorganise the clinics, the schools and the churches. You might even be able to start the hospital again. And contact the missionaries in the area. But your main task is to bring the people back from the bush.' I elaborated on that theme. The restoration of law and order was the most rewarding of my duties. It gave a real meaning to soldiering. One of my most treasured possessions is a photograph of General Mobutu and myself at Aba, taken a few weeks after the incident I am going to describe. On the back he has written:

> To my excellent friend Lt Colonel Mike Hoare, a superior officer of exceptional worth, as much in the military sphere as in that of the pacification of the areas which he liberated from the rebel regime. With all my gratitude for the inappreciable services rendered.

François was highly experienced in this field; he was a district commissioner in normal times and spoke Swahili fluently. He knew the local tribes from long experience. Better still, he loved them. He began his task with enthusiasm.

Two days later he reported to me. His face was ashen and his spirits flattened. He wanted me to come on a tour of inspection of all civil installations in the area to see for myself what had happened to them. We began at the school. In normal times it had housed about three hundred pupils. Now it was deserted. We went into the playground and called out for somebody to come. An old man limped out of a shed. François spoke to him.

'Don't be afraid, *madala*. Tell Monsieur le Colonel what you told me yesterday. Where are the masters and the pupils?'

He hesitated, then decided he had nothing to lose by talking.

'The political commissars made them line up here,' he said, and pointed to a long wall. 'The professors here, the boys there. They asked everybody who could read and write to step forward. Some of the boys did. The soldiers took those boys and those masters away . . . and killed them. Their bodies are in the bush. Come, I will show you.'

Deep in the forest we came across an open trench filled with stinking bodies covered with bloated flies. It was reminiscent of pictures I had seen of Auschwitz. With handkerchiefs over our faces we looked carefully at some of the bodies. Many of the boys had been shot. Some of them had been maimed and left to bleed to death. We staggered back to the cleansing sunlight.

'Why, François? Why did they have to kill them?'

'The intelligentsia must be destroyed. It is part of the basic doctrine of communism.'

'But, for God's sake, man, how can you call kids of eleven and twelve the intelligentsia?'

'We cannot, but they can. They could be tomorrow's intelligentsia, couldn't they? Destroy the civil administration. Kill those in authority, particularly the hereditary chiefs. Encourage terrorism. Disrupt law and order; create confusion; then everything is ripe for revolution, the mob is leaderless and easily controlled. Here you see that doctrine in actual practice. My intellectual friends in the Luvanium have no notion how ruthless communism is in the field. The dogma is plausible enough. The theory is acceptable if you are sitting in your drawing-room surrounded by rational intelligent human beings. The idealism seems noble. The reality is hideous. Come, I will show you something worse.'

The clinic and the hospital had been wrecked and vandalised. The dispensers and the doctors had been killed, one as he was actually carrying out an operation. At the mission a half-crazed priest was the sole survivor of a flourishing monastery which had spread the Word in these parts for over seventy years. The mission church and all its buildings were destroyed.

'But why the church, François?'

'Communism teaches that there is no God. Religion is a superstition and has no place in modern-day living. The State is supreme.'

The catalogue of misery was complete. That these things could be done in the name of a political doctrine I found impossible to accept. But there was no other reason for the mass murder and the wanton destruction of a complete town and its administration. Today when people talk to me about communism and the growing threat to Africa I see that scene again in all its misery and I know who will be the first to suffer – the unfortunate 'intelligentsia'. God help them.

In 1975 I was asked to speak to a very large audience at the Elangeni Hotel in Durban. I was to be one of a platform of rightwingers known as the National Forum. Understandably, my sponsors did not take me very seriously in the arena of South African politics, in which of course I was a child. My sphere of interest was known to be central Africa; in any case I regarded myself as a *citoyen d'Afrique*. They had invited me, I was told with alarming frankness, solely as a drawcard in order to boost attendance. I took this to be some sort of backhanded compliment. I was expected to tell one or two stories from my Congo experiences to amuse the audience. Nothing more. I told the one above. It was received in shocked silence. I went on to say that in my opinion, judging by my experience in the Congo, the real sufferers in South Africa would be the Blacks if communism ever made inroads into the country. I posed a solution. Improve the lot of the Blacks. Create a solid middle class who would have something to lose, some reason to fight against communism. I had seen these tactics succeed in the Congo. Fight communism with the weapons of capitalism, I said. Encourage free enterprise and the small businessman. Spend vast sums on Black education. Invest in tomorrow. If it cost ten cents in the rand on the income tax (my very words) to raise the living standards of the Blacks, it would be money invested in the stability of the country when the crunch came as come it most certainly would.

On the day of reckoning South Africa's lines of communication would be most vulnerable. Never mind the borders; those would look after themselves. There was no force in Africa which could match the South African Defence Force in manpower or equipment.

Unless assisted by a Western power, no African country could defeat South Africa militarily. The danger did not lie in that direction. The real danger was in communist agitation among the Black population. The real danger was in a communist-inspired Black enemy athwart the lines of communication. The real tragedy was that they would be the ones who would lose in the end after appalling bloodshed and misery had decimated the country. They would lose because they were only a pawn in a much bigger plan. They would be manipulated by the political commissars and the Marxists who would pretend they were aiding them today when they knew full well that revolution and the overthrow of the existing order were their real aim. The treasure-house which was South Africa would be added to the Soviet Union, through a Black Marxist government. That was their ultimate goal. To deny its mineral riches to the West was a bonus.

The tumultuous applause which had greeted me earlier on in my speech evaporated. This was not what my audience wanted to hear from me, and my warning fell on deaf ears. Even the press were unable to discern its real meaning. The next day the *Rand Daily Mail* – somewhat disappointed, I suspect, in what I had said as being not right-wing enough for it to criticise adversely – contented itself with an article headlined 'The Day Mad Mike Went Off the Right Rails'. It concluded:

> But then the Colonel went off the rails a little. Sheer White solidarity was not in itself a permanent answer to the Communist threat – far better for Whites to help improve the economic and social lot of the Blacks. This was vital, even if it led to a lower standard of living for the Whites, Colonel Hoare said. Blacks must have something to lose. There must be a stable black middle class. Whites must realise every privilege is accompanied by an obligation.

But here once more in the Seychelles were the unmistakable signs of the Marxist machine at work, and in this case it was more sinister than in the Congo. There the communists were using a spontaneous uprising to further their aims via the traditional route of disorder and chaos; in the Seychelles issues of global significance were at stake, and much had happened recently to turn the Indian Ocean into an area of strategic importance.

The ninety-two islands of the Seychelles archipelago lie about a thousand miles due east of the port of Mombasa in Kenya, on about the same parallel of latitude, roughly 4 degrees 40 minutes south of the equator. The population of the Seychelles is approximately 62,000, the majority living on the principal island, Mahé, which is about twenty-two miles long by seven wide in places. Victoria is the capital. The islands became self-governing in 1971 and received their independence from Britain, the colonial power which had ruled for nearly 165 years, on 28 June 1976. James Mancham, who became the first President, was the leader of the Seychelles Democratic Party. His Prime Minister, Albert France René, was the leader of the Seychelles People's United Party. They agreed to form a coalition government.

The foreign policy of the new government at the time of independence was non-alignment as between East and West. The President saw advantages in continuing the commercial and cultural ties of the past with Britain and France; the Prime Minister saw advantages in the African socialist way of life as espoused by President Nyerere. But both factions agreed that political differences must take second place to the demands of the island's economy, which for years had been barely viable and was now in a parlous state. The President's solution was to encourage tourism, and in this he was hugely successful, putting the Seychelles on the tourist map worldwide.

The population of the Seychelles might be tiny, and its area far-flung, but its strategic importance had not escaped the attention of the superpowers. The islands lie athwart the oil-tanker routes from the Persian Gulf to the west, via the Cape of Good Hope. Their central position in the Indian Ocean gives them a potential as a base for naval surveillance of the African coast, the Persian Gulf and the Indian sub-continent. Acting on the assumption that such a facility was indeed desirable, the United States established a naval and military base on an island in the Chagos archipelago about 1200 miles east of Mahé. The island, Diego Garcia, was leased from Britain or, more correctly, the British Indian Ocean Territories in 1965 for a period of fifty years. Since then the United States had developed it into a major naval base capable of supporting an Indian Ocean fleet of two aircraft-carriers, twenty warships and seven merchant supply-vessels, all essential to the Rapid Deployment Force of which the Marine Amphibian Brigade on the island formed a part. The island was perhaps a little too far to the east to be considered ideal as a base for the speedy surveillance of the Persian Gulf, but this slight disadvantage was offset by its proximity to Singapore, the Philippines and the Far East. Over all, the United States tactical position was greatly improved by an agreement entered into with Kenya which enabled the United States Navy to use the port of Mombasa. Another agreement with Somalia gave them naval facilities at Berbera, her port on the Red Sea.

A glance at the map at this stage might make you wonder why the Americans did not opt for the island of Aldabra, instead of Diego Garcia two thousand miles further east. Its strategic position at the northern end of the Mozambique Channel would seem ideal for their purposes. It was generally thought at one time that Britain had intended to lease this island, the largest in the British Indian Ocean Territories, to the United States, but a small point had been overlooked in the planning stage – Aldabra is the home of the giant tortoise and as such almost unique in the world. Each year thousands of them emerge from the sea to lay their eggs deep in the sands of the foreshore. A naval base or whatever would have disturbed them out of all conscience. Conservationists throughout the world voiced their objection to the planned base vociferously and it was dropped forthwith in favour of Diego Garcia.

In the nature of superpower strategy the Soviet Union found it necessary to counter the advantage which Diego Garcia conferred on the United States by creating one of her own. She immediately set up submarine-bases halfway down the Red Sea on the island of Dahlak, and complemented these with a military facility on the South Yemeni island of Socotra off the Horn of Africa – an island superbly situated to survey the southern Arabian coast, the tanker routes from the Gulf and the northern Indian Ocean. Further well-placed submarine-bases were established at Nacala, a port in northern Mozambique (the *quid pro quo* for Russian assistance to FRELIMO in the past), and at Diego Suarez, an excellent harbour at the northern tip of Madagascar.

Within this context the Seychelles islands began to assume a new importance. If the American and Russian bases were on the rim of a wheel, you could say the Seychelles were at the hub. The fact that Mahé boasted an airport capable of taking the largest airliners and that there were six other airfields on nearby islands enhanced its value. The Russians now began to pursue a vigorous policy of friendship with the new nation. An over-large diplomatic mission from the Soviet Union was installed in Victoria and began to give René advice. Work began on the construction of a military base on Coetivy Island, a remote coral outcrop of ten square miles some 180 nautical miles south-west of Mahé. As the work was being supervised by fifteen or more Russians, assisted by Cubans, it was assumed by Western intelligence sources that this was intended to be the Russian answer to Diego Garcia. They claimed that work had begun in November 1979 on the building of a jet runway on Coetivy long enough to take large freight aircraft, together with underground silos of the type from which long-range intercontinental ballistic missiles could be launched, presumably in the direction of Diego Garcia. Or South Africa.

This development pleased the Russians. They had obtained more than just a foothold in the Indian Ocean. In February 1981 at the 26th Soviet Communist Party Congress in Moscow a Russian naval strategist hailed the establishment of the Russian presence in the Indian Ocean and its littoral states over the last decade as a stupendous achievement. He claimed that in the countries of the Indian Ocean and southern Africa 'truly grandiose events' were taking place. There is no reason to contradict him.

After some weeks the handsome and likeable Gonzague D'Offay returned from London. He had seen the ex-President, who was sympathetic to his personal plight but was disinclined to make any decision with regard to a counter-coup. Furthermore, he gave Gonzague the general impression that he was not really all that interested in such a project. I felt that perhaps Gonzague had misled me inadvertently in our initial interview when he had said that the ex-President was prepared to meet me anywhere in Europe. However, I wrote this off as natural enthusiasm for his cause and a not unnatural blurring of the facts in an effort to gain some support. It did not worry me overmuch. It might have done so, if I had realised how fundamental this matter of the ex-President's intentions really was. Had I known that vacillation on the part of Mr Mancham was to be the bugbear in nearly all my dealings with the Seychellois exiles in the future, I might have been more concerned. As things stood they were incapable of accepting the brute fact that the ex-President was simply not interested in making a comeback at this moment. In their view this was illogical, if not wholly unacceptable. Possibly even disloyal. Had they been assured of Mancham's wholehearted support and leadership from the start, things might have turned out very differently. But for the moment, and on many occasions thereafter, they acted as though he was, or would be, entirely behind them.

But, more to the present point, he brought a message. The London group of exiles would like my military opinion as to whether a counter-coup was feasible or not. If it was, would I make a plan and support it with a detailed budget? Almost fifteen months had gone by since the coup of 5 June 1977 and things would be very different now, I said. This would make a personal reconnaissance of the island even more necessary. Gonzague said he would raise the funds needed to defray the expenses of the trip but regretted they would be unable to reward me for my services. I said they must not worry about that; it was no great matter.

I began to consider what stance I should adopt. In the past I had always held that mercenary soldiers should be used only in support of the armed forces of a legally constituted government, overlooking the difficulty that sometimes posed in Africa. This, however, was an exceptional case. The legal President was James Mancham. That was beyond dispute. The exiles had a righteous and a legal cause. And it was manifestly anti-Marxist.

I decided I would give them all the help I could. Further, if they were unable to pay me for my services, I would give them for nothing.

CHAPTER 2

A Visit to Mahé

I HAD VISITED Mahé once before in 1956 as a tourist. For two months I sailed its blue waters, goggled over its coral reefs, and climbed Morne Seychellois, its 3000-foot peak. Those were happy carefree days when the islands were off the beaten track and could only be reached by a British India steamship which plied between the east coast of Africa and India. Now it was a new name in the tourist world and attracted visitors from all parts of Europe, who arrived by air in droves. I thought it might be wise to have a second opinion on the situation there and decided to ask Gerry Puren, a friend since my Congo days, to come with me. Over a three-Martini lunch I put a proposition to him. He accepted at once.

I had seen Gerry in some hairy situations in the past and been impressed with his courage. In 1967 he was given a *Message to Garcia* type of mission – reach Colonel 'Black Jack' Schramme at all costs; tell him to hold on, help is on its way. The Colonel was besieged in Bukavu with a thousand Katangaise and mercenary troops defying the might of General Mobutu's Congolese army. The only way to get to him was to ditch a plane on Lake Kivu and swim ashore. Gerry made it. That spark of adventure had by no means abated; he was as keen as mustard for any new challenge.

On the debit side Gerry was inclined to be woefully indiscreet on occasion, largely as a result of his almost uncontrollable enthusiasm for any adventure of this nature. But what influenced me more than his previous career was his genealogy. Gerry's great-grandfather had been a master mariner from France who had settled in Mahé at the end of his days at sea. One branch of the family had emigrated to

South Africa, the other had stayed in the Seychelles. Gerry had often told me of his Seychelles cousin, Frank Puren, who had been active in east African politics as a socialist. Naturally enough, as soon as the new regime took over and transport was nationalised Frank was appointed managing director of the Victoria Bus Company. He was thus a person of some consequence – or very nearly. Regrettably the company had not flourished under public ownership, and Frank had been sacked. But all was not lost; he still had considerable clout with the Party. A friend at the centre of things might be just what we needed. We left for Mahé on 24 September 1978.

At this time British Airways provided the only air link between South Africa and the Seychelles. South African Airways had lost this valuable concession – it had been a convenient stop on their route from Johannesburg to Hong Kong – as soon as the new regime seized power. One of the first decrees issued by President René cancelled South African Airways landing rights on Mahé and stopped all tourism from South Africa to the Seychelles. This embargo did something for him with the OAU no doubt, but was nothing short of economic suicide for the island. In one stroke he had reduced tourist traffic practically by half. Some years later he saw the error of his ways and reversed the edict, but by then it was too late, the damage had been done and the island of Mauritius had substituted itself as a more attractive alternative for South African tourists. Even in the political world you cannot have it both ways.

Things had certainly changed since my visit of 1956. For a start there was now an airport on the east coast, some six miles south of Victoria. This had been built in 1971 at a cost of £5¼ million sterling. It had a runway nearly two miles long and had been built out into the sea parallel with the coast. Apparently it had been financed by ceding the islands of Aldabra, Desroches and Farquhar to the British Indian Ocean Territories, which had upset a few of the Seychellois, but unquestionably the airport had changed everything for the better and brought the islands into the twentieth century at long last. Several first-class hotels had been built because of it, and tourism, which had flourished as never before during Mancham's brief reign, spilled over into the building industry and improved the economy. Neat wooden houses were to be seen everywhere in place of those I remembered, many of which had walls made from flattened paraffin-tins. The centre of Victoria now had a stadium and paved roads, but the minute one moved away from the capital things didn't seem to have changed very much after all.

We stayed at the Reef Hotel close to the airport, hired a small open car and explored the island thoroughly. We contacted Frank Puren, Gerry's long-lost cousin, who was affable and helpful but not as well acquainted with those in power as we had hoped. Gerry met one Gerard Hoarau (pronounced 'War-rowe'), whose name had been given to us as a man who might be useful to us in understanding the local scene. Hoarau was a man of about thirty, small and athletic, and the captain of the local first-division football team. He worked as the Chief Immigration Officer, an appointment he had secured on his return from Rome where he had studied for the priesthood for seven years. He was not happy with the way things were going. In his view the new Marxist regime had brought nothing but misery to the ordinary easy-going Seychellois, and it was high time something was done about it.

The reconnaissance was soon done. I formed the general impression that, if the exiles moved themselves quickly, a counter-coup could be staged in a matter of six months. Hardly any opposition existed at this stage.

The new Seychelles People's Liberation Army had an establishment of 200: ten officers and 190 other ranks. The rank and file were mostly illiterates and recently released convicts, mainly of Negro ancestry. A reserve, known as the militia, might number as many as 400, mostly boys of twelve to fifteen. They patrolled secluded beaches at night. The barracks overlooked the eastern end of the airport runway. Two 20 mm anti-aircraft MMGs were sited above it.

The army was being trained by about fifty Tanzanian instructors who lived in Liberation Road, previously Duke of Edinburgh Way. Instruction comprised foot drill and weapon training. There was no rifle range. The men were issued with the AK47 Kalashnikov assault rifle. There were no support weapons, mortars, and so on.

Morale was reported to be high among the recruits, although their turnout was poor, discipline lax, and loyalty to the President in doubt. To counter the possibility of any movement against him by the army the President had raised an élite force of thirty men as his palace bodyguard. This unit was being trained by a Frenchman reputed to be one of Bob Denard's ex-mercenaries.

On the political front the new President was ruling by decree through a six-man Cabinet of doctrinaire Marxists, the most powerful of whom was one Hodoul. Elections had been promised within six months, but this was thought highly unlikely. A communal work-centre had been set up, Marxist propaganda was disseminated by radio and poster, and the achievements of the previous administration denigrated. The memory of the first President was vilified and his house at Glacis vandalised.

On my return to my home in Hilton, Natal, I formulated a plan for a counter-coup which could be executed within six to nine months at a cost of US$5 million. The main items were:

(1) A force of 200 men would be needed on a six-month contract. They should be recruited in Europe and America. It would be politically unwise to recruit in South Africa.

(2) The force should be based in a friendly Arab country in the Persian Gulf. An isolated training camp should be set up in a remote coastal area where training for an amphibious assault could be carried out in complete secrecy. A period of four months should be allowed for this phase.

(3) A fleet of six fishing trawlers would be required, one of which would be fitted with a helicopter and a helicopter-pad.

(4) Zodiac inflatables would be used as assault landing-craft.

Those were the broad details. The plan was simple and feasible, but it required immediate action before the enemy were alerted or Cuban or Korean troops were imported. The firm base required in Arabia was known to exist and was available; the main problem would be the funding of the project. I sent off the report to London and Australia via Gonzague, and waited.

But for the moment I was needed elsewhere. My good friend Euan Lloyd, the producer of *The Wild Geese*, a film about mercenary soldiers in the Congo starring Richard Burton, Roger Moore and Richard Harris, had an interesting proposition for me. Would I accompany him to the United States to assist him on a promotional tour for the film which was to have its première in New York? I had been technical adviser to the director, Andrew MacLaglan. We would appear on innumerable television and radio shows from coast to coast. I said yes. For the next four weeks I met the American media face to face, a harrowing experience at times, but educative. I enjoyed seeing that great country with all expenses paid, and in unaccustomed luxury; but I certainly earned my money! The suave and debonair Euan is a seasoned professional at this sort of thing, which he takes in his stride, but for me a lot of it was unmitigated agony. I lived through some anxious moments in front of the microphone and the television cameras, but none perhaps quite as bemusing as the afternoon I was faced by a famous New York comedian who had misread his script and mistook the word 'mercenary' for 'missionary'. To my horror he then asked me to tell the world exactly how I had brought the Gospel to the heathen in darkest Congo. I had an irresistible urge to say I did it with an FN rifle, but a stern look from Euan curbed me of that nonsense.

As I was on the point of leaving New York for home I received a call from the spokesman for the London group of exiles. He introduced himself as Eddie Camille. We had often spoken over the telephone prior to that, but now he wanted to know if I could route myself via London as the ex-President had said he would like to see me. In any case, it was time Eddie and I met.

I stayed in London for eleven days, at the end of which I was informed that the ex-President had had a change of heart and did not now see any point in a meeting. I surmised from this, accurately, that Mr Mancham was by no means as keen to return to the political arena as the exiles would have had me believe. This uncertainty as to the ex-President's real intentions bedevilled my relationship with the exiles from then on. Obviously it was in their interests to have me think Mr Mancham was as enthusiastic about his return to the island as they were, but this was not always the case.

But I did meet Eddie Camille. I took a great liking to him from the start. Like many colonials before him he had settled in England to become more English than the English. At first glance I would have said he was the typical English squire, but it was his very slight but attractive French accent which gave the lie. He had left the Seychelles some twenty years before, but his heart was still there. He was low of voice and gentle in manner, a typical Seychellois gentleman, held in high esteem by his countrymen, who elected him unanimously to co-ordinate their efforts to oust the René regime.

Over one or two delightful meals at Mumtaz Mahal, an excellent Indian restaurant in Baker Street, I got to know Eddie. It was pleasant to deal with a man who was so balanced and temperate in his outlook. In those early days I was particularly interested in the motivation behind the exiles. Was their sole aim in life merely the restoration of their possessions and their privileged positions – they were after all *les grands blancs* – or were they more concerned about the unsuitability of the communist way of life for the easy-going and indolent islanders? Eddie satisfied me that whilst the former attitude was a very natural one amongst the dispossessed exiles it was not the fundamental one. We had to remember they were the traditional leaders, he said, and had the welfare of their people at heart. René had overturned the way of life of the ordinary Seychellois. The concept of compulsory weekly lectures at which they would be indoctrinated in Marxist theory was an outrage, and the forced removal of their children to nearby island camps for this purpose would be resisted, he felt sure. To say nothing of the changed status of the country *vis-à-vis* the Western world, of which they had always been a loyal part. And to think that they had aligned themselves with the Eastern bloc, and had entered into treaties with Russia, Libya, Algeria and Cuba! The mere idea was repugnant to them. And all in the name of five or six Marxist theorists who had seized power in Victoria and were determined to impose their will on the people, come what may. Eddie grew heated as he denounced the horrors perpetrated on the island by the trusted Prime Minister who had stabbed his President in the back as soon as it was turned.

We discussed possible lines of action. My advice at this stage was that they should do their utmost to enlist the aid of a big power. The obvious one was the United States of America, who had something to gain by having Seychelles in the Western camp. A glance at a map of the Indian Ocean was all that was needed. Another big power – big in this context anyway – whom they ought to approach was the Republic of South Africa; but my advice, even at this early stage, was that any assistance they might possibly get from them might prove to be the kiss of death at the OAU after the event. They must tread warily. But without the aid of a big power, I assured Eddie, they were doomed politically and financially.

The first three months of 1979 saw the beginnings of an underground movement in Mahé. Newsletters of a scurrilous and libellous nature were passed from hand to hand in Victoria. Albert René was said to have rigged the recent election in which he had been returned to office by an overwhelming majority. Furthermore, the letters declared, he had embezzled state funds! I could not see what all the fuss was about. Par for the course in Africa, I would have said. In addition there were some titillating comments on his sexual proclivities, the disclosure of which, in my view, did little to enhance the credibility or moral tone of the broadsheets. I presumed the publishers knew what appealed to their own people best. The reaction was not slow in coming. As the letters became more virulent and damaging they culminated in the arrest of over sixty people, chosen apparently at random from those who might conceivably be anti-René. The most noteworthy casualty was Bernard Verlaque, the popular editor of the only newspaper on the island. Another was Gerard Hoarau, the man Gerry Puren had met during our preliminary reconnaissance last year. Both were destined to languish in gaol without charge or trial for some 240 days before being released and expelled from the country.

René then moved swiftly to protect himself against a possible counter-coup. Tanzanian soldiers were brought in hurriedly. An appeal to France resulted in the gift of *Topaz*, an armed fisheries protection vessel complete with French crew. This ship patrolled the approaches to the harbour at Victoria, and restricted the movement of yachts to day sailing only. All this activity generated much excitement among the populace and punctuated the steadily deteriorating quality of life. Tourism began to drop off drastically, and the proprietors of first-class hotels and other tourist attractions began to worry. The socialist way of life, which knows how to distribute wealth but not how to create it, ground on relentlessly.

In early April, Eddie asked me to present a case to the South African government on behalf of the Seychelles exiles in an attempt to gain support for a coup which would reinstate the legitimate President, Mr James Mancham. Accordingly I wrote to Mr Alec van Wyk, the head of the National Intelligence Service in Pretoria, formerly known as BOSS, the Bureau of State Security, when it was headed by the much feared General Hendrik van den Bergh. Once more I warned Eddie against this type of initiative on political grounds – not, may I say, from any anti-South African bias, which I did not possess. Again I suggested that a better alternative would be for Mr Mancham to approach the Americans in London in view of their interest in Diego Garcia, the build-up of their naval forces in the Indian Ocean, and their need to protect the oil-shipping route to and from the Persian Gulf. That this obvious step was never taken indicated to me once more that Mr Mancham was not keen to get into the show.

Mr van Wyk said he would see me on 17 May 1979. This of course meant a trip to Pretoria some 350 miles away. Perhaps I should just mention at this point that as the Seychelles anti-René group were without any funds whatsoever for activities of this nature I was expected to carry them out at my own expense, aided occasionally by a generous Johannesburg businessman. That I did this for a period of nearly three years may indicate either my stupidity or the degree of enthusiasm I felt for their cause.

I presented myself in Pretoria on the appointed day and was given a courteous reception by Mr Alec van Wyk. I stated the case for the Seychelles exiles briefly and referred to my *aide-mémoire*, which read:

1. What is the attitude of the South African Government likely to be towards the proposed coup?
2. If favourable: Would the SA Government be prepared to give any assistance before the event? And, in particu-

lar, finance up to a maximum of 3 million US dollars.
3. In exchange for such aid you may suggest that the new
    government will provide:
    (a) A sympathetic voice at OAU in favour of RSA.
    (b) Preferential landing rights for South African Air-
        ways at Mahé together with certain other tourist
        rights.
    (c) Special trade links between the two countries; for
        example, agreement in connection with the new oil
        fields about to be developed off Platte Island; joint
        investment in the vast fishing industry of the islands
        about to be exploited, etc., etc.

Mr van Wyk listened attentively to everything I had to say, examined somewhat perfunctorily the documentation I presented and
promised it would all be scrutinised by his Indian Ocean experts. He
was an Afrikaner of the old school, charming and correct. The documentation in all truth did not amount to very much. There were the
names of the shadow government (Mancham's conspicuous by its absence), the promises of reciprocal treatment, copies of the subversive
news-sheets mentioned above, the names of Chinese and Russian
embassy staff in Victoria, the plans for the building of flats for 105
Russians in Mahé, and so on. Not enough to have caused a fluttering
in the dovecotes, I would have thought. Even so Mr van Wyk, who
was due to retire very shortly, said the matter would be presented to
the National Security Council of the Cabinet when it met the following
Tuesday in Cape Town. I would get an answer in ten days.
   On the tenth day I got the answer. It was No.
   In the summer of that year I took my wife and two youngest sons to
Europe, bought a Ford Transit motorised caravan and toured
England, Scotland and the Continent for three months – a pleasant
adventure which I heartily recommend to all families who want to
develop togetherness. I met Eddie on several occasions and on one was
introduced to an arms dealer/financier who was plainly disappointed at
the scale of the proposed operation and the smallness of the demand
which might arise for his wares. He reminded me, with a whiff of
nostalgia, of the occasion a few years back when I had met a notorious
French arms dealer in Lisbon. The Biafra affair was in full spate at
that time and I was on my way to meet General Ojukwu in Port Harcourt. The dealer was keen to supply arms to the General.
   'Persuade him he needs these 250-pound bombs,' he said, 'and let
him know I can let him have these 18-pounder guns very cheap.'
   He handed me some photographs.

23

'Why?' I asked.

'Well,' he answered, nothing abashed (arms dealers as a rule are not noticeably shy), 'I've got hangars full of those bombs and the bloody things are going stale on me. And there's a generous mark-up on them, too.' He winked.

'And the guns?'

I had recognised them as something which became obsolete with the Boer War and had probably been discarded by a museum.

'A job lot I got from Korea. Trouble is I've got no blasted ammunition for them!'

More than a year had passed since I had first been approached by Gonzague D'Offay, and so far the exiles had got nowhere. They were virtually leaderless and without financial resources. I recalled wryly the very first question I had put to Gonzague: Have you any money? Money in this context meaning millions of American dollars. As far as leadership was concerned, the only man of stature and the one to whom they should have been able to look was the ex-President, Jimmy Mancham. With vigour he could have unified the several anti-René factions and given their plans a decisive impetus. Without him they had found it impossible to attract a big power or an entrepreneur. Hence the impasse.

I was all the more surprised, then, to be told at the end of January 1980 that the ex-President had undergone a dramatic change of heart and now wanted definitely and irrevocably to return to his country as President! But with reservations. He did not see himself as fulfilling that role for very long; his main purpose was to re-establish himself as the true leader of his country and to reassert his place in history. After a period of a few months he would hand over gracefully to a carefully trained understudy, and once he had overseen a peaceful transference of power he would withdraw to Britain. I received this scenario with some scepticism: a consummation devoutly to be wished, nothing more. The only voluntary resignation of high office which I could recall in Africa in recent times was when General Gowon departed the hurly-burly of the presidency of Nigeria for the secluded cloisters of Oxford University and the pursuit of learning for its own sake. Real wisdom.

But here, at any rate, was a solid proposition. Could I come to London for discussions with the ex-President? If I could, there was a condition. Mr Mancham must be assured, said Eddie, of some Big Power participation on his side before he made a final commitment. Would I please contact the South African government once more in the light of the changed circumstances? If so, I was authorised to state the *quid pro quo* as before.

Well, now, that gave a new buoyancy to the plan; it had a firm reassuring ring about it. But a three-week trip to London and negotiations with the South African government must cost a few thousand rand, frugal and monastic though my life-style was known to be. I mentioned this small but embarrassing point to my masters in a shy tone, whereupon a sympathetic and generous businessman in London offered to finance half the expenses – but only on condition that we should first obtain a favourable reaction from the South African government. Would I finance the other half? With pleasure, I said.

Once more, even at the risk of being a bore, I detailed the obvious objections to this course of action, pointing out in tiresome detail the inevitability of discovery of any such assistance by the South African government, and the obloquy which must ensue from members of the OAU after the event. Much better, I suggested again, that you get Jimmy Mancham to approach Grosvenor Square. The affair of the Iran hostages was at its nadir; Russia had recently invaded Afghanistan. Surely these events would encourage the Americans to take a more aggressive view of their role in the Indian Ocean? Surely an appreciation of Russia's new position in that area within striking distance of a warm-water port – the great Russian dream for generations – and its potential threat to the Persian Gulf must influence their thinking when they were approached for assistance? But they still wanted me to march on Pretoria. I took steps in that direction.

I asked a man I knew in the National Intelligence Service to come and see me. I had met Martin Donaldson (as I knew him) in 1974, just after my return from the Mediterranean where I had spent three years with my family on a hundred-ton Baltic trader converted to a yacht. (The story is in my book *Three Years with Sylvia*.) Donaldson, despite his name, was an Afrikaner and not, I judged, very high up in the hierarchy of the NIS. He had previously been in the South African Police and attained the rank of sergeant before transferring to the NIS. He was a pleasant enough individual, very conscientious, filled with his own self-importance and rabidly nationalistic in his outlook. On the social side he lacked a certain finesse, perhaps the result of his farm-boy upbringing; but if he lacked something in elegant behaviour he made up for it in the quaint Continental way in which he would bow and click his heels on being introduced. Later I discovered he was not in fact a fully fledged Afrikaner but was half Yugoslavian on his father's side, and that his name was not Donaldson but Dolinchek, which I supposed accounted for that engaging little extravagance.

25

Even so, I enjoyed his company; I lean towards enthusiastic people, and Martin certainly carried the banner with wholehearted devotion. South Africa, man, was the only country in the world, misunderstood of course but still the greatest; those blerry *rooineks* were a pain in the arse and didn't understand us; kaffirs must be taught they didn't own the country; we were here first; Buthelezi was a good coon, he wanted peaceful change; and the blerry Progressives should be allowed to go multiracial in their own blerry suburbs and see how they blerry well liked it. At least you knew where you were with him! From time to time Martin would vanish from the local scene for two or three months, presumably on a course of instruction or some such. At our next meeting, after a couple of beers no power on earth could stop him telling me and everybody else within earshot of his latest exploits in Zambia or Mozambique, top secret though they undoubtedly were. I shuddered at the implications for the country in employing such an indiscreet agent, but for the moment he was my conduit to the people I needed to see in Pretoria.

After some weeks a meeting was arranged, but not with the NIS. According to Martin, the Durban office of the NIS considered that as their chief was in the process of being replaced it was unlikely he would make any far-reaching decisions about anything. They also had some unflattering remarks to make about the new man, who was an academic and had not come up the hard way via the South African Police. They thought it might be wiser if I met a senior officer in the South African Defence Force, and arranged for me to meet a Brigadier Hamman.

I travelled up to Pretoria by train and waited for the Brigadier to show up at the appointed rendezvous. An hour or more passed by, after which a breathless character dashed up to apologise and say he was replacing the Brigadier, who had been called away unexpectedly at the last minute. He suggested we should conduct our interview amidst the charm and secrecy of the station cafeteria. I was not particularly pleased at the turn of events. For a start, the stand-in did not impress me with his manner, which was brusque and overbearing. I graded him as an assistant to the Brigadier, probably a sergeant clerk in the Army. It seemed inappropriate to discuss matters of secrecy and importance with a man who appeared to have little authority, and bridling a bit at the seeming lack of courtesy on the part of the Brigadier I drew things to a close after fifteen minutes' fruitless conversation. Without being touchy or prima donna-ish, I assumed this was the brush-off.

Notwithstanding this failure I arrived in London on 11 March to be pierced through by that abominable east wind which travels all the way from the Steppes with the express purpose of chilling cockneys to the marrow. It was my first meeting with the chief. Eddie ushered me into the presence after meticulously observing every security precaution in the book.

James Mancham is an extremely handsome man. Moreover, he has an imposing presence. His eyes are brown and soft, and there is a sensitive quality in his greeting. He is said to have the soul of a poet. He is a little under six feet tall and well proportioned. With his black beard and engaging smile I could understand why women were captivated by him. On closer acquaintance I found him to be astute and fun-loving, a formidable combination. It is not, however, a combination which produces great leaders. Great leaders are usually self-centred, supremely confident in their infallibility, and conscious of their superiority over circumstances. James Mancham was none of those things; his charm lay in a different direction. He was the man the hour had produced, like Nkrumah, Kaunda or Kenyatta, all unifying forces in their country's transitional stage from British colony to sovereign state; but he gave me the impression that he was sincere, that he had the real interests of his people at heart and that he could inspire loyalty and devotion in those he led.

We discussed the situation in the Seychelles on each of the three occasions when I met him and he listened carefully to my alternative plans for a coup. He saw at once that everything was contingent on raising the large sum of money needed if the proposed coup was to be carried out efficiently. He thought it possible that his old friend Adnan Khashoggi might be able to help him fund the project. Khashoggi, it appeared, had been shabbily treated by the René regime simply because of his friendship with Mancham. His property had been confiscated arbitrarily and he himself declared *persona non grata*. These things on their own were persuasive factors if he was to make an appeal to him for financial aid; but, then, there was also their great friendship and, after all, what was US$5 million to a man like Khashoggi! *Tiens!* In any case, he was to visit the United States shortly and would be seeing Adnan in California. He would let us have a decision by the end of May at the latest. In the meantime he could assure me he really was eager to return to the Seychelles as President once more. If it was a volte-face, it was long overdue. I felt now that at long last we were getting somewhere.

But we were due for yet another disappointment. Early in June a somewhat disconsolate Eddie informed me that Mancham had met Khashoggi in New York and drawn a blank. His friend was sympathetic but, regrettably, he was too involved in defending himself against a massive divorce suit which his wife had brought against him in

America to enter into any new adventure of this kind. Mancham returned to London, and by the end of June his resolve to return to the Seychelles had evaporated. He told Eddie he saw no likelihood of his going back and that 'frankly he was not anxious to expose himself to the dangers he must face as a re-elected President'.

As one door shuts another one opens, says a trite but comfortable little saying. A new star shone in the east. Robert Frichot, a Seychelles exile, previously Attorney-General in the Mancham administration, who was now resident in Australia, came forward at this moment and took over all efforts to oust René, still using Eddie as co-ordinator in London. I had not met him, but from his actions now, and later, I judged him correctly to be a man of courage and ability. His first directive was that he would like me to visit Mahé to attend the Independence Day celebrations on 5 June at which the Army's recently acquired Russian weaponry and equipment would be on display to the public for the first time. They were keen to know what it amounted to.

This time I went alone but, again, at my own expense. Gerry Puren had been dropped from the team on orders from London. It had come to their attention that he had been alarmingly indiscreet in an address he had given to an old soldiers' club. Obviously this could not be allowed. Since my previous visit with Gerry in September 1978 the economy of Mahé had deteriorated rapidly. Tourism had dropped off by a further 40 per cent, largely as a result of the recession in Europe and the high cost of air fares to the islands. More serious was the sudden and unexpected decline in the fishing industry. For the first time within living memory the public were unable to buy fish, their staple food, in the market – and for a good reason. Fishermen were forced to sell their catch to the newly established co-operative at a very low price. The Mahé fishermen, always an independent breed, said they would rather sweep the streets for twenty rupees a day than be robbed of their catch. Their boats remained idle.

The general atmosphere on the island was tense, although the curfew had been abandoned and security was more relaxed. A witch-hunt was in progress for the pilferers of a consignment of Russian-supplied radio sets and other desirable hardware destined for the Army, but apart from that things seemed peaceful enough. I attended the parade, examined the arms, equipment and personnel at close quarters, took over fifty photographs and made an appreciation which I submitted with a report on my return to Durban. Some of the items were:

1. The Parade. A crowd of some 5000 people watched the parade on 5 June 1980. Members of the government and other dignitaries arrived at a saluting-platform by car, accompanied by a little polite hand-clapping. The parade was led by the Police Band followed by various para-military units armed with new FN rifles.

The SPLA marched past in six platoons of 30 men. The troops were dressed in jungle camouflage with steel helmets, Russian pattern. They were well turned out, marched precisely and gave a general impression of smartness. These troops carried much used AK47s with bayonets fixed. There were three RPG7 Russian-made rocket-launchers per platoon.

The infantry were followed by three Russian-made armoured cars, each armed with a heavy and a light machine-gun mounted in the turret. There are a further 9 of these 4-wheeled Armoured Fighting Vehicles in barracks. None were fitted with radio. Followed by six anti-aircraft quick-firing guns of the Bofors type, each towed behind a Land-rover. The guns were loaded with a clip of five rounds. The guns were of an obsolete pattern and probably of Russian manufacture.

Then came six medium anti-aircraft machine-guns, .50-inch calibre, towed by jeeps. These were in better condition but also of obsolete pattern. They were loaded with a short strip of link belt and mounted on tripods. These MMGs could also be used in an infantry-support role.

Followed by six Mini-Mokes each carrying a 75 mm Recoilless Rifle. These appeared to be brand new, were mounted on tripods and looked as though they had never been fired. No ammunition was carried.

After the Army came about 200 men and women of the militia, many out of step, literally an armed rabble. They carried 1914 Mauser-type bolt-action rifles with bayonets fixed. The magazine probably holds 5 or 6 rounds.

This genuinely impressive array of equipment – for the Seychelles – passed by the crowd with not so much as a clap or a murmur of approval. Nor for that matter very much interest. As soon as the tail end of the parade had passed much of the crowd dispersed instead of congregating, as one might have expected, around the platform to hear the President's speech.

The speech itself was well delivered, simply phrased and clear and audible to all. The content of the speech was received without applause or other emotion but a murmur of disapproval – barely audible – arose when the President announced that National Service for children would begin in 1981. [He had tried to introduce this in 1980 but the proposals had met with unexpected resistance from the children themselves, who had staged a spontaneous protest, joined by their parents, to demonstrate against it.] The speech lasted 40 minutes and ended with light applause.

2. Small arms. The AKs were noticeably scruffy and typical of the low-grade but lethal weaponry with which Russia is flooding the African continent. The ancient rifles carried by the militia are probably ideally suited to their purpose, which seems to be to terrify the naïve population.

The Russian RPG7 rocket-launchers appeared to be new and were the most formidable weapon on parade. Noticeable by their absence were pistols, revolvers and machine-guns of the Bren, Russian RPK and PK series. No grenades were seen, neither were any 60 mm or 81 mm mortars or grenade-launchers.

3. Defence. The defence capability has been drawn up to resist some form of conventional attack, either airborne or seaborne. Hence the preponderance of anti-aircraft weaponry and the (presumed) lack of basic infantry weapons.

The armament seems more suitable for a different theatre of war, Europe for example, rather than the hilly terrain and narrow roads of the island. The armoured cars are too big and cumbersome for anything other than airport runway defence. It is doubtful whether they could make a complete turn on any of the local roads. Being roadbound they are at a severe tactical disadvantage in what amounts to ideal ambush country. With no radio control their use must be confined to semi-static situations. The AFVs looked a minimum 20 years old, but in reasonable condition for their age.

[Little did I realise how accurate these observations on their armoured cars would prove to be. The AFVs were in fact the BTR-40 family which went into production in Russia in 1951, and were fitted with one

KPVT 14.5 mm and one 7.6 mm SGMB or, more probably, a modified version of the LMG in the KP series. I learned these facts the hard way a year later when on the receiving end of their fire power.]

Included in the parade was a unit of young boys and girls under fifteen, all very serious and unsmiling, carrying plastic make-believe weapons. For some reason they were drilled to perform a type of ceremonial goose step which looked difficult and not very attractive. On the other hand the Navy, by which I mean the crew of the *Topaz*, the 500-ton vessel donated by France, marched by with Gallic *éclat* and spats, French-style uniforms, French 9 mm submachine-guns, probably the Mat 49, and berets with side badge, all admirably French – ship-shape and Toulon fashion one might say. Without a doubt the smartest unit on parade, although by this time the original French crew and instructors had long since returned to France.

The remainder of my week was spent making a detailed reconnaissance on foot of all possible targets and in preparing an operational plan for the execution of the coup. The principle of war uppermost in my mind was surprise, probably the most decisive element of all. The enemy were not a formidable force, were largely untrained, and were gentle people at heart with no military tradition in their history or character. The plan, I decided, must take cognisance of these facts. Furthermore it could be executed, given local assistance on a generous scale, without a drop of blood being shed; but always subject to total surprise and security. Henceforward these two considerations were uppermost in my mind.

The report was sent to Eddie for distribution and ended with a military appreciation of the situation. Robert Frichot got moving at once. In July he visited Britain and Germany, ostensibly on his annual holiday, and began negotiations with people he referred to as his financiers. He telephoned me from Germany to ask me urgently for a revised budget, suggesting that one at US$3 million would be more likely of acceptance than one of US$5 million. I despatched an amended budget pointing out, not for the last time, that as the budget was successively reduced the risk factor must be correspondingly increased.

Robert was partially successful. Subject to being able to secure a certain political backing for the coup the finance was assured, he said, but perhaps not quite as much as US$3 million. Later I discovered the nature of the political backing that was required: the

Kenya government must support the project (tacitly, I presumed); must undertake to give instant recognition to the new government after the coup; and must agree to provide armed support after the event as soon as called upon by the new government to do so. I mulled that over. None of these political requirements seemed to me to be in the realm of fantasy. The outlook was rosy.

At the end of September 1980, President René released about twenty political prisoners from gaol in Mahé. They were instantly deported. Amongst these was Gerard Hoarau, whom I met in Durban a few days later. Gerard, despite his seven-year apprenticeship to the Church in Rome, was seized with a most unecclesiastical desire to burn René at the stake. He brought with him a refreshing zeal and commitment to the cause. At last, I thought, here is a man with the singleness of purpose needed for the task. At the same time I was a little disappointed in his lack of personal charisma; he was by no means a Mancham. Leaders, particularly rebel leaders having no funds out of which they can distribute largesse to their followers, must rely to a very large extent on promises against the day when they come into their glory or, more accurately, their treasury. A magnetic personality, in these circumstances, becomes a *sine qua non*. Gerard's attributes, which were not inconsiderable, lay elsewhere. He was enthusiastic, energetic and brave, and instinctively I knew he would bend up every spirit to his full height. Revenge is a potent force and eight months' imprisonment without trial a grievous spur.

It was not long before he acted, and acted independently, some of his actions running counter to the general plan which was now forming in Robert Frichot's mind. But this was better than the inaction of recent months. Gerard's first initiative was to fly to London to see the chief, confident he would be able to galvanise him into action with a first-hand account of conditions on the island and a report of how keenly his supporters anticipated his return. Fourteen days later he was back in Durban sadder and wiser. The chief was not to be moved. In truth he had lost all desire to return to Mahé as President. But elsewhere there was a ray of hope. Bernard Verlaque, the capable editor who had been imprisoned with Hoarau for criticising the René government, had also been released from prison and was now in Nairobi, Kenya, where he had been appointed Reuter's correspondent. He had been active in political circles.

In November a meeting was held between certain Kenyan government officials and a delegation from the Seychelles exiles headed by Robert Frichot. Included in the latter were Gerard, Verlaque and David Joubert, a former Minister of Tourism and Aviation in the

Mancham government. The outcome was highly satisfactory, Robert reporting that he had obtained all the backing he required and certain other concessions unspecified. This meeting was the turning-point in the negotiations to date. A green light was now shining brightly at the end of the tunnel. Robert's financiers in Germany were equally pleased at the outcome but asked for yet another amended budget, indicating this time that one at about US$2 million might be acceptable. I complied again with increased misgivings.

At this time, November 1980, momentous happenings were shaking the world. Mr Ronald Reagan had just been elected President of the United States. That great country was now assured of a firm and decisive leadership more in keeping with their proud traditions. The weakness of the Carter administration, which had saddened America's friends abroad, had passed. We who see the United States of America as the only sure bastion against the steady encroachment of communism worldwide rejoiced when we heard the new President declare he 'was going to put America back to work'. That he made good his promise in his first term of office was cause for even greater rejoicing.

In Africa, Libya had occupied the northern half of Chad, the desert state in the centre of Africa. France, in compliance with treaty obligations to her ex-colony, immediately despatched 3000 soldiers to defend an arbitrary line across the desert, south of which the Libyans were warned not to move, whilst negotiations for their withdrawal took place. Large numbers of ex-Foreign Legionnaires were enlisted for this French force on a year's engagement together with some mercenary soldiers of almost the same high military standard. In this way a number of men known to me as possible recruits were spirited away overnight. I removed their names from my register with regret.

Locally I had cause for some annoyance. I had been informed by my men in Johannesburg that an ex-mercenary officer, whom we shall call X, had approached them with a view to recruitment for a coup to be executed in the Seychelles! This bombshell could only mean that security amongst the exiles was criminally lax or, worse still, that they were dealing with X as an alternative leader. I immediately told Eddie that the involvement of X represented a grave security risk which could prove fatal to the operation, that he was unacceptable to me, and that unless I had Eddie's assurance that he was not dealing with him I must resign. For the moment I suspended all action.

Early in February 1981, Robert Frichot visited South Africa. Despite an elaborate smokescreen I became aware that he had come to negotiate with X, who was to introduce him to Brigadier Hamman of the SADF. X appeared to have some influence with the Army, being himself an Afrikaner and an ex-corporal in the Parachute Regiment. He had already persuaded them to bring David Joubert out from London to Cape Town at their expense some days earlier to discuss the proposed coup, which proved to the exiles that he did have considerable clout. Robert's failure to show any interest in my operational plans, or to discuss the thrice-amended budget, filled me with misgivings, and after his departure for Australia I concluded I had been double-crossed. I sent in my resignation to Eddie. Later they were at pains to reassure me that whatever negotiations had taken place with X were of no importance and had not jeopardised the security of the operation. Despite a nagging feeling in the pit of my stomach which told me I was making an error I soldiered on and agreed to overlook what was without question utterly disloyal behaviour on their part. It was an error. Now that all the facts are known to me, I realise that this was the moment when I should have washed my hands of the whole affair. In the event X was dropped shortly afterwards, took it badly and, I have been told, passed information to the enemy about our plans. How true that is I cannot say, but I doubt it.

Two points which were raised in my talks with Frichot were of interest. The first is one which invariably occurs when dealing with politicians involved in a proposed coup. What is to be done with the present office-bearers? Are they to live or to die? Or to go to prison? Most of the insurgents I have known are inordinately fierce at this stage. Being far from the battle they invariably counsel sudden death for their hated rivals. This, they explain, is the most humane thing that can happen. But naturally they want no hand in the actual shedding of blood. In practice these things are somewhat different and seem to be governed by a set of Queensberry Rules unique to the African scene. It very seldom happens that a president or prime minister removed from office by a *coup d'état* is killed out of hand or brought back from exile to face the music. There seems to be some unwritten agreement that allows him to retire gracefully to a foreign country where he may enjoy the fruits of his Swiss bank account in peace for the rest of his days. In the past, whenever my opinion has been asked on this point, I have taken pains to point out that the fate of their political opponents falls strictly within their purview and is not a matter for mere soldiers. If it was not so, I could assure them there might be a drastic reduction in the muster roll of politicians fouling up the scene in Africa today!

One of my fondest memories in this connection occurred during the negotiations I was having with some senior Portuguese army officers just before Angola succumbed to the MPLA, assisted by 25,000 Cuban mercenary troops, in 1975. These highly placed gentlemen were trying desperately to raise a small force of mercenary soldiers – even one hundred, they said, could turn the tide at that critical moment – and asked me to assist. We spent a day examining the possibilities and came eventually to the subject nearest and dearest to rebel hearts. What was to be done with Señor This and General That once we (meaning you) had captured them? A list was prepared showing who was to be eliminated (meaning murdered), and who spared, with reasons.

On this occasion a weedy-looking specimen insisted that the name of Señor X must be added to the short-list of those deemed worthy of death. His compatriots looked at him with astonishment. Señor X was unknown to them.

'But why Señor X?' they asked. 'What's he done?'

'That son-of-a-bitch,' came the reply, 'he seduced my wife!'

The second item was more mundane. Robert had heard that there was some possibility that Indian troops would be stationed on the island in response to an appeal made to Mrs Gandhi. It didn't surprise me, although I thought Koreans might be more likely. Sadly, it now looked as though Robert's German-based financiers had lost interest. This, I presumed, was why Robert was negotiating with his South African connections via X.

But, at long last, in early June came news of a decisive nature. Robert reported that a sum of US$200,000 had been promised to the cause and would be made available towards the end of August. At the same time the situation in Mahé was deteriorating fast. Shipments of arms were arriving weekly and rumours that foreign troops were to land in the new year abounded. Time was running out fast. Once the newly indoctrinated youngsters returned from their instruction in Marxism attitudes in Mahé would change. The older folk, the only ones to have known life under a democratic system, would be ignored. With additional military muscle provided by the communist bloc, the Marxist way of life would become so deeply entrenched as to be implacable. Already the Roman Catholic Church was coming under increasing governmental pressures and losing its influence among the young. Time was against them.

If the exiles were to remove René, they must do so now. Even a few months' delay would prove fatal. The only stumbling-block was the chronic lack of finance with which to stage the coup. Was there any way around that? I thought there might be.

I set to work on an idea – a cut-price coup!

CHAPTER 3

A Cut-Price Coup!

BARRISTERS ARE WARNED, I have been told, never to become emotion-
ally involved in their clients' cases. Inevitably, they say, it leads to
a clouding of one's judgement. The same thing could be said of
mercenary leaders, I imagine; but here I was doing just that, depart-
ing from the accepted norms when all the evidence was against them.
I realised I had become completely obsessed with an ambition to
help reinstate Jimmy Mancham in his rightful office, and was throwing caution to the winds.

I remembered having a similar experience a few years back. My
good friend Ian Colvin, doyen of Fleet Street foreign correspondents
of that time and one who had covered the African scene for the
Daily Telegraph with distinction, once introduced me to the ex-King
of Buganda. We dined at the Savoy Grill. The ex-King had been
recently ousted from his kingdom by Milton Obote. Now he was
anxious to get it back. Could I help? Good manners precluded my
asking the all-important question too early in the proceedings, but
by the time the dessert was served it was unavoidable. Had he the
funds for such a project? Very few people understand the incredible
cost of setting up and paying a mercenary force of, say, 500 men for
even as short a contract as six months. Certainly King Freddie, who
I may say was one of the most charming and captivating gentlemen
I have ever met, had no notion of the cost. Ultimately we were
obliged to examine that problem more closely. We made an estimate
on the tablecloth, Ian acting as scribe. The figure ran into some
millions of American dollars; I forget how many.

'No difficulty there,' said His Highness, swilling some Napoleon

36

brandy in a balloon glass and adding grandly: 'Well within our resources.'

That set my mind at rest.

'Thank you, Sire. May we go into details of the actual payment?'

I hate these ugly direct questions which seek to tie a man of honour down to vulgar financial undertakings.

'The minute you capture the Treasury in Kampala you may take whatever you need to defray expenses.'

Collapse of eager lieutenant-colonel.

But to return to the present day. I decided to confide in an old friend and comrade-in-arms from my Congo days. Tullio Moneta was now living in Johannesburg where he was well known as an actor in the film and television world. He specialised in manly roles which showed off his magnificent physique to perfection. He stood 6 feet 6 inches in his socks and weighed a solid 220 pounds stripped. He always reminded me of Yves Montand, but I remembered him best as an exceptional soldier and a great leader of men. In his last action in the Congo a large chunk of anti-personnel mine had hit him in the stomach but, severely wounded though he was, he still managed to drag one of his men out of the minefield. It took Tullio a year to recover.

I placed the whole position before him and sought his opinion on this one question: could we find fully trained men at very short notice to take part in a coup, *men who would agree to payment after the event*?

In the financial world this is the equivalent of getting a substantial loan from a banker without security. Tullio thought it might be possible but he doubted if it would interest more than thirty or forty men he knew. And of course the rate would have to be much higher than normal to compensate them for the risk of failure, when they would get nothing at all. I said I would make the suggestion in London. Prior to this I had been trying to raise the wind through my financial contacts throughout the world but with no success. Encouraged by Tullio's opinion that men could be found who would accept payment after a successful action I formulated a plan which could be put into operation for a mere US$300,000. It bore no resemblance whatsoever to the conventional attack which prudence had dictated was the correct military solution. Even so, in my opinion, it was sound enough. I wrote to Eddie accordingly:

> I regret that we shall be unable to raise the necessary finance through normal investment channels. Potential investors are thinking in terms of a return of between

300% and 500% for a venture as speculative as this, with repayment within 14 days of completion. Repayment by way of concession or participation in development schemes does not appeal to them either. So I am calling a halt to any further effort in this direction in favour of another plan for your consideration. It is feasible and acceptable to those taking part and may represent our sole remaining chance of success.

In this plan the *preliminary* expenses involved can be met in the sum of approx. 300,000 US $. The only item outstanding will be payment to the employees. They are agreeable, under certain circumstances, to being paid after the event providing the delay is not more than 10 to 14 days. The sum required will be higher than if a cash payment was made prior to the event. We are looking at something in the neighbourhood of one and a quarter million to cover wages alone, making the cost of the whole operation approx. one and a half million.

Under this plan there will be improvements in security and the time-frame can be as short as 30 to 45 days, subject to the situation being more or less the same as it was a few months ago, and subject to there being no foreign involvement in the area.

The suggestion was well received in London. A meeting was convened in Durban at which Gerard Hoarau presided. He was emerging fast as the new leader and had struck out on his own in the last few months believing that the London and Australian groups lacked the resolution and energy needed to get things moving. He informed us that he had made valuable contacts with the South African government through the National Intelligence Service in Pretoria. Later I discovered that it was he who had initiated the negotiations with X, which, unbeknown to me, were still in progress. He handled the meeting confidently and considered the seven-point paper which I laid before them and upon which my suggestion was conditional. The paper read:

The employees are prepared to accept payment after the successful conclusion of the operation subject to certain conditions:
1. Payment: 90% of the agreed amount to be paid within 14 days of the event in US $ transferred to a

Swiss bank account. 10% to be paid after 60 days, as above, subject to conditions regarding discreet behaviour etc. to be defined by employers.

2. Indemnity: a sum of 172,000 US $ to be set aside as a fund for indemnities against death or wounds received in action, or hospitalisation. The scale of payments to be fixed prior to the operation.

3. The new government must arrive in the theatre within one hour of the coup. They are to be accompanied by 1 Officer and 9 men of my Reserve.

4. The Government of Kenya must be prepared to recognise the new regime within 48 hours of the coup and to send 100 armed men to Mahé within that time.

5. That there are no other employees involved in the coup and that no negotiations are to be carried on with other employees, in particular X and TP.

6. That the employees will be returned to their point of embarkation within a stipulated time – say 14 days.

7. That the Principals involved in the financing of the operation should be made known to the Commander.

Comments followed. There would be no difficulty about raising the amount required to pay the men *after* the successful conclusion of the coup. This could be done in several ways: by obtaining loans to the new government from the banks in Mahé; by personal appeal to certain wealthy citizens who would be obliged to comply; and so on. It seemed a reasonable risk to take, but I warned them not to underestimate my men. I would not like it if they were obliged to pay themselves. I said it with a smile, but they got the message.

Yes, they agreed, the 10 per cent retention was a good idea. Mercenary soldiers were prone to brag after the event, they said, and this might prove damaging in the period immediately following the coup when the new government would prefer it to be known that the uprising was spontaneous and carried out by citizens oppressed beyond endurance, and so on. As my plan for the actual coup envisaged the use of several hundred of the local resistance movement this was substantially true. But in any case, said Gerard, the minute the news leaked out that a coup was in progress the main problem would be to stop the people dancing in the streets! Ninety-five per cent of the population were behind them and would flock to our support. There was wide agreement on this point. It was an expression I had occasion to remember.

They saw no problem about indemnities, which could be funded from the same source as the wages. If we were not successful, there would be no fund on which we could draw. This was a risk to be faced.

Much consideration was given to point 3, and now that we had almost arrived at the nitty-gritty of action I discerned a certain lowering of enthusiasm for actual physical participation. You know, a man can get killed! Gerard, however, was foremost in his resolve to be on the plane and undertook to give me the names of a representative government who would travel with him. He bridled at the implication that it was necessary for me to send an officer and nine men to make sure they boarded the plane and did not scarper when the chips were down. The point was not resolved entirely to my satisfaction. The years have taught me that there is a great gulf fixed between the board room and the coalface.

Yes, he could assure me the government of Kenya would be prepared to give instant recognition within the time mentioned but subject of course to it being evident that the new government were in *de facto* control. Yes, he had their assurance that they would send a hundred men within forty-eight hours of a request from the new government.

Points 5 and 6 were swept away. Point 7, probably the most important and intriguing item on the paper, was not dealt with at the meeting. Upon my insistence I was told the answer would be given to me later. When it finally came I was not surprised. It was the South African government acting through the National Intelligence Service.

Things now began to move fast. At the beginning of September, Eddie flew out to Durban. The group met at the Royal Hotel. Two hundred thousand dollars was available immediately and a further hundred thousand was promised in a month's time. Could we make a start? I said we could but the first thing must be a final reconnaissance of the island, and for this I would need Tullio Moneta and another friend whom I hoped would act as custodian of a safe house which I intended to establish in Victoria. The bulk of their talk centred on political appointments, which, whilst it was a nice example of positive thinking, did not really concern me; but I was sorry to see Gonzague D'Offay excluded from the list of those to be awarded portfolios. For some obscure reason he was deemed not to be acceptable.

As an ordinary soldier I have scant respect for all the nonsense which surrounds politics and politicians; the jockeying for position, and the grubbing around for privilege strike me as less than dignified. But the present situation in the Seychelles was positively Gilbertian. The entire population of the ninety-two islands does not amount to more than 62,000 souls all told, but nevertheless the politicians, acting, as they say, in the name of the people whom they represent, have seen fit to surround themselves with all the trappings of a vast nation, ministers of this and that, ambassadors in every major country, secretaries and under-secretaries coming out of every nook and cranny. Ridiculous. And apparently the new regime-to-be did not intend to alter this rewarding state of affairs. What reduced it all to the absurd was that this tiny nation had a vote at the United Nations no whit less than the mighty United States with its 240 million inhabitants.

I raised what I considered to be the fundamental issue. Was Jimmy Mancham prepared to go back as President or was he not? To me nothing else was as important. He was the only home-grown figure capable of doing the job; all the rest, with respect, were lightweights. But, more important, taking a global view, Mancham's unequivocal written undertaking that he was prepared to return as President would give the coup a basis of legality. He was, after all, still the constitutionally elected President. René was a usurper; that much was incontestable.

Happily Gerard was of the same mind and decided to fly to London expressly to get this matter cleared up once and for all. He would ask for a written commitment. A few days later he telephoned me to say he had obtained it unconditionally! The other big news was that he had been nominated Vice-President elect by the chief and was to be groomed for the Presidency over a period of six months. Frichot was informed and pledged his loyal support to Mancham. Work then began on the selection of the new administration. Frichot's name was mentioned as a probable ambassador to Australia.

Tullio and I set out for Mahé the day after a freak snowstorm hit Johannesburg. An unhappy omen. My original plans had been entirely on conventional lines and envisaged an assault landing by some 200 men from ships, probably trawlers, using Zodiac inflatables as a form of landing-craft, supported by a helicopter gunship and a simultaneous uprising of the resistance by way of diversion. An untrained enemy not in excess of 200 would be overwhelmed provided surprise and security were maintained. This plan had been successively emasculated through lack of funds. From an initial US$5 million it had been scaled down to four, to three, to two and finally to a derisive one-third. Now I was faced with planning something completely unconventional. But even in a minuscule operation two basic problems would still have to be solved: (1) how to get the arms to the island; and (2) how to get the men to the island.

The first problem was solved during our reconnaissance. A member of the resistance imported certain bulky goods in crates from South Africa. I visited his warehouse and inspected them *in situ*. He explained that it was exceptional for the Customs ever to open his merchandise. In any case, he had a working arrangement with them which involved. . . . He rubbed forefinger and thumb together suggestively. All the arms we needed could be imported in this way if packed unobtrusively and spread over a large number of crates. Our armament would be about a hundred automatic rifles with, say, ninety rounds per weapon. Grenades, rockets of the RPG7 type, mortars, and so on, would not be needed. This was to be a small show. In my mind I saw the coup as being rather like the Dahomey affair in 1967 where thirty soldiers overthrew the government. But at this stage I was planning a coup to be executed by about a hundred men assisted by three or four hundred men from the local resistance movement. After delivery at the warehouse the weapons would be unpacked in secrecy and removed *pole, pole,* to a safe house nearby to await the arrival of the men. On D-day, an hour or two before they were needed, they would be issued. Simple and workable.

Once the arms were on the island the second problem, the arrival of the men, would be relatively easy to solve. Small advance parties would arrive several days before the main groups. Their task would be to make a detailed study of the specific target – for example, the broadcasting station – which their group had been assigned in the plan for D-day. The men could then arrive in batches over a fairly short period posing as tourists. They would stay in hotels well separated from each other. That would be the broad outline of Phase 1. The entire force would be highly mobile, the open Mini-Moke being ideal for the transport of two or three men and their special baggage.

Tullio and I examined every facet of the plan for the actual coup. We met the head of the local resistance, who impressed us with his dedication to the cause. He was most unlike the normal Seychellois, the majority of whom are cast in a timid mould. This man was prepared to stand up and be counted. Indeed, he had already served a prison sentence for voicing his conviction too openly. He had courage and fortitude, and didn't give a damn for anybody. I wondered if there wasn't a bit of old Ireland in him somewhere. At any rate, he took Tullio under his wing and showed him the island whilst I returned swiftly on an Air India flight to Salisbury, Rhodesia, now

Harare, Zimbabwe. My object was to contact my old friend Jack Malloch and enlist his aid.

Jack was the head of an air transport company called Affretair. It was a sizeable concern but, as Jack explained, already coming under pressure from the new government, who wished to nationalise it. Amongst other things, I wanted Jack to provide an aircraft to fly in the new government on D-day, probably from Nairobi. Jack suggested Libreville. We quickly came to terms but regrettably they proved moribund, the Zimbabwe government taking over the company a few weeks later. But Jack introduced me to a man who put me in touch with the local arms market and told me where a number of ex-SAS men did their drinking. I was not idle.

In matters of aviation there was no man like Jack Malloch. Over the years I had seen him in action in various parts of Africa, and Europe, too. We talked of the days when he ran 'freight' into Biafra out of Lisbon at $10,000 a throw. Jack was the most fearless aviator I had ever met. His record was scintillating and began when he was a Spitfire pilot during the Second World War in the same squadron of Rhodesians as 'Smithy' (Prime Minister Ian Smith of Rhodesia until it became Zimbabwe). I reminded him of the time he was transporting a highly unstable cargo of arms and ammunition, mortar bombs, rockets, that type of thing, in a DC7b into Port Harcourt during Biafra's war of secession in 1967. I had been summoned to meet General Ojukwu in Aba, his headquarters at that time, and Jack was to fly me in from Lisbon.

The first take-off had to be aborted. The load was too great or the fans not strong enough, I forget which. The second was successful, but after flying out into the Atlantic for some hours the engineer judged it prudent to return to land. The oil-pressure gauge was on the blink or the sump plug had dropped out, he said with a fiendish delight, damn him. By this time my nerves were more than a little jagged. I hate air travel. I was disappointed when they did away with that aircraft (I think it was called the Moore Brabazon) which had six engines on either side; but I had this ridiculous manly image to maintain so I put a brave face on it.

Our third time was lucky. We took an illegal route across potentially hostile countries, expecting fighter planes to come screaming out of nowhere to force us down into the desert. But we arrived at Guinea-Bissau without incident and later at San Tomé, a dinky little airport just long enough to get into with a shoehorn. Jack was in the left-hand seat for the final approach to Port Harcourt at a little before three in the morning. We were all on edge as he waited to pick up the beacon which was to be switched on for exactly thirty seconds at 0300 hours Zulu, on the dot. I stood in the cockpit behind Jack's seat; none of that fasten-your-seatbelts nonsense on this trip. He found the beacon and put her nose down. A few miles onwards a sudden flare-path erupted into flame. We were dead on course, thank heaven for that. I felt good to be alive as we began to lose height rapidly. Good, that is, until the awful truth dawned on me. Not for nothing have I soldiered with African troops.

'Hell, Jack,' I said, 'you know what's going to happen, don't you? The minute we touch down our own troops will open up on us. It's the normal drill.' I mumbled on incoherently, my spine rigid with fear as the parched brown earth rushed up to greet us. The moment the wheels touched firing broke out along the length of the runway, exactly as predicted. Bullets crashed through the fuselage and only by the grace of God failed to ignite the explosives we were carrying. We juddered to a halt. We were safe.

'Well done, Jack,' I said thankfully, wiping the sweat from my brow.

'Bastards,' he said, 'they do it every time!'

I only saw Jack once more after this visit. The last time was when I returned a few weeks later to talk arms and aircraft. Some months later, during my trial, I received the awful news that Jack was missing. He had been flying his Spitfire aircraft, the love of his life, which he had restored to its original glory, and was last seen entering a bank of cloud. A day later they found the wreck. It was never established exactly what happened, but a great man and an outstanding pilot were gone for ever. God rest you, Jack, old friend, wherever you are.

Back in Natal I decided to place a ninety-day time-frame on the operation: end of November/beginning of December was what I had in mind. I instructed Tullio to go ahead with some very careful recruiting for key men only; it would be an error to recruit too early and have the men hanging around creating a security risk. Tullio contacted some men he knew in Pretoria who were members of a Citizen Force unit called the Recce Commando. Their first reactions were enthusiastic but they needed prior approval from SADF headquarters before they went any further.

I considered a short-list of other probable soldiers. The market for potential mercenary soldiers has grown enormously in recent years. This is due in part to the Vietnam war, and other local disturbances, which produced a surplus of trained men. Paradoxically, the absence of any large conflict in recent years has also contributed in its way and, as we are seeing in Central America today, there are men who will fight for a cause, financial reward not being their paramount motivation. I maintain a register of this potential and recently have found it necessary to computerise it.

I rang up my old friend Peter Duffy. Duffy had been with me in the Congo as an officer and I could think of nobody more suitable for this little junket than him. Furthermore, we were personal friends of long standing and he would never have forgiven me if I had left him out. To my astonishment he turned it down flat. He was doing very well as a freelance photographer in Durban, he explained, had just won a prestigious award for his press work, and had recently inherited some money in his native Scotland. A short-term contract would only prove unsettling. I saw his point but was naturally disappointed. After all, a man who has crossed Siberia, spent two years in Japan qualifying as a black-belt judo instructor, farmed in east Africa, worked as a film stunt man, and was a physical fitness fiend to boot, ought not to be thinking about mundane things like a settled existence. It's getting so you can't rely on anybody, I thought to myself. 'When are you going on pension?' I asked him, riled. But he ignored the barbed jest. I presumed there was a girl in the equation somewhere. The handsome and athletic Duffy had a well-thumbed little black book, the envy of all the young bucks in town, so I forgave him this traitorous behaviour, wished him well and told him not to forget to invite me to the wedding. His reply was unprintable.

I then contacted another Congo hand, Barney Carey. Barney had been working in London in the hotel business as an innkeeper. His genial manner, ready smile and 'mine host' manner told one nothing of his adventurous spirit and his lust for life. At weekends he jumped out of aeroplanes to stop the blood from congealing, he said. Was he available? Like a shot he reported to the Old Vicarage. He knew that a number of ex-Rhodesian soldiers frequented a bar in Durban at the Riviera Hotel, so I asked him to test the water there as far as recruits were concerned. In a day or two Barney reported that he had met a small number of ex-SAS types who had seen a lot of action in bush warfare, and these would welcome an offer. Most of these chaps were in financial straits, having left Zimbabwe with nothing but a hearty handshake. As the labour market was very dull in South Africa at this time they were finding it hard to get a job. After a bit more research Barney reckoned the pool of would-be recruits was four or five times greater than our need.

I began to think in terms of US$11,000 per man as being reasonable remuneration, having regard to the high risk involved. More, perhaps, for those with greater responsibility. On engagement I would give them an advance of US$1000. This was meant to tide them and their dependants over the two or three weeks in which they would be away from home. On successful completion of the coup they would get the balance due, that would be US$9000 with a further thousand after sixty days subject to good behaviour. If for some reason the coup was not carried out, they would keep the advance, but if – perish the thought – the attempt proved unsuccessful they would only get the original advance. I designed a contract which I would require every man to sign to give effect to this agreement. In addition he would state his personal data and military record. But at this stage the whole thing was exploratory. Nobody was to be signed up and everything was to be discussed under a pledge of secrecy. In the mercenary world this is pie in the sky. I realised that once we had enlisted a single man we would have to move swiftly to the actual operation. In the event nobody was recruited prior to 8 November. My plan at this stage envisaged the immediate transfer of every man recruited to a remote private training camp near a place called Naboomspruit in the Transvaal, owned by a friend of mine. There he would be free from the dangerous attentions of his friends and the press.

Meanwhile, despite promises made, the money for the operation had not appeared. I was in no doubt that it would, eventually, so I decided to liquidate my own private portfolio of investments in order to finance necessary expenditure in the interim. Regrettably the Johannesburg stock market was depressed at that moment so that the sale resulted in a hideous loss. The villain gold was down in the basement where nobody loved it, and when gold is down in South Africa nobody smiles. Some don't even eat. However, after I had explained the necessity for this action to Eddie he assured me that when a reckoning was made my loss would not be forgotten. As it amounted to some US$14,000 I was comforted.

A small truckload of arms arrived at my house without incident from a Rhodesian source. This had been arranged on my last visit to Jack. My next task was to organise the delivery of these arms to the island. For this I had to raise a company which would be seen to deal, on an agency basis, in the type of goods which my Mahé contact imported. He had already provided me with a specimen *pro forma* invoice. Being a chartered accountant myself, this side of things gave me no problem. I then ordered the goods, which totalled an astronomical figure in rand and looked as though they would involve fifty or sixty packing-cases, which was precisely what was required. The shipping agents told me my consignment must be at their warehouse in Point Road, Durban, by 10 October for shipment in SS *Range*, which would leave five or six days later and arrive in Mahé around the end of October. That sounded just about right.

I engaged a discreet carpenter friend to construct the crates for export. We packed them all to hold the goods as per the bill of lading and concealed the arms and ammunition within them. Short of tearing the crate apart there was no way the arms could have been detected. So far so good, but time was flying and my next delivery from the same source would have arrived too late for this consignment in SS *Range*. I decided to confide in Gerard and explained the dilemma. He had the answer. During the last few weeks he had developed his connection with the NIS and now volunteered to ask them for help in procuring the balance of what we needed. I restricted my list to seventy-five more rifles (AK or FN, I was not fussy), with a hundred rounds of 7.62 ammunition per rifle. In addition I asked for fifteen walkie-talkie radio communication sets. He flew off to Pretoria to see what he could do. I wished him luck but I really did not expect we would have any luck with our request. But on 25 September he rang me to say that a high-level conference of NIS officials was being held in Durban that weekend and that he and I were invited to meet with some of them at eight o'clock on the Saturday morning at the Elangeni Hotel.

The meeting was headed by an official named Rothman. He went into the plans for the coup minutely and questioned me on various items. My indent was then discussed, after which Rothman took it to an adjoining room – presumably for someone's approval. He returned and announced with obvious pleasure that as far as his department was concerned they saw no problems. The next step must be to submit their recommendation to the National Security Council of the Cabinet, which met on Tuesdays in Cape Town. We would be informed of their decision on Wednesday. And that, I thought, will be the last we shall hear about it; whilst they, the NIS, will be possessed of all our plans. An old dodge in the intelligence business. But this time I was wrong.

On the following Wednesday morning a strange voice announced that he was ringing from Pretoria in connection with the Elangeni meeting and his name was J. Y. Claasens, Jimmy to his friends. He had some vital information for me. Could I fly to Pretoria at once? I said I could be at Jan Smuts Airport at 1300 hours that day. He said he would meet me.

A summons to Pretoria has a special significance in the South African context. Pretoria is the real seat of government, the place where decisions are made. Cape Town is the legislative capital right enough, but Pretoria is the hub of the political scene and the heart of the Afrikaner élite who run the country. It is also a well-planned city with many magnificent buildings, some of them designed by Sir Herbert Baker in the style of Sir Edwin Lutyens. And, if that fails to tempt you, may I say it is also the home of some of the most beautiful girls in the world.

Mr Claasens turned out to be the second-in-command of the National Intelligence Service, second only to Professor Neil Barnard, the academic who had succeeded the courteous Mr Alex van Wyk. He was a man in his early sixties, heavily built, greying hair, loquacious and personable. He had an infectious enthusiasm for this project, his country and Afrikanerdom. We made our way in silence to the basement carpark. Jimmy drove his official car, a three-litre Ford Cortina, to the outskirts of Pretoria where we pulled up at a small roadhouse café for something to eat. At a carefully selected and isolated table he delivered his bombshell, conscious of its impact. The Cabinet had examined the recommendation and had approved it! His exact words were: 'The Cabinet has given it the OK and the Prime Minister himself is right behind it!'

That was too much for me. Surely not the Prime Minister. . . .

'You mean . . .', I prompted, 'in principle?'

'No, no, no! Not only in principle. He is right behind the whole project. All the way.'

It was still too much for me to accept. Things like this only happen in novels.

'You mean they will give us everything we have asked for?'

'Yes, everything.'

'And the cost?'

'I'm not sure, but it's probable you will get it all for nothing.'

Lady Luck was smiling after all.

Our next stop was at the Burgers Park Hotel, near the centre of Pretoria. In the lounge we continued our discussion, although Jimmy was watching the time closely. We talked about the impending operation, its importance to South Africa, the Seychellois personalities involved, and the security aspect. He took out a box of matches, extracted two and laid them side by side on the table in front of us.

'That's you and me,' he said. 'When I tell you a secret how many people know about it?'

'Two.'

'No. Eleven!'

He placed a third match next to the other two.

'Now how many?' he asked.

'Three,' I said obediently.

'Wrong again! One hundred and eleven.'

He knew his Africa, too, and instructed me for fifteen minutes on the political situation in the Republic and southern Africa generally. I could have listened to him for hours, but suddenly he glanced at his watch and excused himself to make a phone call. On his return his face was less jovial. Something had gone wrong. 'Damned annoying,' he said, 'but we have just had a directive from Cape Town. By order of the Prime Minister we (meaning NIS) have got to back out of this and hand everything over to the Defence Force.' He muttered something to himself in Afrikaans.

We drove back to an airport hotel where I was to spend the night. Plainly this latest instruction was a disappointment to him. I had the feeling that he had been nursing the whole Seychelles project as his baby and that he and Gerard had been in collusion for some months. The order to hand it over to the Army came hard. But there was more to it than that. It was common knowledge in these circles that the Defence Force and the State Security department were deadly enemies, had been for years. It was one of the wounds which it was hoped Prime Minister P. W. Botha, himself an 'army' man and previously Minister of Defence, would heal. The order was, in effect, a sort of capitulation.

'Tomorrow at ten o'clock I have to introduce you to the people in the Defence Force who will handle the whole affair from now on,' he said resignedly. 'I'll send a car for you at 9.30.'

The next day Jimmy drove me to Zansa Building in Proes Street, Pretoria, which was the headquarters of that department of the Defence Force which dealt with clandestine operations. We took the lift to the tenth floor. Security was annoyingly severe, and it took some time before we were shown into a waiting-room and then into an office where Jimmy introduced me to Brigadier Danie Hamman and Brigadier Martin Knoetze. Knoetze was in fact the 'sergeant' who had deputised for Hamman at the railway station the year before. It never pays to judge a book by its cover, does it?

Jimmy explained his mission. Certain arms, ammunition and equipment were to be made available to me at once by order of the Cabinet.

The two brigadiers needed more than a minute to absorb the meaning of this amazing order. Hamman, I discovered later, apart from being a fine soldier, was also a polished diplomat and had served one tour of duty as military attaché in the South African embassy in London. Knoetze was more the homespun whiz-kid who had gone far in a very short space of time. What he lacked in suavity he made up for in directness of approach.

'Wait a minute, wait a minute!' he said. 'We can't go issuing arms and ammunition to any old Tom, Dick or Harry just on your say so.

We must have an authority. We've got to have something in writing. Have you got a letter of instruction?'

Perfectly reasonable, I thought, even if voiced a bit tersely. But Jimmy was in no mood to be crossed by a junior officer.

'Nobody's asking you to trust me, for Pete's sake. Ring Cape Town now, go on, and speak to the Secretary to the Cabinet. She'll give you the number of the minute in which this instruction was authorised.' He rushed on in Afrikaans, which I did not understand. Jimmy was damned annoyed.

After a few minutes' discussion I was asked to wait in an adjoining room whilst they made certain enquiries. When I was asked to come in again everything had apparently been explained to their satisfaction, and Jimmy bowed out. I never saw him again, although he kept in contact with me over the telephone from time to time.

Brigadier Hamman, who was the senior of the two, began to interrogate me as to my general plan, which I outlined. I explained my urgent need for certain arms, ammunition and hand-held radios. I wanted them delivered to me not later than 7 October as I had a consignment of goods leaving Durban in SS *Range* on 15 October, and I needed time to crate them, and so on. He said this could be done.

We discussed the types of arms available and I selected the para-type AK47 with four magazines per weapon. I asked for a number of thunderflashes – dummy grenade-type explosives usually used in training and in no way lethal, merely noisy – but these they could not supply. There would be no problem over the walkie-talkies; they would buy them for me. The cost? Not a cent. The arms were not new, they said, most of them were ex-enemy and had been captured in Angola. Everything was arranged in a most efficient manner, but they asked me to stay over that night just in case there were any snags.

The following day I was asked to go further into the details of the operation. I told them it involved a hundred men, and a small reserve; that the arms were to be shipped to Mahé and then trans-ferred to a safe house; that the men would arrive in small groups as tourists and stay in hotels all over the island; that each group would have a specific target; and that on D-day we would be assisted by about three hundred men of the local resistance. I did not go too deeply into my actual plan for D-day, which was no concern of theirs. Asked about the security aspect of recruiting a hundred mercenary soldiers, I said it was absolutely essential to the plan that on recruitment the men should be whisked away to a remote training camp. There they would be out of touch with the rest of the world, the press in particular, and they would be able to get to know each other, and me, and to rehearse to a certain extent the actual operation. Had I such a place in mind? I said I had a friend who owned a private game ranch in the Naboomspruit area which might do. Knoetze said he thought we could have a Defence Force training camp in the north-western Transvaal for this purpose. I agreed that would be better.

The two brigadiers visited me at my hotel later on, and this time they were accompanied by their senior officer, whom I took to be General Westhuizen, although we were not introduced formally. The visit could be termed a social one, and nothing of importance was discussed. I then returned home to await events.

The first event was a visit from the NIS man Dolinchek, who was now very keen to get himself into the act. He offered his services as a security man, suggesting he could report secretly to me on the behaviour of my men on the island prior to the coup. There was something distasteful to me about that, although I have no doubt it was a reasonable suggestion, and I brushed it off. But he persevered in his desire to take part in the affair, so that I assumed he was under orders from his headquarters. Some unofficial representation in the operation could very well be in their interests. He wanted to come ex-officio, he said, and would get special extended leave for as long as it took. I said I would consider it.

In his enthusiasm he jumped the gun and began to interfere on his own account. He made the cardinal error of ringing up Tullio in Johannesburg late one night pretending he was calling from New York, complete with phony Yankee accent. His object was to warn Tullio, authoritatively, about the dangers of recruiting an American whom Tullio was interviewing as a possible recruit. This made Tullio angry and then alarmed at the ham-fisted antics of the amateur sleuth. 'James Bond *manqué*,' Tullio nicknamed him and threatened to pulverise him if he annoyed him again. But it didn't stop him. Gaffe succeeded gaffe. There was something reminiscent of Peter Sellers's famous Inspector Clouseau about Dolinchek, but I must say in all fairness that he had his uses. One of them arose almost immediately.

A warning telephone call advised me that a delivery was about to be made to my house at eight o'clock one morning. The deliverer was speaking from Howick, a village about ten miles from my home. Was the coast clear? I made sure it was, gave the servants jobs elsewhere, and waited. An hour later a five-ton truck drove into my mist-shrouded drive and then across my lawn leaving deep indentations in the grass. Sergeant-Major van der Merwe and a co-driver had driven all through the night and now began to offload their potent cargo into my wine-cellar, a spacious vault under the back of my house. The SADF were certainly efficient. I gave a hand with the offloading while my wife prepared a substantial breakfast for the two hungry men.

The delivery was far in excess of what I had requested and included hand grenades, RPG7 rocket-launchers, rockets, AK47s, and crated 7.62 ammunition sufficient to sustain a small revolution. Whilst I was very grateful for the prompt delivery of this vast quantity of arms, I was embarrassed by its richness. I estimated there must be about a million rands' worth of stuff in my cellar, excluding the radio equipment. I wondered what the old vicar who lived in this house until just after the war would have thought about it! And just as I was musing thus I heard my dog barking at somebody who must have entered the open gates and was now fast approaching the cellar where we were as busy as old-time Cornish smugglers burying their loot. It was an old lady and her grandson. 'Ah, my dear Vicar,' said she, 'I've come about the confirmation of little Harry. . . .' I led her politely in the direction of the New Vicarage. I mention it only as an example of how the best-laid plots of mice and men can gang the way Robbie Burns said they could. And it also gives me a chance to tell you that despite my fierce reputation – totally unwarranted, may I say – members of the rude public often mistake me for the Vicar. What the moral of the story is, if any, I am not sure.

Whilst the sergeant-major and his co-driver were having breakfast I wrote out a detailed copy of my operational plan and handed it to them for personal delivery to Brigadier Hamman, who had requested it. The plan, in essence, was the one already described, but gave details of two alternative plans which I would substitute if for any reason the first plan had to be aborted. The second plan envisaged the purchase of an ocean-going yacht into whose false bilges the arms and ammunition would be stowed. The third plan spoke of a way of getting the arms to the island *with the men* but gave no specific details. In turn the sergeant-major handed me a signed copy of an official SADF delivery-note itemising the weapons, etc., just delivered. Whilst this may be common commercial practice as proof of delivery, it cannot be recommended where clandestine operations are concerned. I placed the delivery-note carefully in my safe, never guessing the destiny which awaited it.

Before crating the new delivery of arms it was essential to test them. One never knows with captured enemy weapons, even though they look serviceable on casual inspection. And this is where I made use of Dolinchek. The testing of a large number of arms presents an abnormal problem to a layman, one that is by no means easy to solve. Secrecy and all the facilities of a rifle range are prerequisites. Dolinchek was able to solve the problems and arranged for the rifles to be tested on a sugar farm belonging to Natal Sugar Estates to the north of Durban. He must have told some lies in arranging this because I heard subsequently that the management of that very correct corporation were justifiably furious when the news leaked out that they had inadvertently aided and abetted, albeit unknowingly, an illegal operation. Once the arms were proven to be in perfect order I stripped them down and began the laborious process of secreting them, surrounded by the other items for export, deep in their crates.

It was then that the first bombshell exploded. Brigadier Hamman telephoned me urgently two days before the consignment was due for delivery to the agents.

'Have they gone yet?' he asked.

'No, not yet. They go down to Durban tomorrow. Why?'

'Don't send them. We have just received some highly reliable information from an immaculate source in Mahé warning us that the consignee is under suspicion and everything he imports from now on will be examined in detail. Sorry, but we advise you to abandon that part of your plan forthwith.'

I mulled over that bit of bad news for a few hours before making any decision to cancel the arrangements I had made for delivery. My experience in the past has been that official intelligence agencies very often draw wrong conclusions, or distort their information, or deliberately give one a bum steer for reasons which suit their own book best. Even in the most prestigious organisations, in concerns which you would swear were wholly above suspicion, even in government departments, there are enemy agents quietly and unobtrusively working away to frustrate plans of an anti-communist nature. It is naïve to suppose otherwise. But this advice placed me in a hell of a predicament. Time was flying, a large sum of money had been spent already on furnishing the goods for export, not to mention the crates, and it would mean abandoning all that and starting from scratch on a new plan.

I decided to ignore the warning and take a chance. The worst case would be that the consignment was searched on arrival and the weapons found. Would that incriminate the consignee? Prima facie, yes, one supposed, but he could plead total ignorance of any intent to import arms, couldn't he? What could they prove? The worst that could happen was that we would lose the entire shipment and the money spent on it. On the other hand, if I aborted the shipment, I could return the goods and I might get the money back. Or would they give me a credit note? As mine was a brand-new company with no trading record I imagined the best I would get would be a credit note. These wretched alternatives had to be considered.

But what finally made up my mind was a totally unexpected call from a friend of mine in another intelligence service, part of a foreign embassy in Pretoria. I had previously contacted him for assistance, financial and political, in this venture, but his country had deemed the affair too small to meddle with. He had described the sum of money requested by me as 'chicken feed', God bless him. Although they were definitely not interested on an official level, they wished me well privately. Now he was ringing to say that their agent in Mahé had passed some vital information to them that morning. This turned out to be substantially the same as the news Brigadier Hamman had given me earlier. I wondered if there had been any collusion between the two but decided it was improbable. The possibility of a plant also existed. But this definitely put a different complexion on things. To fly in the face of one warning might be forgivable, but to disregard two must be considered undeniably imprudent.

Reluctantly, and with serious misgivings, I abandoned the shipment. The unpacking was a tedious process, long, laborious and costly. The suppliers – fortunately for me a very large Durban house – eased my discomfiture and took pity on what they deemed to be an error on the part of a beginner in the business. They took everything back and charged me a handling fee. I was grateful to them for this consideration but I was now back again at square one.

The second bombshell arrived the next day. The training camp which Brigadier Knoetze thought could be allotted to me was no longer available. Somebody had had second thoughts. Any possibility of my getting to know the men taking part in the operation vanished with that decision. Soldiers will know that it is extremely hazardous to go into action with people one does not know intimately. It is a well-accepted principle in warfare that leaders must know their men, men must know their leaders, and men must know each other long before the trauma of battle begins. Absolute rapport is essential. It is the lack of this vital ingredient which makes polyglot forces, such as the United Nations peacekeeping force in the Congo in 1960–4, for example, inefficient, unworkable and impossible to unify. In the present instance it was to prove the major cause of disaster. When the chips were down and a decision had to be made as to whether we would fight or not, the total lack of cohesive thought or close understanding of one another proved fatal.

There seemed to be no alternative; I must press on with the second plan. But, first, I must organise the safe house in Victoria which would be needed whatever plan I used. I offered the job to my brother-in-law, Bob Sims, and gave him twenty-four hours to consider it. Bob, who had been a jockey in his youth, was at that time working with Brian Cherry, one of South Africa's foremost racehorse-trainers at Shongweni near Durban. Brian agreed to let Bob go at short notice. Fortunately, Bob was a small-arms buff and a fanatic on all weapons. He had a small armoury of his own and a workshop in which he could do adjustments, altering the pull on triggers, adjusting sights, fitting new stocks, that sort of thing. This love of weapons, a strange phenomenon in many men, was to prove his undoing. He answered the next day that he was game for the adventure and would like to take his fiancée with him. A day or two later he set out for Mahé armed with introductions to people who might be willing to rent him a house for a period of six months. This proved to be no problem and he soon established the safe house and began to live the life of a normal tourist until such time as the arms would begin to arrive in dribs and drabs.

The fact that I could trust Bob implicitly led me to carry out an experiment which was to have far-reaching consequences. Bob was just the man to test out a plan which I had been considering for some time. He had the guts and indomitable spirit it would take; years of sailing with him in *Colin Archer* as my crew off the difficult Natal coast had shown me what he was worth in a tight spot. If I was able to strip down an AK47 and pack it in a bed of polystyrene not more than two inches thick, could it be made to look like the base of a piece of hand luggage? I made a prototype. Without the butt, which in any case was of the folding para type, it fitted perfectly. But then there was also the question of weight. I looked at the relative weights of various weapons. I append these for those who may be interested:

Romanian AK47	8.5 lb
Bulgarian AK47	8.25 lb
Heckler & Kock, HK54, a first-rate West German submachine-gun	5.5 lb
Schmeisser, MP40, 9mm, German, one of the finest Second World War weapons	8.87 lb
UZI, Israeli, the prince of all submachine-guns	8.9 lb
One AK47 magazine, empty	12 oz

| One AK47 magazine with 30 rounds | 29 oz |
| Carton of 20 rounds | 12 oz |

After a lot of thought I reckoned the AK47 was probably the best in the circumstances. My decision turned largely on the availability of ammunition. If it came to a shoot-out and we had to capture enemy ammunition, I knew they had plenty of it! So that clinched it for me.

I showed Bob the prototype and gauged his reaction to taking it through Customs at Mahé. He was impressed with the appearance of the hold-all grip; it was not too heavy, had plenty of room for clothing above the false bottom, and he was confident he could carry it through Customs with no let or hindrance as required on his passport, he said with a grin. I suppose tearing around racetracks at thirty miles an hour perched precariously in the saddle fits you for life's little gambles like this. Anyway, off he went with one of these babies secreted in the bottom of each of his two cases and arrived safely.

As soon as he had set up the safe house he unpacked the weapons, and others which I now sent by other willing carriers, assembled them with care and secreted them in a vault below the house safe from prying eyes. In the meanwhile he enjoyed the life of a tourist. Nobody bothered him.

The second plan called for the purchase of an ocean-going yacht. I began my search immediately. I had owned a 36-foot yacht here in Durban harbour for some ten years, so the scene was not new to me. I was looking for a vessel not less than 45 feet on the waterline. That would be the minimum if she was to carry my cargo in her bilges, but primarily she would have to be seaworthy without a lot of preparation. I could afford about R80,000 for such a ship. Then there would be the cost of delivery. This would entail hiring a competent skipper for the 2600-mile voyage plus a crew of four, victualling the yacht for thirty days, and paying return air fares from Mahé to Durban, and incidentals. It began to look as though it would be out of my reach. I inspected a few yachts in the yacht basin and found one which seemed ideal. It was a ketch with a concrete hull, had a good seagoing record, and the bilges were spacious and just right for my purpose. The asking price was R120,000, but I imagined that could be whittled down. The owner was a rich and well-known businessman and a sportsman to boot. But before making an offer I had to see what the skipper and crew would ask for their services, always supposing I could find chaps game enough for this affair.

The voyage from Durban through the Mozambique Channel to the Seychelles is in normal times a fairly easy one, but the voyage must be timed to take advantage of the south-east monsoon so that it will blow conveniently on the starboard quarter. But at certain times of the year the whole area is subject to the Indian Ocean cyclonic system, which can spell disaster. The cyclone season has been known to begin as early as November, so the crew I needed would have to be experienced sailors as well as agreeable to a spot of gun-running. In fairness I would tell them exactly what they were doing to earn their money; it was not just another yacht delivery.

Finding the right man for this job proved impossible in the short time I had allowed myself. The most likely yacht skipper, and the one who had experience in these waters at this time of the year, asked a fee of R50,000 for himself alone. Regretfully I had to abandon my second plan solely on the grounds of expense.

But I was not going to give up too easily. I made one last effort in Pretoria and visited my special friends, the ones who had thought the whole show was too small for them. They did their best for me but could not help financially. As my friend and I parted he wished me well, told me not to take things too easily – 'It's not a game you are playing, you know' – and ended with a sinister warning: 'Watch out, Mike! Make quite sure you are not being set up!' I pondered that deeply on my way back to Hilton, but I could not see that I was in any danger or that anyone would want to sabotage the effort, or me. Looking back on it now, I am not so sure. The world of international politics is weird, devious and despicable. Was somebody interested in stopping the coup? Certainly, America had an investment of over $14 billion in its tracking station on Mahé, but how could that fact militate against us? I dismissed it from my mind.

It was now the beginning of November, and the news from the island spoke of possible reinforcements of Cubans and Koreans in the near future. Something would have to be done very soon or the opportunity would be gone for ever. I discussed the dilemma with Gerard. I showed him my dummy luggage, told him I had already passed a number of weapons through to the island in this way, and explained that while this was satisfactory it was proving too expensive and time-consuming to be continued indefinitely. Some other means must be found to get the balance of the arms to the island. Could he help?

Once more Gerard said he would consult with his friends in the NIS. We had the arms; all we needed was the means of transporting them to the island. But in addition a further unforeseen problem vexed us. There was only one flight a week to Mahé from Johannes-

57

burg and it would be too risky to put more than eight or nine men on each flight. This meant that men who went on the early flights might have to stay in Mahé for as long as seven or eight weeks before the last group arrived. Apart from the security aspect this would involve further hotel bills, and so on.

It began to look as though we would have to abandon the project until we could raise sufficient funds to do the job properly. I thought wistfully in those days of my original US$5 million budget! The fact is, as I have always known, and was discovering again now the hard way, war, insurrection, attempted coups – call them what you will – cannot be carried out on the cheap. The unexpected beats you. It is horrifyingly expensive, and when things go wrong, as they must when you have pared the budget to an absurd degree, your principals will not remember that you were trying to do your best to make the plan feasible on the money available. They will only remember that you failed. Loyalty you must not expect of them. *Elle n'existe pas.* That is life.

On the other hand, one should be warned by the inability of one's principals to raise the funds necessary for the project. Perhaps this is a sure indication that their cause is not as popular as they may imagine it is.

CHAPTER 4

The Final Plans

AT THIS PRECISE MOMENT Gerard's contacts with NIS proved fruitful. They had a plan, he said, which would enable us to solve our fundamental problem: the delivery of the arms and the men to the island. From this moment onwards the guiding hand behind the final plans was that of the NIS; Gerard was the conduit, I turned the tap. For me this was a great relief.

Their first directive put me in touch with the owner of a travel agency in Johannesburg with whom they had often worked in the past. When I met this gentleman in his Johannesburg offices he laid before me a complete plan, all cut and dried, for getting the men to the island in one group. It was simplicity itself: a charter flight for fifty men flying out of Manzini Airport, Swaziland. Somebody had obviously given the idea a lot of thought. The men, according to this plan, were to be members of a club. The club was to be called 'The Chauvinist Pigs'. Each man would wear a tie with a distinctive motif. He would provide these. There would be no problems getting the men to Swaziland. He would organise a bus. Formalities at the border would be taken care of. And getting our special baggage through Customs on both sides of the border? Not to worry, every-thing would be arranged.

But fifty men? That would reduce my force to an effective sixty, including the advance party. Well, that wasn't so bad. Hadn't twenty-five brave Frenchmen seized the whole of the French Cameroons in 1942? Yes, fifty would be enough, always supposing we had the element of surprise. And if there had been a leak we could abort the coup before it started.

59

But could I do it in time? In the remaining three weeks before take-off I would need to recruit the men, send off the advance parties, prepare sixty or more pieces of special luggage, arrange transport for the men to an assembly-point, and hold briefing sessions in Durban and Johannesburg. I decided it could be done.

But I baulked at Chauvinist Pigs. True, the name was meant to convey the idea of a group of hearty beer-drinkers out on a spree, but it rang hollow. I came up with a counter-suggestion. How about 'Ye Ancient Order of Frothblowers'? In my youth in England the AOFB were a famous order and frequently the butt of music-hall jokes. I rang my sister in London and asked her to research their background. She sent me the following from the *Daily Telegraph* of 19 November 1979:

> With the death of Albert Powell, for many years the Keith Prowse manager at the Carlton Hotel, Haymarket, there can be few surviving members of Ye Ancient Order of Frothblowers, who flourished briefly between the wars to help deprived children.
>
> The charity was founded in 1924 by Herbert Temple, after his friend, the eminent surgeon Sir Alfred Fripp, refused a fee for an operation. Temple thought the old 'Tiny Tim' style of appeal for waifs and strays was 'threadbare', so he arranged for members to buy for five shillings a pair of cufflinks which had cost him 2s 8d and gave the balance to the fund.
>
> With fine recruiters like Powell, the worldwide membership reached 700,000 and raised 100,000 pounds, despite carping from critics who, said Fripp, 'resent conviviality in any shape or form'.
>
> A member who recruited 2,000 others became known as a 'Cloudburst', while the penalty for not wearing the cufflinks at official functions was a contribution to the 'hostbox'. Women members were admitted – they had to wear a brooch or scarfpin – but were not allowed to use the name of Frothblower. The alternative, 'Fairy Belle', may help to explain why the order was wound up in 1931.

When I heard later that the original AOFB was also staunchly anti-communist I was delighted. It seemed the right name for us, and I liked the idea of providing toys for the children of Victoria. So that we could be seen to be members of a club I ordered a sterling-silver lapel-badge for each man, a bit of uncharacteristic extravagance, and had large stickers made which showed a foaming tankard of beer overprinted with the letters AOFB. These would be attached to our luggage. On delivery I was disappointed to see that the letters were carelessly printed and off centre, but by then I had more serious things to worry about.

The leader of the Mouvement pour la Résistance on the island now paid a visit to South Africa. He informed us about the state of airport security at Mahé, and the efficiency of their Customs officials. Formalities at this moment were noticeably lax, he said. British Airways, who had a vested interest in tourism to the island, had just held training sessions for airport staff, teaching them how to be pleasant to visitors, how to avoid causes of friction, and so on. If he was given sufficient notice, he could make sure that his own men, many of whom were Customs staff, would be on duty. I became more confident about the idea of taking the weapons with us in dummy luggage. It looked like a reasonable risk. There had been no problems with the people whom I had sent already, which was encouraging, and with some inside help it looked as though we could work out a plan for sending the arms over at the same time as the men.

Recruitment now began in earnest. Tullio had gathered a group of about twenty men, nearly all Afrikaners, to meet me at his house in Bryanston. They were led by Pete Doorewaard, a man in his late twenties, for whom they had a marked respect. Doorewaard was a very correct leader, and wanted everything done formally. Once he knew what was afoot he said he would have to have permission from Defence Force headquarters before his men could take part in this operation. They would also require leave of absence from the country, but he did not anticipate any problems. I liked the way his group responded to his firm leadership.

Before our next meeting at Tullio's house Brigadier Hamman asked me to visit him. It was essential, he said, that the force I was raising should not be predominantly South African. I must try to confine the number of South African nationals to no more than fifteen. If this caused problems, would I consider recruiting in Europe? If so, he might be able to assist financially, perhaps with as much as R30,000. I turned down the offer – it was far too late in the day for that – but I refused it with considerable heart-searching. Wasn't this exactly what I had advocated right from the start, a force to be raised in Europe, free from any obvious association with South Africa?

At the second meeting in Bryanston we got down to business. I was impressed by the quality of the men. They were all members of the Recce Commando, an élite unit which has a reputation in South Africa equivalent to the Green Berets in America or the SAS in Britain. They were highly experienced in combat and many of them had taken part, they told me, in clandestine operations in Mozambique, Zimbabwe and Zambia. But what surprised me most was their high standard of education. The majority of them were university students or were employed in executive positions. This is not to say that I expected them to conform with the image of the typical mercenary soldier as foisted on the public by the leftist press, which depicts the mercenary soldier as a boorish lout whose only ability is to carry arms against a defenceless adversary; *les affreux* in fact. These men were politically aware and anxious to help their country in whatever manner they could.

At a briefing a few days later I described the operation in broad terms, gave details of the contract, and began to enrol the volunteers. I was delighted to find among them two old Congo hands: Kurt Priefert, a German in his late thirties, and Peter Rohwein, half Russian, half East German. Both had served with me before, and I knew them as first-rate soldiers. Kurt was a fitness addict and in great physical shape. He was also an expert on small arms and a collector of unusual weapons. Peter had owned a coffee plantation in a remote corner of Rhodesia but had decided to leave Zimbabwe with the advent of the new Marxist regime. He wanted no more of the communist way of life, he said, and opted for South Africa to make a new start, even though it meant leaving everything behind him.

I interviewed the men privately and explained that this would be a high-risk operation with an abnormally high rate of pay, but of short duration. The timing of it was of particular concern to Johan Fritz. He was twenty-three, had already graduated at Pretoria University and was now about to sit his exams for a second degree. I noticed that he was held in particular esteem by his comrades not only for his academic prowess but also, as Pete Doorewaard told me, for his courage and determination in action. Johan had served three years in the Parachute Regiment and loved soldiering. When he came to fill in the answer to 'next of kin' on his enrolment form he wrote: 'Friend'.

'Yes,' I said, 'but who?'

He then wrote: 'Vic de Beer.' Vic was his buddy in the unit.

To name a friend as one's next of kin is not all that unusual in mercenary soldiering. In the past I have seen it happen many times. Frequently a man will nominate his girlfriend as his next of kin, prompted perhaps by some romantic notion or maybe out of sheer bravado – none of us really think we are going to be killed, do we? – without realising the possible consequences of his actions. I recall one young lady in Cape Town who inherited $20,000 in this way; the money was the indemnity payable to her as next of kin on the death of her boyfriend in action. She refused to accept it, saying she had only known him for a few days! But in Johan's case, of course, it was not for me to pry into his private affairs. I assumed it was the usual one of a son having some difficulty obtaining parental approval for an adventure of this sort, and thought no more of it. I learned later that his father was a very prominent and well-respected businessman, and a director of General Mining Corporation, one of the biggest public companies in South Africa.

On the whole I was well pleased with the recruitment so far, but I am not infallible and I made an error which I lived to regret. One of the men introduced himself and mentioned that he was a doctor. We had already signed on a Doctor de Wet, but I believe that a mercenary unit can never have too many doctors, like the crew of an ocean-going yacht, so I took him on although I was a little disturbed by his very cautious and halting manner, and, more particularly, by his noticeably scruffy appearance. These things are important in this context. Anyway, I gave him the thousand-dollar advance and hoped for the best.

I had signed up all the men I needed and promised to return for a final briefing a day or two before we were due to start. Tullio then asked me, privately, if I would consider the recruitment of an acquaintance of his despite the fact that he was not a soldier. His friend, Sven Forsell, was an Austrian, the son of a High Court judge, and well known in the film industry as a producer and director of motion pictures. He wanted to come, said Tullio, to experience action as a mercenary soldier so that he could make an authentic movie in a similar vein! That did not strike me as a very sound reason for risking one's life, but I agreed to talk to him. He impressed me with his enthusiasm for his art and I signed him on, not as a soldier, but as an admin executive whom I would need, after the coup, to help with the travel arrangements of over sixty men and the myriad complications which commanders are heir to in circumstances like these. I look forward to seeing the film one of these days.

Back in Durban, Gerard had put a holiday flat at my disposal for the purpose of recruitment. I interviewed a large group of men whose leader appeared to be Ken Dalgliesh, a most intelligent Scot (no relation to the famous footballer of the same name) who was also the owner/manager of the Riviera Hotel where ex-Rhodesian soldiers used to meet for a drink. Among them was a sprinkling of American soldiers of fortune and one or two Britons. Most of them had seen action in the Rhodesia bush war against Robert Mugabe's ZANU and Joshua Nkomo's ZAPU guerrillas, some as members of the famous Rhodesian SAS. Many of them were genuinely attracted by the opportunity to do something helpful for South Africa; but the money to be earned, let it be said, was their fundamental reason for enlistment. Some of the more politically aware also saw the importance of the coup from an anti-communist point of view.

I explained the strategic importance of the Seychelles to the West to both the Johannesburg and Durban groups and pointed out its commanding position athwart the tanker route from the Persian Gulf to the Cape of Good Hope and points west. Was it not bad enough having a 'Hadrian's Wall' of Marxist states stretching from Angola on the Atlantic, through Zimbabwe in the centre, to Mozambique on the Indian Ocean, without adding to the potential Russian threat by having a Marxist regime controlling Mahé? The majority, particularly the Afrikaners, were well aware of the benefits which would accrue to South Africa from a successful coup, and intensely interested in the recent power-play over the islands which the Russians seemed to be winning. For many of them our attempt began to take on the spirit of a crusade. Within a few days I had all the men I needed and was sorry to refuse a number of good types who clamoured to enlist.

The time had come to send off the advance parties. There would be three pairs, each pair representing one of the three groups into which the main force was to be split for the actual operation. The primary task of the advance parties was to make a detailed reconnaissance of the target which their group would assault on D-day. For this purpose they were given aerial photographs and maps of their objectives. When their groups joined up with them later they would share the detailed information they had gathered. In common parlance they were to 'case the joint'.

I examined the nominal roll closely and selected Ken Dalgliesh and Aubrey Brooks as the first pair. Aubrey had served in the Selous Scouts and the Grey Scouts in Rhodesia and was a well-balanced and thoroughly experienced officer with a first-class combat record. He also had that ability to compromise, to use whatever materials were on hand, even though they were not the best ones, which distinguishes the mercenary soldier from his regular counterpart. There is regrettably no well-calculated G1098 or War Establishment in a mercenary unit, a fact of life which the majority of regular officers would find insupportable in a mercenary unit.

The second pair were an American named Charlie Dukes and his buddy, an Englishman named Roger England. They had both served in the SAS unit in Rhodesia. Charlie was the screen prototype of the mercenary soldier, devil-may-care, lean, tough, and ready for action at the drop of a silver dollar. His mate Roger was a quiet thoughtful man, a thorough professional, hard as nails, and one who had lived through more action than he cared to remember. I felt instinctively that, come what may, that man would never crack. And I was right.

Finally there were Barney Carey and Desmond Botes. I needed Barney on the island to tie up a number of administrative details, the hiring of cars, the drawing of a large sum of cash to pay the men a per-diem allowance in local currency; and liaison with the safe house, the only person to be entrusted with that knowledge. Des Botes had been in the South African Police for five years and was well known throughout the country as a teacher of judo, which he had learned in Japan. His mature outlook on life and his unflappable nature and sound judgement impressed me.

The construction of the special baggage proceeded in my workshop with meticulous care. Every item was checked and double-checked before the false bottom was finally glued into place. It would be fatal in the event of an emergency to find the breech block was missing or the firing pin had fallen out! The magazines were loaded with precision, and all possibility of a cross-feed eliminated. I was happy with the final product and subjected each case to a searching examination before I passed it fit for action.

It was at this point that I had another visit from the egregious Dolinchek. He insisted on being recruited as a member of the force and came prepared with a false identity and back-up data to support it. He had certainly done his homework. His name was to be Anton Lubick, and his brand-new South African passport suggested that he had official approval for his scheme. I took him on after he had signed the enrolment form but explained to him that he had no official role to play in the operation as far as I was concerned. The men who would execute the coup were all highly trained soldiers, and the last thing I wanted was a fumbling amateur fouling things up at a critical moment. He could come, I told him, if he came purely as an observer. I surmised this was the probable intention of the NIS anyway. I decided to send Dolinchek to the island on his own, more or less at the same time as the advance parties, but unbeknown to them. Bravely – and I must give him credit for that – he volunteered to take a piece of the special baggage with him.

But to be merely an observer was not his entire thinking. He laid before me a plan of action to be carried out by himself and three special experts, whom he would tell me about, which left me flabbergasted. His intention was to burgle the Russian embassy in Victoria, no less! This was to be done immediately after the coup and during the confusion which would follow. I very seldom use swear words, but I used them then. Was he completely out of his mind? Did he not realise that a coup against a minuscule nation of 62,000 people with a 200-man amateur army was one thing, but to take on the might of one of the world's two superpowers was another? Had he considered the implications of what he was suggesting?

Yes, he said, he had. Not only that, but he also saw it as a golden opportunity to glean secret information about the entire communist network in Africa. Their embassy in Mahé, he was convinced, was where plans for Africa were co-ordinated; hence the overlarge diplomatic staff, and so on. Furthermore, he had already taken some preliminary steps. For a start he had persuaded Peter Duffy to volunteer after all. His purpose here was to use Duffy's skill as a photographer of secret documents. In addition he had arranged for me to recruit two other men, who worked full-time for the NIS, as ordinary members of my force. These types would do the strong-arm stuff. Of course these little details were not known to me at this interview, but I turned down the burglary caper flat and expressly forbade any such nonsense. I summed Dolinchek up as some sort of anti-communist fanatic, probably a little unbalanced. A nut, but an entertaining nut. I hate to curb a man's natural enthusiasm for his cause, particularly this cause, but this was ridiculous. And on that discordant note we parted. That Dolinchek subsequently went through a complete change in his political allegiance and strove after his arrest to join the Marxist commissars on the island is for me one of life's great unsolved mysteries! I never saw him again.

Meanwhile a suitably large plane and a courageous pilot had to be found, one who would be prepared to fly in the new government on D-day within one hour of the end of the coup, as agreed. Gerard was to arrange the passenger-list, and I imagine he had to do some tough talking before he could produce a manifest. He asked me to discard my original plan, which was to provide him with a bodyguard from my reserve who would accompany them on this flight. Instead he asked me to deliver a small number of pieces of my special baggage to his flat in Durban. He would then provide for his own protection from certain Seychellois living in Durban.

The take-off point was to be Nairobi. Gerard had visited the Kenyan capital in the last few days and made all the necessary arrangements for the assembly of the new government and for permission for the plane to take off for Mahé at minimum notice. Plainly he was dealing with somebody at a very high level who was sympathetic to his cause. I never knew who it was, neither did I ask. It was sufficient for me to know that such a splendid fellow existed.

Peter Duffy found the pilot, an old friend from his east Africa days, who was not only highly experienced but also courageous and thoroughly reliable and, I may say, a legend in his own lifetime as an aviator of outstanding ability. He confirmed that his plane was ready, that it could be in the right place at the right time, ticking over, just waiting for the word to take off. I sent him the codewords he would need to identify himself on his approach to Mahé once we were in control. At the same time I telexed a draft to Eddie of US$25,000 as part-payment of the US$40,000 we had agreed to pay for this flight. Whatever the cost, it was going to be worth it. To be in sole command of the political situation in Mahé after the coup, awaiting the arrival of the new government, was not my intention. *Chacun son métier*. But I never doubted Gerard would arrive within the hour to install his administration.

The next important step was to develop the general AOFB idea and to make sure all the members understood it. We were a Johannesburg beer-drinking club. We met formally once a week in our favourite pub in Braamfontein. We played Rugby. Once a year we organised a holiday for our members. We obtained special charter rates. Last year we went to Mauritius. In the best tradition of the original AOFB we collected toys for underprivileged kids and distributed them to orphanages. We were good guys, *lekker ous* in the vernacular. It sounded reasonably plausible.

Following this line of thought I bought over a thousand rands' worth of toys for children in certain convents in Victoria. I made sure the toys were as bulky as possible and weighed little. Rugger footballs were ideal. These were packed in the special baggage above the false bottom to compensate for the weight of the weapon. It was a nice thought that some little ones would get some fun out of it.

But I was not to forget that a club like this would undoubtedly have a tour leader, somebody who was popular and had the respect of the members. These clubs are like that. Of course he must be typical, about the same average age and knowledgeable. The obvious choice was Peter Duffy, a man famous for his wit and bonhomie. Good old Peter, just the chap! I rehearsed him in his role and laid on him the duty of shepherding the baggage through the Customs at Mahé. He was to make a big production of the toys for the children. Create a diversion, I said.

All that remained were the final briefings in Johannesburg and

67

Durban. At these I produced an AK47 and passed it round to make sure that everybody was absolutely certain how it was stripped and assembled. I timed a few of them and found they could assemble it in twenty seconds flat. I checked that everybody had the right documents and that their cholera shots were current. I showed them a scale model of the island made in plaster, about two feet long, which showed all the objectives in detail. I passed around wall posters and photographs of the six members of the Seychelles Cabinet and described the gentlemen concerned. One who was known to be a homosexual aroused some ribald comment. For the last time I explained that the Seychellois were a gentle people and that it was my intention that the coup should be carried out bloodlessly. This could only be done if we maintained the strictest security and acted with the greatest speed and surprise on D-day. The actual operational orders would be issued in Mahé. This was Phase 1 – the approach to contact, as it were; but for the moment we were only tourists and must act as such. I explained that if things went seriously wrong at the moment of our arrival the advance parties would be there with weapons to cause a diversion. The deepest question came from one of the Durban group, a highly intelligent man named Simon Willar, who had been a captain in the Rhodesian Army. 'Is there a way out?' I replied that the plane which would bring the new government in would provide the means of escape if that was found necessary on D-day.

Final instructions were issued for both the Johannesburg and the Durban groups to assemble at Jan Smuts Airport at 1400 hours on 24 November. A railway bus would take them to Ermelo in the eastern Transvaal which was to be our assembly-point. Ermelo was about 180 miles from Johannesburg and close to the Swaziland border. We would spend the night there at a Holiday Inn and leave for Swaziland early the following morning. The Durban boys were given air tickets to enable them to join the bus from Jan Smuts Airport in good time. I went through my checklist several times before I was satisfied that I had forgotten nothing.

My one outstanding problem was at what stage to tell the men that I expected them to carry an additional piece of luggage through Customs which would contain arms and ammunition. If I told them at the final briefing I knew that without a shadow of doubt somebody would talk and the whole plan would be wrecked. I felt justified in my decision – tell them an hour before they were due to board the bus for the Swaziland border and give them a chance to back out if they did not want to take the risk. We had the reasonable expectation that our own men from the Resistance would be manning the

Customs, which in any case I had been assured were lax. To my mind it was a calculated risk. Nothing but the sheerest bad luck would wreck it.

Meanwhile the men had been warned to bring an additional piece of hand luggage which would be taken from them at Ermelo and substituted by a piece I would give them which would contain toys for the children of Victoria. I imagine the more astute of them must have realised there was something deeper in this than met the eye, but no questions were raised on this point.

Another thing was worrying me. I had felt bad that I was leaving Gerry Puren out of the operation. My original plan had given him a specific role, but he had been very indiscreet some months back in addressing a South African old soldiers' club meeting when he had actually broached the whole question of an attack on the René regime, and intimated that he would be looking for recruits at some time in the future. When this news reached Gerard he had ordered that Gerry should be dropped from the planning team at once. But as there were only forty-eight hours to go the risk of any further indiscretion could be ruled out.

I asked Gerry if he would still like to take part in the operation, and explained why he had been left out of recent planning. Just as I had expected, as soon as the old warhorse heard the trumpet he started pawing the ground. On his way back from the Drakensberg where he had been spending the weekend he called at the Old Vicarage. I went into the specific role which I wanted him to play; it was based on some information Gerry had given me years ago. He was not to come as a soldier; he was to have nothing to do with the actual coup. I had highly trained soldiers for that. His task was only to neutralise a certain party and keep him out of the way at the actual moment of the coup. Both of us had known Bob Noddyn, a Belgian mercenary soldier in the Katanga and later in the Congo, who had served with Bob Denard in 6 Commando. In some action or other many years ago Gerry had saved Noddyn's life, and Bob had vowed he would never forget it. If at any time Gerry needed him, he would welcome a chance to repay him. Now was the chance. Noddyn was actually on the island of Mahé employed as the trainer of a special bodyguard to protect the President. In addition he ran a restaurant called La Sirène in Victoria. On the day of the coup all I wanted Gerry to do was to make sure that Noddyn was kept at home and out of the fight. Could he do that? He reckoned that would be comparatively simple. On that basis I enrolled Gerry as a member of the force, paid him his advance and sent him off to break the bad news to his wife.

I paid a final visit to Gerard, who was preparing for his flight to Nairobi. Before going he gave me the original tape-recording of a special message to be broadcast to the people of the Seychelles within minutes of the coup. This message had been recorded in London by Jimmy Mancham, or so I was told by Eddie, and flown out just in time to reach me before I left for Ermelo. The ex-President's message was followed by one from Gerard himself as heir apparent. Both messages were in Creole. I had to employ a special courier to rush the tape to a Johannesburg studio to get it rerecorded on to a reel suitable for broadcasting at 15 inches per second. I would carry this bulky item with me in my luggage. The chances of a Customs official asking to hear what was on it were infinitesimal.

In deference to popular tradition the messages were to be followed by martial music. For this purpose I selected *The World of Military Bands*, well-known marches played by various bands of the Brigade of Guards; *Massed Bands of the Parachute Regiment*; and *On Parade with the Band of HM Royal Marines*. What a pity that the public of Mahé had to be deprived of that musical treat! One of the vicissitudes of war, I dare say.

For the last time I ran through my checklist. All those things which ought to have been done had been done. And nothing had been left undone which ought to have been done. At least, I hoped not. I got myself to bed early that Monday night, as is my wont, to prepare myself for the adventure ahead. I slept soundly. It was the last time I would sleep like that for nearly three and a half years.

CHAPTER 5

The Operation

———

IT WAS TIME TO LEAVE HOME. The VW Combi I had hired was loaded with the fifty holdall-type bags which we had prepared so carefully. Each one had a number to correspond with the ones I had given the men. Pasted on their sides was the AOFB logo. I carried the fifteen radio sets loose, and these would be distributed among the men. A label on each stated it was for delivery to a yacht in Victoria yacht basin, just in case questions were asked.

I walked round my orchard for the last time. The Methley plums were ripening fast and promised abundant fruit. It looked as though it would be an early summer this year. My bulldog Cadwallader savaged my hand in his peculiar form of farewell before I made tracks for Ermelo, three hundred miles away across the Natal Midlands.

I reached the Holiday Inn at Ermelo about 5 p.m. Peter Duffy was waiting for me in the lobby, looking worried. The bus from Johannesburg had arrived a little earlier than I had expected and some of the men had begun drinking hard in the bar. Peter startled me out of the drowsiness induced by the nine-hour drive.

'We're going to have to call it off, Colonel,' he said flatly.

'Why? What's up?'

'One bloody idiot has got himself stoned in the saloon bar and hit a civilian!'

'So what?'

'So he's laid him out cold, unconscious, that's what. As soon as he came to he threatened to call the police and lay a charge for assault and GBH and God knows what else. Trouble is he's one of the local nobs. I've talked him out of it for the moment, but he's

71

mad as a snake; his best suit is ruined and his girlfriend is having hysterics.'

I cursed myself for not having thought of this probability in advance. Heaven knows I have had enough experience of this sort of thing with mercenary soldiers. This type of boisterous behaviour is entirely in keeping with the character of very many of them. The truth is you cannot have it both ways. If you want men who are tough, adventurous and ready to take an almighty risk, then you are going to get the type that is difficult to handle and prone to take a drink. Spirit and circumstances and tensions have to be taken into account.

But that didn't make matters any better. It was a poor start to the show, and we would have to move fast if our cover was not going to be blown. Duffy was right. As soon as the South African Police showed up awkward questions would be asked and our drunken friend would spill the beans without a shadow of doubt.

'What do you suggest, Pete?'

'Don't know. It's a long shot, but money might pacify the unlucky little bugger.'

'Like two hundred rand?'

'Like five hundred rand! Suit wrecked, evening messed up, loss of face with the doll. . . . Not less than five hundred. I'm not saying he'll take it, but I'll work on him if you say so.'

I said so – what else? – and peeled off the notes. Half an hour later Duffy reported success. Oh, well, these things happen.

Just before dinner Duffy presided over an AOFB meeting in a special conference room. He reaffirmed the objects of the outing to the club members exactly as though we were respectable Froth-blowers. He cautioned them about heavy drinking and warned them to be ready to leave the hotel at 0400 hours the next morning. The bus would take us to the Swaziland border at Oshoek sixty miles away. We had to cross it by 0700 in order to reach Manzini Matsapa, a further seventy miles on, in time for our 0930 hours take-off.

Gerry Puren and I dined together and shared a quiet bottle of Grundberger Stein. At eleven that night Eddie rang me from London to say there had been a last-minute hitch with the plans for the assembly of the new government in Nairobi. I had half-expected some of them would cry off when the chips were down, but it was not fatal to my plan. I had a few days in hand, although the quicker we moved after arrival the better. I had received news that René was leaving for Paris on 28 November to visit the French Minister of Finance – complete, of course, with begging-bowl. That would suit my plan admirably. A coup whilst the President was out of the country was altogether in the finest African tradition. He might even be happy at the outcome. A comfortable Swiss retreat, *maningi* American dollars in the bank, ex-President status, not such a bad scenario after all. And from my point of view it made the possibility of a bloodless coup all the more likely.

I called an O group of officers at midnight. I gave orders for our movement the next day to Swaziland and issued the bombshell. They were to tell their men at reveille the next morning that they were expected to carry a holdall through the Customs at Mahé which would contain a weapon and ammunition. If any man decided that he did not want to go through with it for any reason, he had my permission to withdraw. In the event only one man made that decision. It was one of the Recce Commando, the rather scruffy individual who had signed on as a doctor and had been so evasive with his answers on enrolment. One of his mates told me later that he wanted to gain some credit from the South African authorities by telling them all about it before it happened. The chump did not appreciate, even though he had been told, that the NIS not only knew all about it but were also the prime movers in the organisation of the whole affair!

We went through the Swaziland border-post at Oshoek without incident, taking our place in the early-morning queue of heavy trucks waiting for the Customs to open. On arrival at Matsapa the Fokker Friendship was waiting on the tarmac just outside the arrivals hall. Our luggage went on board without any problem. So far so good.

Just after take-off I noticed with some annoyance that there were three or four passengers on board in addition to our party. That was not in the original plan; we were supposed to be the sole charter party. It would not have mattered, but I had counted on being able to address the men in the air prior to our arrival in Mahé, and this put paid to that. After several hours flying over the Mozambique Channel we sighted the Comoros Islands in the distance, dark volcanic outcrops ringed with white surf in a perfect setting of deep blue sea. We touched down on a strip of flattened lava apparently miles from anywhere. This was the island of Moroni, the capital of the Comoros. We did not disembark, but two of the extra passengers got off and a young Frenchman got on. He carried the Sword of Damocles in his baggage but I was not to know it. We took off after forty minutes' wait in the torrid heat.

The air hostesses, two very attractive Swazi girls, announced that Seychelles regulations strictly forbade the importation of fruit of any kind into Mahé. Just an official warning of no concern to us, of course. I sat next to Gerry Puren in the front of the plane and passed the time solving the *Financial Times* crossword. By the time I finished it Mahé was dead ahead. The pilot flew low along the east coast, so that we saw the airport buildings and the barracks at the end of the runway to the south of them quite clearly. I wondered if our plans had leaked and looked carefully to see if there was any sort of welcoming committee surrounding the airport. My plan in that event was to have the advance party waiting at the airport ready to create a diversion during which we could grab our baggage and assemble our weapons. But everything appeared perfectly normal. I glanced at the men. They seemed pretty calm, if a little tense here and there.

I headed the queue to pass through Immigration. No problem. Then we hung about waiting for the baggage trolley to bring the heavy luggage. I picked up mine and passed through the green door without being stopped, followed closely by some of the men. Everything was going well. I waited in the Customs hall to see how it would go with the main body. Excellent, excellent. Duffy was superb. He began cracking jokes with the stewardesses and distracting the attention of the Customs officers whilst the men passed through the green doors in a steady stream. An occasional bag was examined, and the toys raised a smile, but apart from that everything was going normally. It looked as though the men from the Resistance were on duty as arranged. That was a great relief. I breathed freely and passed through the glass doors and crossed the forecourt into the parking area whilst Gerry went back in to hire a car for the two of us. In another five minutes the most hazardous part of the operation would be behind us.

I looked around casually and spotted the men of the advance party sitting quietly in their cars as though waiting for friends off the plane. Barney Carey got out and approached me, surprise to see an old friend written all over his face. We chatted for a few minutes. Yes, everything was quite normal. No, there had been no leak. The man Dolinchek had made himself known to the others against my orders. This had been an embarrassment for them. They were not impressed with his behaviour; he boozed too much. I looked around casually and saw Dolinchek sitting in a car on his own. Bob Sims was in another. Aubrey Brooks and Ken Dalgliesh gave me a sign of recognition. So did Charlie Dukes and Roger England. Everybody was in place, armed and ready for any contingency.

By this time nearly all the men had passed through Customs and had seated themselves in a small bus standing in the forecourt which would take them to their hotel. Their luggage, including the holdalls, was stacked on the roof. Suddenly one of my men rushed up to me

74

and shouted: 'For God's sake, Colonel, stop him! Stop him! He's gone mad.' I ran to the bus. Gerry Puren was on the roof throwing the baggage down to the men as fast as he could and screaming at the top of his voice, 'Get out the toys! Get out the toys!' But Gerry was far from mad. This was his way of getting immediate action. To anybody who did not know Gerry like I knew him it would certainly seem as though he had lost his head and was completely out of control. (Later this understandable display of panic was ascribed to me, with some glee, and not a little venom, I suspect, by the South African press.) Gerry was doing the right thing; he was reacting at once to the situation as he saw it. Perhaps if time had permitted he should have spoken to me first before taking such drastic steps, but I do not criticise him for what he did. Action, in these circumstances, is invariably better than inaction.

The unbelievable had happened. Inside the hall only three people were left to pass through the Customs; all the rest were safely through. One of the three was the Frenchman we had picked up at Moroni. Customs had found fruit in his baggage and were making a big issue of it. A supervisor, seeing the altercation, intervened and confiscated the fruit. As luck would have it, the supervisor was not one of the Resistance men. The next man in line was one of mine. He denied having any fruit, but the supervisor demanded that his luggage should be searched. The hardness of the bottom of the holdall aroused his suspicion, and he insisted that the bag should be stripped. Discovery of the weapon was inevitable. A fight then broke out between my man and the supervisor. Tullio Moneta, who was standing close by, monitoring the passage of the men through the checkpoint, realised that the game was up and seized the supervisor in both hands and flung him bodily against a wall where he collapsed like an eggshell.

The airport security officer standing nearby made a dash for his office about thirty yards away. One of my men, an American, assembled his AK in less than fifteen seconds and took a snap shot at him as he ran through the crowd. He missed. The security man bolted his door and telephoned the duty guard at the barracks to raise the alarm. The bullet shattered the plate-glass door leading out of the hall. I heard the shot and saw the hole it made at the same time. I ran to the door and pushed my way in. Just inside a man was lying on his back, mortally wounded. It was young Johan Fritz. The shot had struck him by accident. Dr de Wet, one of the Recce Commando, was kneeling over him examining the wound. Johan was unconscious and dying fast, the bullet must have penetrated his heart. I held his hand and asked the doctor if there was anything we could do. He shook his head sadly. In another minute it was all over. The shock of his death in these circumstances was catastrophic.

I ran outside to get things under way. I had no choice. We must start the coup now, at once. The first step must be to seize the barracks and the airport. These were our two most vital objectives. They must be in our hands before we could rally the Resistance and advance on Victoria six miles away. There was simply no alternative.

The officer who was to command the group which was to take the barracks in the planned coup dashed up to me for orders.

'Seize the barracks. Take your seventeen men. Use that bus.'

He ran off to muster his group. They boarded the bus and screamed off down the road in the direction of the barracks two miles away.

Vernon Prinsloo walked up to me swiftly. Vernon is one of the finest soldier sportsmen I have ever served with. He had been welterweight champion of Rhodesia in his time.

'Take the tower, Colonel?' he asked calmly.

This was to have been Vernon's role in the bigger plan, and he had prepared his mind for it. Good soldiering; I am sure he had anticipated all the probabilities.

'Yes. Take three men.'

I shouted to Barney to bring up his car. We must get down to the barracks quick. At this moment bursts of fire broke out between us and the barracks. Must be the Tanzanians, I thought. I knew they lived in a private house about halfway between the airport and the barracks. I hoped none of the barracks assault group had been hit.

A young Irishman, Standish-White, intercepted me on the way to the car.

'Roadblock, sir?'

'Good lad,' I said. 'Use ten men. Block the Victoria side.'

He ran off to do it. I looked at my watch. Fourteen minutes had elapsed since the shot was fired which started the whole thing off.

Tullio stopped me just before we pushed off. He knew all about small warfare: don't wait for your CO to come to you with orders; it's your duty to find him.

'Orders, Colonel?' he asked.

'Put the terminal into a state of all-round defence, Major,' I said. 'Nothing to land. Use barrels. I shall be at the barracks. With luck we'll seize it. See you.'

He patted me on the back and grinned. I never knew a man who enjoyed the excitement of action more.

Barney and I raced off towards the barracks. As we came opposite the house used by the Tanzanians a few bursts of fire passed harmlessly over the top of us. 'Why do African troops always shoot high, Colonel?' he asked me nonchalantly as he steered around some ruts in the road. 'Don't know,' I said. 'Just thank God they do.'

We drew up fifty yards from the barracks gates and put the car under cover of some palms. Force of habit, I suppose. We ran forward and hid behind the trunks of two thick palms not more than twenty yards from the gates, which we could see quite plainly. Barney had an AK. I was unarmed and felt indecently dressed, even though I have always believed that a commander should never use his personal weapon in action. His job is to command. He cannot do that if he turns himself into a rifleman. Of course, if he is attacked, that is another matter; but command is what he is there for. But in this case I would like to have altered my own rules. A further demoralising factor was that we were not in uniform. Civilian clothes seem all wrong. Don't ask me why.

Some of my men were coming up through the undergrowth to my left and were shouting to each other to keep contact. I could see that they were not going to get very much further once they came up against the high-security fence surrounding the barracks. But what I did not know was that the assault group had already put in their attack on the main gate and been beaten back and suffered two casualties, both wounded. The whole group had withdrawn into the dense bush on the far side of the gates. I could see a high-tension wire lying crazily across the road – severed, I suppose, by a bullet. The smell of cordite hung acrid in the air.

Kurt Priefert was dodging from tree to tree and finally made it to where I was standing.

'Four men, Colonel, and I'll take it,' he gasped.

As he said it, I heard the sound of a mortar being fired; the hollow boom of a ballastite cartridge is unmistakable. Then another, and another.

'Eighty-one,' said Kurt as the three of us dropped to the ground as one man.

'Didn't know they had any,' I said, with a hint of apology.

'Correction,' said Kurt, 'sixty-mil.'

Kurt was the expert at all times. He loved small arms. I often told him that the day he was killed his last words would be 'Hit by a 9 mm parabellum fired from an UZI!' or whatever. We heard the dull thump as the bombs hit the ground one after the other about a hundred yards away. Incredibly, not one exploded. Barney laughed.

'Silly buggers have forgotten to prime them properly,' he said.

Some more followed, but their error persisted. Happy day for us, thank heavens, but rather uncomfortable just the same.

The light was beginning to fade fast. Here, a few degrees south of the equator, dark would fall like a curtain in less than fifteen minutes. But now the heavy revving of an armoured vehicle told me something unpleasant was approaching. Slowly, like some prehistoric monster, a BRDM armoured car nosed its way around the barracks huts and stopped plumb in the middle of the gates, blocking the entrance. Its light and heavy machine-guns began to swivel round and round as though searching for a target. Its side-lights flicked on. The driver kept his foot on the brake, his rear lights casting an evil red glow around him. But he was so closed down I was sure he could see almost nothing through his tiny visors. Twenty yards away we froze behind the shrinking palm trees.

'What about it, Colonel?' repeated Kurt. 'Four men, covering fire and we'll blast them out of the guardroom. There can't be more than six in there.'

'Thanks, Kurt, but it's too late. You'd get yourself written off, old son. No way can you get round that armoured car.'

There was nothing for it but withdrawal to the airport. Put that into a strong state of defence and attack the barracks at first light with maximum strength. By that time the Resistance would have rallied to us. I gave the order to withdraw. We clambered into the bus, Kurt driving, and made it back to the terminal building without loss. Some men ran back through the bush, including Ken Dalgliesh, who I noticed was barefoot.

Tullio reported to me as soon as I got back. The airport building was defended all round and he had established an outpost at the northern end of the runway which could command any approach from the sea. De Wet was the section leader. Aubrey Brooks had been wounded in the attack on the barracks and was missing. A search party had failed to find him before they withdrew. Charlie Dukes was wounded in the same action with a gunshot wound in the upper arm. He had lost a lot of blood but had made it back to the airport. He was lying down quietly, nursing his AK. I asked him what happened.

'Gee, Colonel,' he said, 'it was just like the movies. We went in four abreast, all guns blazing, and beat up the guardroom. But a burst of fire from nowhere hit us on one side and we couldn't get enough support to go again.'

I wonder if movie-makers know how much they contribute to errors in soldiering of this sort.

Tullio said that sixty-five people who had been in the airport at the time of the alarm had been rounded up and placed in the reception hall, not as hostages but for their own safety. They were in good shape – particularly, he added, four girls, photographic models who just happened to be here on assignment!

I established my headquarters in a room just off the main reception hall. Two of its walls were made entirely of glass but it had a telephone which was still working. I was just wondering about all that glass when my runner/bodyguard, an ex-Foreign Legionnaire, a Yorkshireman named Don Kenny, ran in to tell me that three lorryloads of infantry were approaching down the main runway. I never saw the action; it was all over before I got there. About two hundred yards from our position the infantry climbed out and advanced in line abreast! Paddy Hendrikse with two men made their way down one side of the runway through the thick bush to take them in enfilade. Unfortunately, some ill-disciplined wretch in the stop section opened fire on the advancing men too soon, whereupon they dropped their arms, abandoned their lorries, leaving one actually on the runway, and fled. We sent out a patrol to pick up the arms, all AKs. That was the sum total of the fight the Tanzanians put up. We never heard of them again.

I examined the defensive position. Pete Doorewaard and his men were controlling the runway side of the building and had an outpost at the northern end of the runway, the one commanded by De Wet. Other sections completed our all-round defence. Gerry Puren and two men were across the road from the carpark defending a filling station as part of our perimeter. This was obviously unsatisfactory, and I went across to pull them back into the main body of the defensive position. I found Gerry on the telephone. He was trying to reach the captain of the Fokker Friendship, who had managed to get away to the Reef Hotel before the balloon went up. Gerry wanted to ask him to return and fly us out to the Comoros! My friend Gerry was never short of cheeky ideas. But he could not contact him. In any case, I could not see the captain risking his plane in those circumstances.

Gerry was in an awkward position. He was not really one of us, he had an entirely civilian role to play, but he could not walk away from the fight. We discussed the possibility of his melting away into the bush and making his way to his cousin Frank. Surely he would be able to shelter him until the confusion died down. I told him I thought we would be able to take the barracks at dawn and be able to subdue all opposition by noon the next day. I left him with an order to report back to the main position with his two men as soon as he had finished trying to raise the captain of the Fokker Friendship.

The two men reported back a little later, but there was no sign of Gerry. They said he had vanished. I never saw him again from that day to this.

A short while later heavy machine-gun fire broke out from the end of the runway not far from the barracks. It was an armoured car firing its 14.5 mm cannon, its target the control tower. Some rounds struck the tower just below the windows, breaking off large chunks of masonry but missing the plate glass above. The cannon was not able to get the elevation required. Soon it was joined by another AFV. They advanced in tandem up the runway. When they were about thirty yards from the tower they opened up again and hit it with everything they had. Inside the tower the two Seychellois air-traffic controllers were close to hysteria. One of them, panic-stricken, got into a dustbin and pulled the lid down on top of him. A fairly normal reaction, I imagine; I remember during air raids the comfort one got from pulling a blanket over one's head. But now it was getting really dangerous and the shells were penetrating the masonry and passing right through the tower. Not surprising, really, as the 14.5 mm cannon fires a tungsten round weighing about a pound and measuring four inches long by one inch thick. At this point Vernon Prinsloo decided discretion was the better part of valour and withdrew his men and one of the civilians by the back door. The gentleman in the dustbin opted to remain there.

The leading armoured car, drawing no fire from us, decided to advance further. He left the area of the control tower and motored round to the forecourt of the terminal leaving the other AFV to withdraw down the runway for a reason known only to himself. This tactical error cost the commander of the leading armoured car his life. It is a fundamental rule that armoured vehicles must never be used singly in a mobile role; they must cover each other at all times and ought properly to be employed in threes, two the irreducible minimum. The BRDM stood now in the forecourt like some gigantic animal pawing the ground, determined to kill his prey but unable to flush it out. This side of the terminal building was in total darkness, and the driver could see nothing even with the aid of his tiny side-lights. Five yards from the swivelling guns fifteen of my men and myself crouched down behind a dwarf wall and held our breath. Charlie Dukes, despite his wound, was at the ready, lying next to me. I considered shooting out the side-lights but decided against it; it would have given our position away. The AFV rolled forward and then stopped, uncertain as to his next move. He was now five feet away. If he had opened fire at the wall with his 14.5 mm cannon, we would all have been killed stone dead. That bullet

80

would pierce six bricks side by side, never mind one, like plywood.

After three or four agonising minutes he reversed out of the forecourt and continued up the main road past the filling station towards Victoria, only to be halted at our roadblock. He opened fire, but my men were well concealed. Nobody was hit. Nobody moved. The BRDM reversed out of it quick. But as soon as his rear wheels hit the mud at the side of the road they started to spin. The driver, panic-stricken, revved up hard, making a fatal mistake. The vehicle began to dig itself in, engine screaming and tyres burning. Seeing they had the AFV in their power, my men emerged from cover and fired on the tyres, ripping them to shreds. He was finished. It was only a matter now of delivering the *coup de grâce*. Under covering fire Peter Rohwein ran forward, picked up some mud with both hands and plastered it on the visors of the armoured car. The crew were now completely blind. They were at our mercy.

'Tullio,' I shouted, 'cease fire! Tell the crew to surrender! Tell them they will be safe. Parle français!' Tullio hammered on the side of the armoured car and yelled at them in French to surrender. There was no answer. He grabbed a Seychellois and made him yell out in Creole that they must surrender, no harm would come to them. In reply they opened fire wildly with both their weapons, bullets ricocheted all over the building. They were not going to give up that easily. Tullio prepared a Molotov cocktail and flung it at the front of the vehicle. It exploded with a flash and burned steadily, but still the men refused to surrender. Rohwein climbed on the back of the BRDM and poured a bottle of petrol around the groove in the lid of the cupola and set fire to it. That did it. The lid flew open, knocking Peter off the back. The commander popped up firing blindly in all directions. Answering fire hit him in the chest and he slumped down dead. The other three crew members surrendered.

The three were brought to me for interrogation. They were not Tanzanians but Seychellois. They were, naturally enough, extremely frightened, and thought they were going to be shot out of hand.

'How many men hold the barracks?' I asked.

'Sixty.'

'Tanzanians?'

'Yes.'

'And the Seychelles army? Where are they?'

'They have run away.'

'We haven't come to kill you Seychellois. We have come to help you change your government and reinstate your legal President, Mr Mancham. You can go. But go straight to your barracks and tell the Tanzanians there are three hundred of us and soon we shall have another three hundred Seychellois from the Resistance. They must surrender. If they do not, we shall be forced to attack them and they will die. If we see you again, you will die also. Go!'

They were off like scalded cats. They could not believe their luck. But Tullio gripped one of them as he ran off.

'Not this one, Colonel; he's a Tanzanian. He's the commander of the armoured car. Speak Creole, you bastard!' He couldn't. But he answered Duffy in Swahili. He was a Tanzanian, all right.

Tullio put him with the civilians. Whatever he was, I salute a brave soldier. Ignorant perhaps, in military matters, but still brave. In the aftermath it appeared we were wrong about him. He was actually the commander of the barracks! He was in fact a Seychellois and not a Tanzanian. Had I known he was actually the commander of the barracks, things might have turned out very differently, but that's the luck of the draw.

The capture of the armoured car gave us an immediate lift. It altered the balance of fire-power decisively in our favour. I gave orders for the vehicle to be crewed and brought into service in the forecourt; but, alas, the tyres were too far gone for that. Worse still, the wiring of the 14.5 was burned out and the gun would only fire single rounds. Regrettably I had to abandon it after placing it tactically at the entrance to the terminal building. The dead man was still inside it. I now hoped that the second BRDM would return to the attack in the same manner. This time we would be careful not to wreck the tyres. But, sad to say, he didn't.

With the upsurge in our spirits I thought this would be a good moment to let my intention be known. We would mount an attack on the barracks at first light. Things always look bad at night, I said, but come the dawn we shall win. We have got nothing against us but a handful of Tanzanians. Come on, lads. It was well received.

But Tullio seemed to be in some pain. When the BRDM had driven into the forecourt some of the men had scrambled for cover in a ditch. In the rush Tullio had been injured, the toenails of his right foot had been ripped out forcibly and his foot was bleeding. He wrapped it around with a handkerchief and carried on without a murmur. What a man! He came towards me, all 6 feet 6 inches of him, his AK47 nestled on his hairy chest like a toy. 'Colonel,' he said, 'you know something. This is the only time a man really lives!'

I knew what he meant.

As soon as the firing stopped, Vernon Prinsloo decided to go back to the tower. He took with him Charles Goatley, a Rhodesian who had flown helicopters in their bush war. Goatley now sent down a message that Air India flight 224 from Harare, Zimbabwe, *en route* to Bombay, had been asking for permission to land. For some reason the air-traffic controller, the gentleman in the rubbish-bin who had been in the tower all this time, had not seen fit to answer them. What should he say? This message came by word of mouth as our radio net was not working at this moment owing to interference. I immediately issued a negative: Do not land! I repeated it three times so there would be absolutely no mistake.

It was obvious to me that it would be madness to allow the plane to land in these circumstances. The enemy were still in the barracks overlooking one end of the runway, and I was certain that as soon as the plane touched down it would come under heavy fire. Naturally enough the Tanzanians would think the plane was bringing in re-inforcements for us and in their minds they would be justified in treating it as hostile. Even if it escaped destruction by enemy fire, what about the lorry the Tanzanians had abandoned in the middle of the runway barely six hundred yards from the barracks?

As I heard no more from the tower I assumed that my order had been received and would be complied with. They had received an order all right, but not one from me. One of the Recce Commando, a man named Alan Mann, saw fit to alter my order to read 'Affirm-ative. Let it land.' (Mann told me this during the latter part of my trial when he was spending the night at my house as my guest. He explained that he had good reasons for taking this extraordinary step, but by then it was too late for me to make use of this startling evidence in my defence.)

My experience with irregular soldiers has taught me that mercen-ary soldiers – and by that I mean those who are not fighting for their country, or a cause, or for the pride of the regiment, or for medals, or whatever – will always consider pulling the ripcord when the alternative looks as though it will be defeat. Their attitude is very hard-headed and contains no element of romance or sentiment or cowardice. 'He that fights and runs away, May live to fight another day.' This sums up their outlook. I would agree that is plain common sense in many circumstances. A live dog is better than a dead lion. But we were not in such an impossible position as might have appeared to Mann and perhaps some of the others at that moment. And this is precisely where lack of communication with my men and my lack of an intimate knowledge of them, or of me by them, proved fatal. Had we known each other as we should have done, I am confident they would have trusted my judgement. I knew what the real strength of the enemy was. I knew there was no Seychellois army and that the fifty or sixty Tanzanians opposing us were no great shakes as soldiers. They weren't the United States Marines or a half-company of the Brigade of Guards, for Pete's sake! And at this stage there was still every hope of the Resistance making an appearance. But one or two of the men, at this early stage, had decided not to take any chances and decided that it would be prudent to keep the back door open just in case.

The last thing I wanted at this critical stage was a plane to land and hold out the possibility of withdrawal – of escape, if you like. Morale would be shattered. Men *will* fight to the last man and to the last round when there is absolutely no alternative; but that was not our position, however much it might have looked like it at a certain level.

As a result Goatley talked the plane down in good faith, thinking that was what I wanted. Later I learned of the actual conversation between him and the captain of the Air India plane in which it was abundantly clear to the meanest intelligence that all was not well on the ground, that it was not the usual controller in the tower but an amateur who barely knew the procedure for bringing an airliner down, and that there must be some very good reason why nobody had answered him for over twenty minutes when he made his first call to the tower. Something was obviously very wrong at Mahé airport. Surely prudence should have suggested that it might be wiser to fly on to the alternative destination in those circumstances: the island of Mauritius.

But it did not. The Boeing 707 pursued its course relentlessly. The pilot, for reasons known only to himself, decided to ignore the fact that there were no lights on the runway, that there was a strange and uncertain voice in the control tower, and that red flares were being fired from the end of the runway warning him not to land. All of this should have told him as plainly as could be not to land. But in spite of this he decided to land. There must have been some compelling reason for this extraordinary decision. There was. It was the first thing I asked the pilot when I met him, as you will read.

But for the moment, after having given my negative to Air India's request to land, I had more important matters to attend to. I found a telephone which was still working and rang up the head of the Resistance. As it was an automatic exchange the chances of interception were negligible. In any event, we had been on the ground for over four hours and so far there had been no sign, no message of any kind, from them. Didn't they owe us some loyalty, too? Where were the hundreds who would be dancing in the streets the minute they knew we had landed? Where were the hundreds who would flock to our support regardless? Conspicuous by their absence. As soon as I got through, a voice told me there was no Mr X there. I left a message for him nevertheless – 'Tell Mr X Mike is expecting him at the airport at once' – and gave it in French so there would be no mistake. He must have been standing right by that telephone. Where else would he be at a time like this? But nothing happened. Even so, I was still not convinced that the Resistance with its several hundred potential soldiers were to be written off as a chimera. Given a rallying-point and a resolute leader I was sure, am still sure, they would have made their way to me.

I had hardly put the phone down when I heard the sounds of a jet plane landing. I dashed to the other side of the hall and through the blackness of the night saw a Boeing 707 landing deep on the runway, tracer bullets fired from the barracks making patterns in the sky around it. The plane was using the searchlights in its wings, two jets of powdery white light stabbing the night. I could not believe it. The damned thing had landed against my orders! I sent for Tullio and asked him to find out what had happened. He reported that my order had been corrupted in transmission; the tower thought I wanted it to land. It was only by the grace of God – assisted by Goatley, I presumed – that the plane had not crashed into the lorry on the runway. It was nothing short of a miracle. But it was obvious that some part of the plane had been damaged by the truck, probably a wing flap. Why the hell did he do it? I would know soon enough. The plane turned and taxied up to us with that high-pitched scream from its jet engines which cauterises the eardrums of anyone within fifty yards. I sent for Duffy and asked him to present my compliments to the captain, to explain that we were in the middle of an attempted coup, that it would be safer to leave the passengers on board for the moment and would he kindly come to my headquarters.

A gangway was pushed up to the nose of the plane, and after a few minutes Duffy returned with the captain and another officer. The captain was a small Indian with the fine features of a high-caste Hindu. His name was Saxena. His co-pilot was a jovial-looking chap named Misra. They were both extremely worried, understandably; but after explaining the position, and trying to put them at their ease as far as I was able, I told them they were in no danger so long as they did what I told them. As long as they co-operated with me they would come to no harm from the enemy; I would see to that. My words were intended to convey that meaning; no more, no less. There was no threat implied.

'Why on earth did you land when you must have known something abnormal was going on down here?' I asked Saxena.

'I had to,' he said simply.

'You mean you were out of fuel?'

At that time I was not aware that this would have been a serious breach of international air-transport regulations. A plane must carry sufficient fuel at all times to enable it either to return to its point of departure or to fly to an alternative airport, in this case Mauritius.

'No,' he said, 'we had enough fuel, but we had already begun our descent.'

'But what difference does that make?'

'Well, once a plane like ours begins its descent it cannot climb again to 35,000 feet and still have enough fuel to reach its alternative airport. It uses too much in climbing.'

It was an answer all right, and who was I to question it? I do now, though. It is my firm belief that Air India flight AI 224 from Harare in Zimbabwe *en route* to Bombay via the Seychelles on 25 November 1981 had insufficient fuel on board to fly to any other airport in the event of an emergency at Mahé which would have made it impossible for him to land. I may mention here that this belief was common among the airport staff and the people of Mahé in the days following this incident. No other reason for taking the appalling risk of landing in those perilous circumstances makes any sense. As the captain said, he had to land.

But, whatever the reason for his landing, I had to get on with it. Our relationship was cordial. Saxena told me his chief concern was for his passengers. I replied that I shared his concern, but for a different reason. They and his plane were an embarrassment for me. If I could arrange for him to take off again, would he go? He answered readily that he would, that was exactly what he wanted. As it was also exactly what I wanted, I said I would try to get the necessary permission from somebody in Victoria. Meanwhile could we refuel him? Could he say how badly the plane was damaged? Again he co-operated readily. I sent for Dalgliesh and instructed him to refuel the plane under the direction of Captain Misra, the co-pilot. Very soon the air was filled with the reek of paraffin and Dalgliesh reported the plane was full. All I needed to know now was how badly the plane was damaged. Everything would depend on that.

I asked Tullio to find someone from among the civilians who could help us get permission for the Air India Boeing to take off. He returned with a slim, unsmiling individual who said he was Mr Loustou Lalanne, the air-traffic controller. He was the chap who had been in the control tower on his own when the Air India plane had made its first call to Mahé for permission to land. Apparently he had extracted himself from the comforting rubbish-bin without doing himself any lasting damage. He began to use the telephone.

Suddenly a shell screamed through the air and exploded on the runway two or three hundred yards from the airliner. And then another, but this time closer. A third shell, nearer still, rattled the plate-glass windows of our room. We threw ourselves to the floor, Saxena and Misra under the table. If the shells didn't kill us, those slabs of glass would. Tullio ran in to report.

'My God, Colonel, if they hit the plane every one of those passengers will be burned to death.'

'I know, Tullio. And, if that happens, there won't be a place in the whole wide world you and I will be able to hide after that. They will say we did it – deliberately!'

Loustou Lalanne held the phone out for me. I introduced myself as Mr Tom and used a moderate tone of voice. I asked for an immediate ceasefire in order to allow the Boeing to take off again at once. But there was a mad dog on the other end of the line. Not only a mad dog but a very frightened mad dog at that. And a mad dog that was as drunk as a skunk to boot. He screamed down the phone.

'Who the hell do you think you are? Who gave you permission to bring that plane down? Yes, I know you are holding seventy hostages. Yes, I know the shells are falling close to the plane. Yes, we are aiming at it. As far as we are concerned, the hostages and the plane are expendable!'

It was no good talking to him. The man was rabid. And his language unprintable. But apparently it was no less a personage than the Minister of Defence. I put the phone down on him.

'No luck, Colonel?' asked Tullio, worried.

'No breeding, Tullio,' I replied.

The shelling began again, more accurately. The gunner must have had an observation post close by as the range improved steadily. The target was unmistakably the Boeing airliner. De Wet, the soldier doctor who was holding the sector at the end of the runway, reported by radio that a boat was approaching his position. I assumed this must be *Topaz*. I knew it had a heavy gun in its armament; perhaps that was responsible for the shelling. But De Wet had taken a bearing on the flash of the gun and timed the flight of the shell. Good man, that De Wet, and a fine soldier, a worthy descendant of the illustrious Boer general of the same name so greatly admired in England, in keeping with that chivalrous tradition of the English which honours their bravest enemies. This new information would put the gun in the hills in the vicinity of the President's house at Sans Souci, about five miles away. If so, the gun must be a 75 mm recoilless rifle. It would certainly have the range. And the distinctive noise of the projectile confirmed it. It set me thinking. If it was a 75, who could be firing it? The Seychellois were not trained to it, I was sure. Was it perhaps our old friend Bob Noddyn? Not a nice thought, that, but we would find out one day; these things cannot be kept secret indefinitely in the mercenary world. Meanwhile I sincerely hoped not, if only for his sake.

Worse was to come. To give us a full hand, as it were, mortar-bombs began to fall on the runway in a haphazard fashion. This time they exploded. Somebody was reading the manual. Nothing to my mind is so demoralising as mortar-fire. It does not announce its impending arrival or its provenance. The first thing you know is that you are within the orbit of its lethal shards, all travelling at the speed of sound and all capable of inflicting instant death or hideous wounds. But in this instance they seemed to have no other purpose than to dent the runway, if that. At all events the mortar-attack stopped as suddenly as it began.

But I still had to stop the 75 mm and get permission for the plane to take off. I turned once more to Loustou Lalanne. This time he had more luck. A secretary put me through to an anonymous voice which was calm and cultured. It was the President.

'Mr President,' I began, 'in the name of humanity I ask you to stop the shelling of the Air India Boeing immediately. The plane and the passengers on board have absolutely nothing to do with this situation. I implore you to stop it at once.'

He said he would consider the point, and continued.

'You sound like a reasonable sort of chap, one I can talk to. Has it occurred to you that you and your men have been grossly misled? The position here is nothing like what you have been led to expect.'

'With respect, Mr President,' I interrupted, 'may we discuss that later? For the moment, we are within seconds of a catastrophe which could shock the world. Please, I beg you, stop the firing and give permission for the plane to take off at once. It has no connection with us whatsoever.'

At this point Saxena indicated by signs that he had something he thought I should tell the President. I cupped a hand over the mouthpiece.

'Tell him I have some members of the Zimbabwe Cabinet on board, including the wife of the Minister of Tourism, Mrs Shimurera.'

I relayed this important item to the President, and added: 'Please allow me to mention, sir, that if that Boeing 707 is blown up by your gunfire your tourist industry will suffer a setback from which it will not recover for ten or fifteen years to come – if at all.'

He said I should ring again in half an hour.

The shelling continued for another ten minutes and then stopped abruptly. I rang the President again to thank him. He still had not reached a decision about the take-off. The minutes of the night flashed by. I was conscious of an annoying feeling that I was expending my energies in the wrong direction. This was the time when I ought to have been planning the attack on the barracks, the time for encouraging the men, for preparation. Instead of that I was tied to this damn telephone and this infernal albatross of an aeroplane.

An hour later permission was obtained for the Boeing to take off. But, first, the President wanted to verify everything I had said with Saxena. I put the captain on the phone and held my hand over the cradle to cut him off if this became necessary. I did not intend to let Saxena give away any vital information regarding our strength. He confirmed that he was ready to take off. The President gave him thirty minutes in which to fuel up, not knowing this had already been done. With a sigh of relief Saxena put the phone down. Then he and Misra went out to make an examination of the plane and the damage done to the flap. A piece about ten feet long had been bent in the collision with the truck but as the flap mechanism functioned normally they decided they could take off. The Captain said he would have to give the engines an abnormal boost to overcome the effect of the damage.

'Sorry to be a nuisance, Mr Tom,' said Saxena, 'but I must make a personal examination of the runway. It is my duty. I cannot take the responsibility of a take-off knowing there may be impediments on the runway.' It was a quaint phrase, but I could see how right he was and thought highly of him for it. He was certainly a most conscientious skipper. I offered to have the truck removed for him. He said that was absolutely essential.

The President rang through again. Permission for take-off was granted subject to one thing. I must assure him that we would not leave with the plane. I gave him that assurance knowing full well he was merely making this statement for effect and that nothing would please him more than our sudden departure. I then asked him in my turn to assure me that the plane would not be fired on from the barracks as it took off, and that Saxena and Misra would be given safe conduct whilst they were examining the runway. He agreed to that.

Saxena got busy at once. Could he have a party of ten men for his protection, two jeeps and a searchlight? I refused him the men. I explained what would happen if the enemy were to see a group of men approaching them down the runway in this manner. They would open fire. I said I was sorry but the best I could do would be to give him one jeep and a searchlight and to phone the President once more to make certain the barracks knew exactly what was taking place. Saxena and Misra then drove off alone into the night, towards the barracks, about a mile or so off. It was an extremely brave action. I was certain they would draw enemy fire and I very much doubted if they would reach the end of the runway alive. We watched the jeep's headlights go down the runway, stopping from time to time and then disappearing altogether in the distance.

It occurred to me that they might never come back. There was nothing to stop them going straight to the barracks and asking for sanctuary. But in another thirty minutes they were back again, all smiles. I was answering the President's call as they approached. He wanted to know why they were taking so long, and how did he know I was not going to take off with them? I said I would speak to him on the phone at the exact moment of take-off when he would hear the plane's engines going by. This seemed to satisfy him.

Whilst I was on the phone Saxena had been talking to some of the men. They congratulated him on his bravery; it was a gallant piece of work. For his part, he said, he was genuinely grateful to me for arranging his departure. On the spur of the moment he added, addressing a group which included Sven Forsell, Don Kenny and a Swede named Jan Sydow: 'Is there anything I can do for you chaps? You saved me; perhaps I can save you.' Sven and Jan brought me this amazing offer. I said nothing, but Tullio was worried.

'Some of the men want to go on the plane, Colonel. They think we should accept the captain's offer.' There was a hint of apology in his voice.

'Who do?' I asked.

'The ones that have been talking to Saxena. If you say stay and fight, Colonel, then that is what we'll do. At least, you can count on me, and Kurt, and Peter Duffy and quite a few of the others. But I must tell you some of them think it would be wiser to go while we can.'

'Well, let's hear what they have to say, then. Get a representative group together and we can have a council of war. Ask Saxena and Misra to be present.'

Five minutes later eleven or twelve of us stood round the two pilots in the dark.

I began: 'Captain Saxena has offered to take us with him. Do we want to go or do we want to stay and fight it out? I know there's a lot to be said on both sides, but hear my advice first. Things don't look so good for us at this minute. They always look bad in the middle of the night. But at first light they will look different. My plan is to attack the barracks with our whole force. There are only about sixty Tanzanians holding it. You saw how they fight. I advise that we stay and fight it out. We must win.'

Pete Doorewaard spoke up.

'I'm sure you're right, Colonel. I agree we would win, but we must also suffer some casualties in the attack.'

'That's right. Most probably we will. But not abnormal ones.'

'How many men do you think we might lose?'

'Who knows? Maybe ten killed and wounded.'

'It's not worth it, Colonel.'

'You have lost the power of surprise, sir,' somebody added.

It was not what he said, which was true enough, but the way in which he said the words '*You* have . . .' which was so revealing. If he had said '*We* have . . .', it would have meant something completely different to me. They were not speaking as a unit. They were individuals. They could not be blamed for that, but they were not a unit. Neither were they being mutinous; they were merely saying what they thought, which was fair enough. They were intelligent men reasoning a problem out. We went on to discuss the strength of the enemy. Some of the men thought the Russians would send reinforcements from their naval vessels, which were known to be in the neighbourhood, within twenty-four hours. It was too late in the day for me to explain the absurdity of this proposition. If I had had time, I could have told them that there is not a single recorded instance of Russia interfering in any situation of this kind *using its own nationals*. But the fact that we had lost the element of surprise was undeniable, and I had told them repeatedly the success or failure of the operation would depend entirely on having it. I had to face that now. I turned to Saxena.

'You told some of my men you were prepared to take us with you. Is that so?'

'Yes. You have saved me, Mr Tom, now I will save you.'

'Thank you. Where can you take us?'

'Bombay?' We all laughed.

'Now, don't be ridiculous, Captain,' I said gently. 'You must know they'll send us straight back here on the next flight, don't you?'

'Well, where would you like to go? I can only fly for a maximum of five hours without refuelling and in any case I must look at my charts before we reach a decision.' Captain Misra went to fetch them from the cockpit.

While he was gone, I remembered that in one of my talks with

Jimmy Mancham he had said the Sultan of Oman was a friend of his and sympathetic to his cause. Eddie had also told me that if I hit trouble the Sultan would help us.

'How about Oman, Captain?' I asked.

'Oman? Where's that?'

'Don't play silly buggers, Captain,' I said. 'You know as well as I do where Oman is. How many hours' flying time is it?'

He said he would have to work it out with his navigational officer. But that proved unnecessary. One of my men, an Englishman who had held a commission in the British Army, had been seconded to the Omani Scouts.

'Permission to speak, sir? Not Oman, please, not Oman. I was stationed there. The place is run by the British. I can tell you now that as soon as we arrive the RAF will put us straight on another plane. We'll be back here in a matter of hours.'

There was a general murmur of agreement. Oman was out. (Months later I discovered by chance that the Englishman had been cashiered from the British Army for disgraceful conduct in Oman. Whether or not this had anything to do with the advice he gave us I cannot say.)

'Well, then, where else is within five hours?'

'Comoros.' It was Kurt.

The pilot said he knew the Comoros. 'No good,' he said. 'They can't take a Boeing 707. We need a minimum runway of two miles.'

'Mauritius?'

I spoke in favour of Mauritius, but the consensus was against it. I was reminded that the communist element under Bérenger was pretty active there.

'How about South Africa?' suggested Pete Doorewaard.

'Hell, Pete!' I said, shocked. 'An Air India plane! It will embarrass the hell out of the government.'

'Yes, I know it will, sir, but it can't be helped. In any case, it will be home. We'll be properly treated. It's a civilised country. We can make Durban in under five hours.'

Undoubtedly the men thought, particularly the Recce Commando, that as the South African government were completely behind us in the attempted coup surely they would do what they could to help us on our return. In similar circumstances the Israelis would act that way to help their nationals, wouldn't they? That was the general supposition. And after we had ruled out Black African countries there really was not much of a choice. Looking back on it now it was surprising that nobody suggested Kenya. Of all the ex-British colonies in Africa, Kenya was regarded as the most advanced, the most civilised and, we believed, sympathetic to the attempted coup. But nobody suggested it.

Saxena said he and Misra would have to consult about the flying time to Durban, but he thought it would be within range. He added, somewhat incongruously: 'I've always wanted to go to Durban.' We laughed, but I wondered if he knew anything about apartheid. The cheerful Misra cracked a joke about a blonde and a bottle of beer and Durban's famous beach which went down well and eased the tension.

I told Saxena I would not be coming with him, that I planned to stay behind and rally the Resistance, and that some of my men would stay with me. In any case, I had told the President that I would telephone him so that he could hear the plane taking off without me. Saxena said he hoped I would change my mind and suggested that at the last minute, after I had telephoned the President, I could climb on board by a rope ladder which he, Saxena, would let down from the cockpit. I thanked him and said I did not think it would be necessary.

I issued orders for the withdrawal. Tullio was to count the men as they embarked. No weapons or ammunition to go on board. All weapons to be destroyed before embarkation. Johan's body was to be wrapped in a tarpaulin and placed in the luggage bay with all respect. Our luggage was to be loaded; nothing need be left behind. Barney and Don Kenny were to destroy the secret codes, the lists of names given to me by Hoarau, and the large reel containing the tape-recorded message by Jimmy Mancham. Anybody who did not wish to go must report to me.

Roger England decided he would stay and take his chances. He would make his own way to the sea and swim the few miles back to his hotel across the bay. He was a hard little nut. If anybody could do it, he could. I shook his hand and wished him luck. Barney also decided to stay. He had examined the Boeing and didn't like the look of the flap. He reckoned the chances of getting off the ground were pretty slim. 'In any case, Colonel, they'll fire on the plane as soon as it gets within range. It's a sitting duck. An RPG7 properly handled could take it out.' I agreed with him that no power on earth would stop the Tanzanians firing on the defenceless plane, no matter what the President might order; but a target moving at 150 miles per hour might not be so easy to hit from one side as he might imagine. It was a gamble.

The sections fell back one by one, De Wet's last of all. Some of the men began to bend the barrels of their guns, not such an easy job as it sounds. Some flung the breech blocks into the bush. Others removed the firing pins and pocketed them. They searched in the dark for their luggage and loaded it into the plane. Pete Doorewaard took a small group of Johan's friends and they wrapped his body carefully and reverently in a large piece of canvas and carried it to the plane. He reported to me that his men were ready to go.

'I'm staying with you, Colonel,' said Barney. 'I've got a few weapons together. Shall I get some more chaps? I know Kurt and Peter Rohwein are game. And Tullio. Anybody else you want, Colonel?' Strange that they were all former 5 Commando men. An answer proved unnecessary. Tullio and Kurt came into my room looking very determined. Kurt had his Colt .45 in his hand, as usual.

'You are coming with us, Colonel,' he said, gently but firmly. 'We can't let you stay.'

'Sorry, sir,' said Tullio, 'but it's the best thing. We don't think you stand a chance. In any case, we are going to need you when we get home. There's a Mini-Moke outside.'

'Put that away, Kurt,' I said. 'We'll walk to the plane.' Suddenly, the whole thing seemed hopeless. Without Kurt and Tullio, my two most able and courageous lieutenants, the chances of raising the resistance would be negligible. Without them it would only be a matter of time before the few of us were rounded up and shot. There was no point in being a dead hero. I had to think again. And fast.

A hundred yards away the Air India Boeing prepared for take-off, its jet engines rising to a shrill pitch. Navigation lights blinked alternately from wings and tail and belly. A young Seychellois joined us as we walked across the apron. 'Sorry you have to go, sir,' he said, close to tears, 'but you'll come back one day, won't you?' 'Maybe,' I said and asked him to tell the 'hostages' not to leave their room before dawn; it could be dangerous for them if they were caught wandering about in the dark.

I said good-bye to Barney. Even at this fateful moment he could not shake off his 'mine host' manner, and saw me courteously to the foot of the stairs. He planned to make his way back to his hotel on foot, he said. Don't worry about him; he'd be all right. Kurt, Tullio and I walked slowly up the gangway and felt our way into the pitch-black interior of the cabin. The step into the dark was symbolic. It seemed to me it was the end of all things.

The cabin door slammed shut. The plane edged forward and picked up speed. The jet engines screamed hysterically as the giant wheels sped along the runway, faster and faster, forcing us relentlessly towards our destiny. The coin was in the air. If it came down heads, we would be OK. If not, a flash and it would be all over; we would never know what hit us. Tracer bullets curved through the sky around us as a parachute flare tried to turn night into day. Nothing had hit us . . . yet.

The Recce Commando men drummed on the floor with their heels, urging the plane to take off – one, two . . . one, two, three! . . . one, two . . . one, two three! – the paratroopers' ritual, and ended in the traditional cheer as the plane lifted off. The wheels locked in with a bang. The Boeing climbed steeply, pressing us back against each other as we sat in the blackness on the floor. We were safe. The plane levelled out and suddenly everything went quiet. The lights came on.

We were in the first-class compartment, and Tullio and I moved into two vacant seats against the bulkhead. We sat silently for a few minutes. I offered up a small prayer of thanks for deliverance from what looked like certain disaster in the air. One bullet in the petrol-tank would have been enough; the plane would have exploded before we were off the ground. But we were safe now. Safe to face the stark reality of failure.

It was just after 2.30 a.m. and two hours ahead of South African time. With a five-hour journey ahead of us we should land about 5 a.m. The captain made an announcement over the public address system, and told us we were headed for Johannesburg. He gave our estimated time of arrival as 5.30 a.m. There was a general gasp of dismay from the passengers when they realised they were going back almost to their starting-point. There were about seven in the first-class section. In the seat in front of me a middle-aged woman was talking animatedly to a gay and vivacious party whom I took to be Mrs Shimurera. She was by no means put out by the excitement of the last few hours. On the contrary, she bubbled over with laughter. None of the others seemed very upset, either. I wondered if they knew how close they had been to an awful death.

I went through to the tourist section and got Duffy to compile a nominal roll of my men on board. Barney Carey, Roger England, Gerry Puren and Aubrey Brooks were still on the island; forty-three men were present; Charlie Dukes was wounded and Johan Fritz dead. None of the men left behind was South African. I had honoured my undertaking to Brigadier Hamman. I looked the men over. They were settling down to sleep or chat to their neighbours in the normal way, but what astonished me was to see a number of them nursing their AK rifles on their laps whilst others were busy stowing them in the luggage compartments above their seats. I asked Tullio to explain how this had happened.

'I didn't have time to refer back to you, Colonel,' he said, 'so I changed your order myself. I had a very good reason for doing so.

If the take-off had been aborted and we had stopped at the end of the runway, we would have been at the mercy of the Tanzanians – no arms, nothing to defend ourselves with. I ordered about half the men to bring their weapons just in case.' I supposed he was right, there was that possibility, but it made things look very different. Now we were armed men aboard a civilian plane, not at all the same thing as unarmed men invited on board by the captain.

Saxena came back from the cockpit with a broad smile on his face. He held out his hand. 'Congratulations, Mr Tom!' he said warmly. 'I cannot thank you enough for getting us out of there.' I returned the compliment and told him I was glad to fly with such a brave man. His recce of the runway and the take-off in the face of small-arms fire needed nerves of iron. He passed it off modestly and ordered up some champagne, fetching the glasses himself. He made a little speech and handed the filled glasses to Tullio and Duffy and me. I didn't drink mine, only because champagne gives me a headache, but I accepted the glass in the right spirit. I then told the captain that I regretted that contrary to my orders some of my men had brought arms on board. Could I jettison them over the ocean? He laughed at my ignorance of pressurised cabins and said the next best thing would be to put them in disposal-bags. He called up one of the two Indian air hostesses – charming girls, one of them was actually a film star in Bombay – and asked her to bring some bags. These proved too small for the weapons, so Saxena suggested we stack the arms in a couple of blankets which a cabin steward placed on the floor near the forward galley just behind the cockpit. Tullio had the arms collected a little later and dumped in the blankets, which were then knotted and re-mained there until we disembarked.

Fatigue and reaction hit me hard. It was sixty-eight hours since I had had any real sleep. I slept fitfully for about half an hour, but the realisation of the sinister position we were in made real sleep impossible. Tullio had been thinking things over, too, it seemed.

'Well, Colonel, what now?'

'Five million dollars and we do the job properly, Tullio. There's no future in cut-rate coups!'

Tullio laughed. He decided to hand me his ultimate accolade.

'Colonel,' he said with feeling, 'you got balls!'

Contemplating the truth or otherwise of this anatomical compli-ment, I fell into a decent sleep.

When I awoke, Goatley, the helicopter pilot, was sitting in the cockpit behind the left-hand seat, chatting amiably to the pilots. Previously he had asked me if he should go there to help them with their approach to the South African coast as this would be strange to them. I thought that would be a good idea and agreed. That little effort earned him a twenty-month sentence in gaol! But for the moment he was swapping yarns with the pilots and learning something about a Boeing. Dalgliesh joined him for an inspection in much the same way as passengers are sometimes invited to visit the cockpit on normal flights.

But time was going and we had to think seriously about our intentions on landing. For my part there was never any alternative to a straight surrender to the authorities and let them make what they liked of it. The fact that the South African government had organised our attempted coup to a very large extent must count for something; but in fairness it was only reasonable that we should try to cover up for them as much as we could. We owed them that out of loyalty. In the last three years, I am sorry to tell you, that word has become rather tarnished in my vocabulary; but that was my thinking then and it was certainly the thinking of Dalgliesh and Duffy. Ken had contacts in the Security Branch and Peter also knew a number of senior officers in Durban. They both thought it would be correct to advise them of our arrival in advance. If they were given enough time, Peter thought they would be able to help us and themselves out of what must prove an embarrassing situation. As soon as we came within radio range of Johannesburg he sent the message, adding that as a result of an international emergency we requested permission to land. The wording, which was somewhat unusual, was suggested by the crew.

Peter was hoping that if the Security people were given enough notice of our arrival they could transfer us to another aircraft immediately after we landed. We would then take off never to be seen again. But in fact we would land at some remote airport in the country and then melt back into normal life after a reasonable pause. That was his theory. It sounded a bit far-fetched to me but at least it was a plan. In my heart I was convinced that things would take their course regardless of whatever we might try to do to help. The fat was in the fire and there would be no way we could stop it spluttering.

As dawn began to break the pilot sent back a note to say that Johannesburg was closed because of ground mist and Bloemfontein was the nearest alternative airport. Had we any objections to that? I said no, but Durban was nearer. The captain preferred Durban as he was running low on fuel. So without any preliminary reconnaissance he dropped steadily down over the city and made a perfect landing with a ten-knot tail-wind at Louis Botha Airport, Réunion, a minute or two after 5 a.m. Peter Duffy went forward to the cockpit to suggest to the captain that a far corner of the field, as far from the public gaze as possible, would suit us best. This would also give the security officials a chance to help us if they wanted to. We taxied up to a distant hangar and halted.

Some twenty minutes passed before the doors were opened, a gangway brought to the forward entrance and the engines switched off. An ambulance dashed up and a doctor came on board. He was a professor from the famous Wentworth Hospital near by. His staff had been alerted during the night and were ready to deal with heavy casualties on board. The doctor fixed Dukes up with a drip, attended to one or two minor ailments and left. We waited. An hour dragged by. Plainly the authorities were flummoxed. So was I. What would their reaction be to this extraordinary situation? 'Blue' Kelly, one of the men recruited by Dolinchek and an employee of the NIS, obtained permission from the captain to disembark and telephone his headquarters in Pretoria. He brought back no news. But after an hour or so a plain-clothes officer from the South African Railways police boarded the plane, chatted with Duffy whom he knew, and discussed matters with the captain in the cockpit. The police officer then took over command of the plane.

It was now past eight o'clock. The passengers were becoming restless and the children noisy. The captain found it necessary to rebuke them over the intercom but later allowed them to disembark and walk around the plane to get a little fresh air. We remained seated and bored to tears. Certain people in Pretoria must have wondered what the hell to do with us, but a decision was finally taken, I imagine, along these lines: it was obviously a hijack; they must in no way be seen to condone the action of hijackers; they must act as they would if the plane had been hijacked, for example, by a gang of Arabs. Their next move was in step with that line of thought: send in the South African Railways Police Task Force at once! Which is precisely what they did.

About ten o'clock – that is to say, nearly five hours after our arrival – a South African Air Force Hercules C130 landed and disgorged fifty policemen dressed in anti-riot gear, steel helmets, body armour, the lot, who now raced towards our peaceful Boeing and surrounded it with a creditable show of military zeal and expertise in keeping with the highest standards of an élite force. I presumed they were putting into action a drill for combating some deadly terrorist threat. But in the present circumstances the drill was singularly inappropriate if not absurd. The men ringed the plane, some taking up the lying position under the wings, some kneeling under the tailplane, some standing, but all pointing their weapons inwards towards the plane with deadly malice.

Thank God they never found it necessary to fire. Without a doubt they would have written off half their own force, not to mention the plane itself and all its passengers, wicked mercenaries and innocent civilians alike. But common sense prevailed after a while, and an officer suggested that it might be wiser if they turned about and made as though to resist imminent attack from without rather than from within. While this was all highly entertaining to our somewhat jaded senses we gained the distinct impression from our ringside seats that this task force might not be, after all, an élite force, but was drawn perhaps from volunteers who had seized the chance to get down to Durban-by-the-sea for the weekend. A few of my men, viewing this sorry performance with alarm, remarked later that their greatest moment of danger was not at Mahé but on the ground at Durban airport. I am sorry to have to add a sad footnote to this story. One of the 'task force' visiting his girlfriend that same evening accidentally discharged his firearm in her living-room killing her instantly.

It was now eleven o'clock, and the charade had almost played itself out. Honour apparently had been satisfied and the South African Police had demonstrated, via the press, that they were perfectly capable of handling hijack situations by whosoever committed without fear or favour. The passengers were told to disembark by Colonel Mouton, the South African Railways police officer in civilian clothes who had taken over earlier, and they left by the after gangway. Many of them had made friends with my men during the flight and there was a touching scene when one of my gay Lotharios bid farewell to a very pretty girl whom he had induced to nurse his imaginary wounds all the way from Mahé. We meet the bold and handsome Lieutenant Nick Wilson again later in the story.

But now there was some positive action. The plane was towed to a hangar close by and we were asked to disembark. The crew lined up at the forward door and shook hands with us as we passed through with many a merry quip. I thanked Saxena and Misra for all they had done and told them I would see them one day in Hornby Road. Who knows, I might. We then strolled over to a hut inside the hangar, accompanied by some Railways policemen, types rather more relaxed than the 'task force', and were ushered into a large room. We took our seats on benches facing a blackboard and were asked to write our names, including our *noms de guerre*, if any – nice touch, that – on a piece of paper. This was taken by a grey-haired officer standing by the blackboard. He cleared his throat and announced in English: 'I am Brigadier J. S. Visser, Divisional Commissioner Port Natal of the South African Police. I arrest all of you on a charge of hijacking an aeroplane. You are now my prisoners. You will remain here until it is decided what is to be done with you.'

I immediately stood up. I was at the back of the room.

'Excuse me, sir. May I say something?'

'Yes. Who are you?'

'My name is Hoare. I am the leader of this group. I wish to protest most strongly. I wish you to note that we did not hijack the aeroplane. An arrangement was made between myself and the captain of the Boeing. Please verify this whilst he is still here.'

The Colonel said he would make a note of what I said.

An hour later we left the room and were directed towards a pile of luggage and told to find what belonged to us. Mine had vanished. We were then escorted to a South African Air Force Hercules C130, very warlike in its khaki livery, and walked up the ramp to find an uncomfortable seat for the two-hour ride to Waterkloof air base near Pretoria. The authorities were taking no chances and had provided armed guards to watch over us. They need not have bothered. Every man slept soundly all the way.

A large crowd of servicemen gathered round the plane as the ramp went down. We marched off two by two to be handcuffed to one another by a policeman at the bottom of the ramp. As the young policeman placed the bracelets on my wrists he said in a very quiet voice: 'Sorry to do this to you, sir.' It was a gentle thought. We climbed into two or three waiting trucks. With a wailing of sirens the convoy of trucks, outriders and official cars whisked us away from the air base and down the road to Pretoria. One or two of the knowledgeable, recognising the road, guessed we were headed for Sonderwater Prison, one of South Africa's four maximum-security gaols, reserved exclusively for Whites.

An hour later we stopped in front of some bungalows almost hidden behind rows of wire-mesh fencing topped with a tangle of barbed wire. It was Sonderwater Prison. At first sight it looked harsh, sordid and utilitarian. In places some flowering bougainvillaea triumphed over it.

It was the end of the road.

CHAPTER 6

The Supreme Court

ANY ILLUSIONS which may have existed in our minds that we were some species of hero were soon dispelled. It was made abundantly clear to us that we were criminals. A series of orders were barked out at us as we lined up for the induction process during which our personal possessions, money, watches, rings, and so on, were taken from us, registered and placed in a small white bag. Then we were told to strip naked to see whether we were secreting dagga (marijuana) or not. A disagreeable-looking Afrikaner in sports clothes shouted at me: 'Hey, you! You in charge of this lot?'

'Yes. I was. Why?'

'Well, don't give us any trouble, hey,' adding a few phrases in a similar vein, all singularly aggressive.

Then it was my turn.

'Are you in charge here?'

'Yes. What do you want?'

'Why do you find it necessary to treat us like criminals? We are soldiers, not thieves and rapists.'

This novel suggestion seemed to be more than he could comprehend at one sitting. He dismissed it and me with a shrug.

We were in the unenviable position of being held incommunicado under Section 22 of Act 62 of 1966, the dreaded Act under which the State could keep us in prison indefinitely without trial – or without a charge, for that matter. Nobody told us this; it was something we found out painfully for ourselves in the next few days. Anything more demoralising than to be kept in prison under this

Act, deprived of the normal rights pertaining to a prisoner awaiting trial, is hard to imagine.

The punishment cells of the prison, known as the 'bom cells', had been specially vacated to accommodate us. We had one each. Kurt was in the next one to mine, but it was impossible to talk to him; a warder was on duty the whole time. It was solitary confinement, no books, no writing materials, no shoes. They even took our trouser belts away. At first it didn't matter. We slept. Not a sound came from the forty-three of us for the next ten hours.

Late the following day I had a visit from General Zietsman of the South African Police. He was the head of the Criminal Investigation Department and had been appointed investigating officer for this case. His attitude was friendly and helpful. I began by complaining that we were being treated like terrorists. If we were to be charged with an offence, why were we not brought before a magistrate in the normal manner when we could apply for bail and have legal representation, and so on? The General seemed slightly amused with my naïveté.

'All in good time, Mike,' he said, 'but first things first. We want to find out exactly what happened. I want you to get all your boys together and ask them to co-operate with us. They have nothing to lose and perhaps something to gain.'

'Like what, for instance?'

'Well, we can let you have books to read, give you your shoes back and so on. Perhaps we can arrange a little recreation for you on the sports field, things like that.'

He went on to explain that the South African Police had nothing to do with the Prisons Department, which was a separate entity and a law unto themselves. It was the first time I had heard that remark but not the last. Little did I appreciate how true it was. But if we co-operated in the making of full and frank statements to the South African Police, then he, General Zietsman, would do what he could with the Prisons Department to ease our lot. As we had no reason to be anything but co-operative the men agreed readily. Early the following morning a team of police officers arrived at the prison and we began to make our statements. Nobody cautioned us that these statements might be used in evidence against us at a later trial. Our general impression was that the authorities were trying to sift the true situation so that they could advise the Attorney-General of the Transvaal. He would then bring some charge against us or set us free. Little did we know how damning our statements would prove to be. With hindsight I thoroughly agree with the old lags who taught me the golden rule in prison: 'Never make a statement without your lawyers; better still, never make a statement!'

I gave my statement to a Brigadier du Plessis, who thoughtfully provided a typewriter. I stated the history of the attempted coup, the involvement of the South African government, the recruitment, the operation such as it was, the arrival of the Air India Boeing, Saxena's offer to take us with him after we had obtained permission for him to take off again, and so on. I ended:

> Of the original weapons supplied to me by Brig. Hamman the balance which were not used for some reason, as for example the RPG7s as being too big for this operation, were reported to the Brigadier. He was to make arrangements to collect them from my house in Hilton. This may have been done by now.
>
> I have been punctilious in my observance of the agreement I made with Brig. Hamman – namely SA interests were to be protected at all costs, hence the reduction in the number of SA nationals taking part; and secondly, that I must not leave any SA Army personnel on the island regardless. This I have also done.
>
> I would like to make a suggestion in this statement. Of the 45 men who formed the main party 20 are SA nationals and 25 foreign passport holders. As the precise make-up of the force by nationality is known only to me I would like to suggest that all the SA passport holders are released and the blame etc. taken by the 25 foreigners of whom I am one. This should be practical as the SA men involved are of a high calibre and understand the importance of this step. The mercenary force would then be seen as 25 men which is an acceptable figure.

The General was as good as his word. As soon as the statements were completed we received certain privileges, books appeared and we got our shoes back. We were medically examined, photographed and had our finger- and palm-prints taken. The food, however, remained almost inedible. It was served morosely by a long-termer who shoved the steel plate under the grille with a flourish and a clatter. Here you are, Fido, good boy, din-dins! Except it was food no self-respecting dog would have eaten.

Then to my surprise I was told to report to the front office where

Brigadier du Plessis and another senior police officer said they had orders to take me to my home in Hilton, some 350 miles away, to search my house for papers connected with the operation. They hoped I would co-operate. I did. We arrived several hours later in their fast car to the astonishment of Phyllis, who naturally thought I had been released. As it was her birthday she persuaded the police officers to stay for dinner once they had gone through my files and removed everything they needed. The wine-cellar was of course still embarrassingly full of small arms and ammunition surplus to requirement, so they made immediate arrangements to relieve me of these. We returned to Sonderwater in the early hours of the next morning. The short excursion into reality had a strange surrealistic quality about it which evaporated as soon as the cell doors clanged behind me.

On the sixth day General Zietsman appeared again to announce that all the men were to be released unconditionally and at once, save five who were to be charged with 'man-stealing'. I assumed this was a direct translation from the Afrikaans for 'kidnapping'. It seemed a strange sort of charge, but I was happy for the men who were to go scot-free. The general mood was that the whole thing was not of any great importance as far as the authorities were concerned. Plainly the Attorney-General for the Transvaal must have studied our statements and presumably those of the Air India crew and decided there was no basis for a charge. Why, the Minister of Law and Order himself, Mr Louis Le Grange, had stated, according to the press, that the episode in the Seychelles was nothing to get fashed about, 'just a few men running around in the bush shooting out a few windows'. Although he was ridiculed for this statement at a later stage, we who had taken part in it were inclined to agree with him. But not apparently the Seychelles government. They immediately put in a claim to the United Nations for compensation amounting to $19 million! A high price for one plate-glass door, several bottles of Coca-Cola, and a couple of high-tension wires which had been severed by bullets outside the barracks. And possibly several pairs of trousers belonging to highly placed individuals in the government. I don't think they succeeded with their claim.

Two days later the five of us – Tullio, Peter Duffy, Dalgliesh, Goatley and myself – appeared before a magistrate in Pretoria. The press were there in full force. We were remanded for a month, no charge was laid and we were allowed bail – R10,000 for myself and R5000 for each of the others. (At this time the South African rand was worth slightly more than the American dollar.) If the South

African Police did not view the affair too seriously, the magistrate obviously did.

On my return home Phyllis brought me up to date with all that had happened since 25 November. The night that we returned from the island in the Boeing was also one of intense drama for her. Eddie Camille had been on the phone from London several times during the night, almost distraught, trying to find a way to bring help to us in Mahé. Whilst we were in the air Jimmy Claasens had rung her from Pretoria with a message of hope and encouragement: 'They are on their way back. Don't worry. Everything is going to be all right. Thank God he's brought the boys back!' But as for Jimmy Claasens in person there was no sign. His telephone number in Pretoria had been discontinued, and he himself had vanished.

And Captain Saxena? What of him? Well, a most interesting development. As soon as we had left the Boeing in Durban he and his crew disembarked and were taken to a VIP lounge where they were medically examined by the British Airways medical officer. Saxena and Misra then made statements to the police, and his crew gave an interview to South African television. Yes, she had seen it.

The navigator was asked: 'Well, Mr Vasan, what was it like to have experienced a hijack?'

'Pardon me, it was not a hijack!'

'How do you mean?'

'No, it was not a hijack. You can say they commandeered the plane.'

I immediately ordered a copy of that interview and had it delivered to my lawyer in Johannesburg. Strange to tell that, although he charged me R165 for it, I never did get to see it myself. Somewhere along the line the video tape was lost in the lawyer's office. Neither did he see fit to introduce it as evidence in my defence.

As dawn broke in Mahé on the morning of our departure the intrepid Tanzanians decided to attack the now undefended airport buildings, without, it was reliably reported in distant Bagamoyo, a trace of fear. From a range of about a hundred yards they opened fire with an RPG7, one rocket smiting the Fokker Friendship squarely on the nose. A hit, a palpable hit! At the sound of this firing the remainder of the Seychelles army still in barracks, convinced that they were under attack once more, scaled the security fences as one man never to be seen again. It was said that they waited not upon the order of their going but went. The Tanzanians then advanced triumphantly to the airport terminal where, meeting no resistance, they visited a terrible vengeance on the duty-free stores. Those that were not busy getting themselves horribly drunk on hard liquor were now looting everything portable in the Swazi airliner including the carpeting. From thence they moved to bigger and better things. On the charitable but improbable assumption that the enemy, ourselves, had moved to Victoria itself, they advanced on the capital, there to indulge in a spectacular orgy at the larger and better-stocked duty-free shop. The rest of that day was spent in looting and rapine on a scale never before seen in Mahé, not even in the days of the privateers of the seventeenth and eighteenth centuries. Perhaps the Seychelles government would have been better advised to address their $19 million claim to Dar es Salaam rather than to Turtle Bay.

But the uproar which followed boded ill for my men on the island. There was never any chance that they could pretend they were ordinary tourists – one of their number saw to that. The army, aided by the police, set to with a spirit of determination born of revenge to round them up. Roger England, who had indeed swum his way back to his hotel and got himself quietly to bed as though nothing untoward had happened, was the first to be apprehended. It was not just a question of simple arrest. The army had to show that they were in command, and this meant beating up the suspects and throwing them into prison with the maximum degree of brutality. After Roger they found Barney. They proceeded to break all his ribs and smash in his face. One by one they picked the others up; somebody had indeed split. Aubrey was found wounded, lying in the bush unconscious, and taken to hospital under armed guard where he received the battering meted out to them all regardless of his wound. Nothing is so senselessly cruel and harsh as a coward in a position of authority, and the Tanzanians and the Seychellois in this case were no exception. Bleeding and knocked about, Barney, Roger and Aubrey found themselves in solitary confinement. Donaldson, who was now unmasked by the Seychelles Police as Dolinchek, alias Anton Lubick, accompanied them but miraculously escaped ill-treatment. Very odd.

There was now a hue and cry to find Gerry Puren. The island was combed from end to end, on foot and from a helicopter, but Gerry had vanished. Obviously he was in one of two places, either with his cousin Frank or with his old friend Bob Noddyn, but of course the authorities were not to know that. He remained undetected for fourteen days, which was a pretty stout effort for a sixty-year-old, after which he emerged on 10 December like John the Baptist proclaiming that he had existed all that while on the wild fruits of the island, bedding down at night on the hospitable leaves of the ubiquitous palm tree.

Phyllis had warned her brother Bob by telephone that the balloon had gone up and that he must dispose of the arms in the safe house at once. He tried but found it impossible to get rid of them all in time. He hung on too long in the belief that as nobody knew him they would leave him alone. Worse still, he just could not bring himself to destroy those lovely weapons! But somebody had split on him, too. He was arrested, beaten up and flung in gaol.

Whilst these arrests were being made the Seychelles government, in the best Marxist fashion, had engaged the services of Rent-a-crowd, who now gathered several times a day at strategic places to shout and scream for the blood of the prisoners. Instant death was demanded, and the clamour reached the prisoners in their cells. Their condition was now so bad that they did not care what happened.

Back in South Africa I set to at once to furnish legal aid for the men. I visited a Johannesburg lawyer, who appointed a Mahé attorney, one Kiernan Shah, to represent them. I tried to find a barrister who was eligible to appear in a Seychelles court. This was trickier than it appeared. The Seychelles Chief Justice had told us that no South African barristers would be permitted to appear in their courts other than those with Commonwealth status. We found such a one, who also had dual Irish and South African nationality, which would prove convenient, but he was not a State Counsel (roughly the equivalent of a Queen's Counsel in the United Kingdom) but a Senior Advocate at the Transvaal Bar. His name was Mike Hannon. The defence of the men on the island was now placed in his hands. Regrettably, Camille, Hoarau and company were unable to contribute anything towards the costs of their defence and showed little interest in their fate, or our fate, from that moment on. The hired hand must face his own consequences. I do not complain of this. It is one of the risks attached to this way of life.

But now I came face to face with one of life's more unpalatable facts. The cost of defending oneself in a court of law must rank as one of the most expensive undertakings which can beset the average man in the course of his life. A barrister may charge a fee for one day's appearance in a high court equal to what an artisan earns in one month! Furthermore, that day may consist of no more than two hours. The fairness of this is completely beyond my understanding, even after taking into account the time he may require for familiaris-ing himself with the brief. However, that was how it was, and I had to get on with it.

It soon became apparent that the men in the Seychelles would not be brought to trial in any great hurry. My main concern was that no arbitrary or barbaric action should be taken against them, no kangaroo courts, no summary judgement whereby they would be taken out one night by enthusiastic citizens and done to death. I have seen this type of justice meted out in Africa before. I suppose I am one of the few to have witnessed a trial by acclamation, where the accused are arraigned before a mob, who then scream 'Guilty. Kill him!' (Stanleyville 1964) or in exceptional cases 'Let him go!' But Hannon was confident the norms of justice would prevail in this case, albeit slowly. In fact the greater the delay in their trial the better the chances would be for them, passions would abate, and a fairer trial might ensue. In the meantime we must do whatever we could to ease their lot. The first thing was to arrange for Hannon to visit the men to assure them they were not forgotten and to see they were being reasonably treated. Ugly rumours had seeped out of prison and found their way back to Britain about the disgraceful treatment the men were receiving at the hands of the prison and army bully boys, and the British authorities had intimated that this must stop. It did not, but that redoubtable leader Mrs Thatcher did not intend to be thwarted by a minor nation in this blatant manner. At a later stage she demanded a proper standard of justice and obtained it. The prisoners were, after all, British nationals.

The pendulum of justice now swung in my direction. At five o'clock on the morning of 5 January 1982 came the imperious knock on the door which has become the dreaded symbol of official tyranny in South Africa. Two police officers, both majors, stated that I was under arrest as from that moment and must surrender myself into their custody at once. I demanded the right to call my lawyer on the phone. They tried to resist this, but I succeeded after some heated argument. I was taken to Durban, placed for several hours in a police cell at C. R. Swart Headquarters, documented and finger-printed, and so on, once again, until joined by nine of my men who had been similarly rounded up. The same scene was being enacted in Johannesburg. Comparing notes later we discovered that the treatment of my men in the Transvaal was markedly less rough than ours in Natal.

To my surprise there had been a reversal of policy. All the men who had been released without charge at Sonderwater on 2 December had now been rearrested together with the five of us who were on the man-stealing charge. At a brief hearing in the magistrates court we were all remanded on bail on fresh charges under the Civil Aviation Offences Act No. 10 of 1972. The charge of man-stealing was dropped. Bail was set at R20,000 for me, R10,000 for the four others, and about R1000 for the remaining thirty-five. Passports had to be surrendered, and we were obliged to report to a local police station at certain times each week. Obviously somebody had had a rethink about the seriousness of our case and was anxious to show the world that the matter was not going to be swept under the carpet. It was rumoured that pressure had been brought on the South African government by the Air Line Pilots' Association to take stringent action against us. It was known in our circle that South African Airways took the dimmest possible view of our government-aided action in the Seychelles, whilst of course they would have been among the main beneficiaries had it succeeded. Any failure on the part of the government to prosecute us, they felt, could jeopardise their operations worldwide. Thus, it was thought, they added their weight to the case for action against us. As far as the general public were concerned, the newspapers had already tried us and found us guilty of hijacking the Boeing. On the day we landed the *Rand Daily Mail* announced in banner headlines 'HIJACK!' It now seemed that the government were only too anxious to appease these lobbies.

I determined to get the best defence that I could afford for my men and myself. I sent out a telegram to all the accused saying that I was arranging this and that those who wished could be included at no cost to themselves. Those who wanted to defend themselves by other means were of course free to do so. Peter Doorewaard immediately informed me that ten members of his Recce Commando group – two others had turned State's witnesses – would be defended by Mr Eddie Stafford, SC, assisted by Mr P. C. Oosthuizen, SC, both members of the Transvaal Bar. As the brief for these eminent barristers was in excess of R100,000 it became obvious that the Defence Force, through some sense of obligation no doubt, was footing the bill. All the rest came under my umbrella bar 'Blue' Kelly, an NIS agent, who decided to defend himself. Prescience is a characteristic of this remarkable Australian.

I had told my solicitor that R50,000 was the maximum that I could afford for my defence and that when that had gone I would be obliged to dispense with all legal representation and go it alone. He assured me that, at this stage anyway, it was highly unlikely that the trial would last long enough to exhaust that sum. How naïve I was. In the end I spent a total of R80,000 on our defence, including the defence of the men on the island, before my advocate retired from the case, leaving me to defend myself, and the men to defend themselves, at our own cost. Of this sum I was able to recover R25,000 from the money entrusted to me by the Seychellois for the operation.

But apart from legal costs we were finding it hard to maintain ourselves with the trial hanging over us. The men were unable to settle to any steady employment and their financial reserves were being rapidly depleted. I motored to Pretoria to ask the Welfare Department if there was any possibility of our being able to 'get a number' as they say, to enable us to appeal to the public for some assistance with our legal and related costs. My lawyers prepared a case, but we were turned down. If they gave us permission, I was given to understand, it would then not be possible for them to refuse it to those Black groups – and there were several of them – who were also asking for permission to appeal for funds from the public to support themselves and their families during trials for terrorism, political offences, and the like.

Later I sought the assistance of *Soldier of Fortune* magazine in Boulder, Colorado, in the United States. They placed an advertisement in their magazine, which incidentally has a readership in excess of 1½ million, telling their readers that I was selling my 5 Commando shoulder-patch for US$5, and that the sale of this item would assist me personally in meeting the costs of our defence. With typical generosity the Americans responded speedily and during the next three years my wife maintained a brisk correspondence with over 3500 Americans many of whom were kind enough to buy the patch.

But my most immediate and pressing need was to engage a barrister for our defence. To this end I was introduced to Mr Hymie Slomowitz, SC, in Johannesburg, a highly respected member of the Transvaal Bar. I attended the famous barrister in his chambers in Pritchard Street. He began with the observation that he was not sure whether he could take my case or not as this would depend on the date of my trial, but if he did he would insist on a certain strategy. He held up the statement which I had made to the instructing solicitor. At the end of it I had written: 'I do not wish to make any reference to the SADF Delivery Note, or the part played by the SA Army, in my defence, unless circumstances are so disastrous that my solicitor advises me otherwise.' This, he said, was not how he saw things.

If he accepted the case, he continued, he would insist on two things. (1) If he was acting for the group of thirty-one men he must have our assurance that we were all of one mind. A conflict of opinion during the course of the trial would almost certainly result in a retrial. How far-seeing this eminent SC was will become evident later on in the story. (2) He would insist on the fullest possible disclosure of all government involvement in the Seychelles affair. In his view that was my only hope. He then went through the case thoroughly and expertly, examined a number of alternative approaches to the defence and ended with these sombre words:

'There is absolutely no doubt in my mind that you will be found guilty and that you will be sentenced to a term of imprisonment. The only thing which is in doubt is how long that sentence will be.'

I don't think I was particularly shocked. It had become obvious to me in the few weeks since the operation that the government was obliged to have us tried in the full glare of world publicity and that they would be at pains to show that South African courts were part of an independent judicial system free from any governmental interference. Despite all else which may be said against the South African government, it would be very hard for an objective and fair-minded observer to find differently. That was certainly my thinking at that time; my subsequent trial did much to persuade me otherwise. But if I was to defend myself by telling all I knew about government involvement, I asked Mr Slomowitz, surely this would be grossly disloyal on my part to people who had tried to help me, and surely this would react to my detriment. When I was found guilty and sentenced surely this evidence would be remembered and they would lock me up and throw away the key. Mr Slomowitz was not disposed to discuss that aspect of the aftermath, but restated that my best defence was to tell the entire truth regardless of any feelings of loyalty I might have towards the government or anyone else. Regrettably, as it transpired later, he was unable to act for me owing to an engagement elsewhere, but as Mr Hannon was already familiar with our case I asked him to defend us as well as the men on the island.

The trial was set down for 10 March and would be held in the Natal Supreme Court in College Road, Pietermaritzburg. This was a disappointment. There could be no doubt that a trial in the Transvaal would have been more to our advantage, if only because of the preponderance of Afrikaners in that province. The Hon. Mr Justice James, acting Judge President of Natal, would preside assisted by two assessors, Mr G. G. Lynn and Mr L. L. Mackay. I recall being unpleasantly surprised that there was to be no jury, which only goes to show how little I knew about the South African legal system. The jury system died out in South Africa just after the Second World War, in practice, but was not legally abolished until 1969. In the ensuing days I had plenty of time to ponder the differences. I presumed the jury system had been abandoned because it did not suit the multiracial character of the nation. Twelve good men and true might be all right in Britain and in America where all men are deemed equal in the eyes of the law, but here in South Africa what would happen if juries were composed, as they would be at present, entirely of White men? In a terrorist trial of Blacks, for instance, an all-White jury would certainly be prejudicial to their interests. So to that extent perhaps a judge and two assessors might be fairer.

But I was sorry that there was no jury. A strict interpretation of an Act of Parliament is not the only consideration in a court of law. Our forefathers who introduced the jury system wrought much wiser and fairer than they knew. Justice tempered by the understanding of one's fellow-men is, in my humble view, much fairer than slavish adherence to a criminal code which allows a judge no latitude, no exercise of plain humanity. Legal experts, the so-called triers of fact, administer the law in all its stark rigidity, and very frequently without the simple understanding which might serve as mitigation in the eyes of the accused's peers, the twelve good men and true.

So, on the morning of 10 March, Tullio and I presented ourselves in good time at the Supreme Court. The case had aroused the interest of the world press and their representatives were there in large numbers. The Supreme Court is housed in one of those old red-brick buildings which were built by the British in late-Victorian times and remain the glory of present-day Pietermaritzburg. But as a modern courthouse it is woefully inadequate, its only attraction lying in its size which enables it to accommodate a large number of accused where it is necessary that they should be tried simultaneously – as, for example, in a terrorist trial.

The scene inside was impressive. The courtroom itself was over sixty feet wide and ninety feet long. The domed ceiling was seventy-five feet high and strutted with wooden rafters from which fluorescent lights were suspended. At one end a bench had been constructed five feet high behind which the judge and the two assessors would sit. To the right of the judge was the witness-box, which was equipped with a microphone. To his left were two benches to accommodate twelve members of the press, which in other times would have seated the jury. In the well of the court sat a lady registrar and a stenographer. Behind them were three tables for the three members of the prosecution and behind them again tables for the counsel for the defence. To one side of these tables were more benches for official observers. In all an imposing array. We, the forty-three accused, sat behind counsel for the defence in three tiers of benches of a type more suitable for a cathedral than for a court. The depth of the seats made it impossible to lean back. Behind us, a good eighty feet away from the majesty of the bench, was the public gallery which might seat as many as a hundred people. A coat of arms of the Republic of South Africa hung behind the judge's bench, draped on either side with heavy crimson curtains. Interpreters and court orderlies were seated close to the witness-box, and two police sergeants, armed, sat on either side of the accused.

Almost a Hollywood setting but for an ugly green box-like contraption just in front and to one side of the accused which housed the air-conditioning. When this was turned on it became virtually impossible to hear what was being said in the front of the court. The acoustics, in any case, were very poor.

From the first day I was doomed to disappointment. I had been brought up on the literature of famous high-court trials at the Old Bailey in London and elsewhere and looked forward to hearing the same sort of superb English, beautifully phrased, from the Attorney-General of Natal and his two assistants, as they developed their case against us. Not an unreasonable expectation. After all, eloquence, good diction, the judicious choice of words, these were the very stuff of courts of law as I had read about them. Judge of my surprise when the Attorney-General rose to address the court for the first time; it was quite impossible to hear him! His voice was low, his enunciation poor, and his remarks addressed entirely at the judge seated a few feet away from him. His manner showed an arrogant disregard for the accused. I immediately asked our counsel, by means of a note, to protest. We simply could not hear. But worse was to come. When we could hear the chief prosecutor his accents were not those of the Inner Temple but plainly those of an Afrikaner who had learned English late in life. Not that there is anything wrong with that, let it be said, but the way he pronounced words such as 'mer-sennerry' did violence to the ear. To add to my misery his name was Rees, which had led me to expect the lyrical cadences of Wales. But these were matters to be borne with patience. We were, it must be remembered, only the accused; the drama being played out up front was what really mattered, or so we were given to understand.

The Civil Aviation Offences Act No. 10 of 1972, which is more or less a copy of similar legislation adopted throughout the world, seeks to protect aviation and aviators in general from any form of interference from the public whilst in the performance of their duties. It has been rightly said that the terms of this Act give the courts power to sentence an offender to thirty years in prison if he be found guilty of brandishing a penknife, for instance, while in the air. I don't think that any right-minded person would disagree with this legislation.

But there is no universally accepted law on the subject, each country interpreting the law according to its needs and in some cases its political persuasion. That is why one reads about hijackings taking place in the Middle East, for example, where the hijackers subsequently surrender to a country of their choice and nothing more is ever heard of them. In 1982 a plane was hijacked in Pakistan and flown to India. The hijackers were released and congratulated! Much depends apparently on where one carries out the crime. Politics plays its part. In our case there was no doubt the authorities intended to bend over backwards to secure a conviction against us if only to show the world they stood behind the legislation wholeheartedly.

A hijack is, by definition, a seizure of a plane *in the air*. This posed a problem for the prosecution as it was known that whatever occurred that night at Mahé airport occurred on the ground, after the plane had arrived and before it took off again. But they brought charges against us under the Civil Aviation Act sufficient to cover every possible alternative. In the main, these were that we interfered with the crew and disrupted the airport at Mahé and Louis Botha. The charges, which of course had nothing whatsoever to do with the attempted coup, may be summarised as follows:

(1) On board the aircraft in flight at Mahé, and from Mahé to Louis Botha Airport, the accused unlawfully by threat of force or by intimidation . . . seized or exercised control of the aircraft. Or, unlawfully and wilfully interfered with members of the crew in the performance of their duties.
(2) Jeopardised the safety of Mahé airport, and/or the aircraft, persons and property.
(3) Jeopardised the safety of Louis Botha Airport, and/or the aircraft, persons and property.
(4) Were unlawfully and without the permission of the captain of the aircraft, in possession of arms and ammunition.

What the whole thing boiled down to, then, was this: the prosecution said we hijacked the plane and interfered with the crew and disrupted the operation of two airports; we said we flew from Mahé to Durban at the invitation of the captain of the aircraft, who made the invitation because we had saved his plane from destruction on the ground by cannon-fire.

The prosecution laid before the court a list of forty-three witnesses, fourteen of them being the crew of the Air India Boeing, the rest being people who had been in any way connected with the arrival of the aircraft at Louis Botha Airport on the morning of 26 November. The case began with the calling of these witnesses; and for us at the back of the court, unable to hear properly and in many cases having everything translated from Afrikaans into English, it was incredibly boring.

But it soon became obvious to everybody that the main prosecution case would depend to a very large degree on the evidence
to be given by Captain Saxena and his crew. Would they come to
South Africa for that purpose? Would they be allowed to come by
their government was perhaps a more valid question. After the case
had been in progress for a few days the prosecution announced that
they had sent the two assistant prosecutors to the island to try to
persuade Mr Loustou Lalanne, the Director of Civil Aviation for
the Seychelles, he of the dustbin armour, to come to South Africa
to give evidence as a State witness. He refused without giving any
reasons for his decision. Meanwhile the government of India forbade
the two pilots to come to South Africa. There was now some
speculation as to whether the prosecution would accept these facts
as insuperable and allow their case to collapse as a result. Certain
political observers saw this as a way out of a dilemma for the
government. If the main witnesses for the prosecution were unable
to come to South Africa, that was all there was to it; they had tried
and failed. South Africa's honour or good intentions could not then
be called in question.

But that was too easy a way out. It was becoming plain to us that
somebody was very keen to have our heads on a platter. The general
feeling among the accused was that this was South African Airways,
who felt their operations worldwide had been jeopardised by our
action.

The State then made an application to the court for the evidence
of Loustou Lalanne and the two Indian pilots to be taken on
commission *in the Seychelles* as the court could not compel their
attendance in South Africa. Our advocate asserted that this would
be unfair to us as the court ought both to see and to hear the
witnesses. The demeanour of the witnesses for the prosecution was
a matter the court should have an opportunity to consider. The
written record was insufficient. Argument followed.

On the application to take evidence on commission in the Seychelles the court held: it was not the prosecutor's fault that these
witnesses had not come forward to give evidence; the prosecution
believed such evidence was important in arriving at a just decision
in this case; it must not be lost sight of that the defence would not
suffer any great hardship during the hearing of the evidence on
commission – the accused could be represented by counsel who had
precisely the same rights to cross-examine as they would have had
in open court; a full record would be kept of the evidence taken in
this way and presented to the court. (As reported in South African
Law Reports, State v. Hoare and others, 24 March 1982, page 306.)

The judge went on to say that even though the court did not actually see and hear the witnesses this factor had to be given due weight; but to a large extent its importance was reduced because the court consisted of three men who were 'triers of fact' and men of some legal experience and not a jury. They were fully aware of the dangers of accepting the disputed evidence of witnesses whom they had not personally heard in preference to the evidence of witnesses who had given evidence viva voce. Nevertheless, they would approach the problems with great circumspection.

With that judgement went any hope that the trial might come swiftly to a conclusion. The government had been presented with a golden opportunity to drop the case against us when the prosecution witnesses refused to come to South Africa. They had a way out and they did not take it. It seemed certain to us now that the government were determined, come what may, to nail us. 'And Aaron shall lay both his hands upon the head of the live goat, and confess over him all the iniquities of the children of Israel . . . putting them upon the head of the goat, and shall send him away by the hand of a fit man into the wilderness.' Was that what it amounted to? It looked like it to me.

Oddly enough, nobody suggested an alternative venue for the commission. Surely, we thought, a hearing in the Seychelles, the scene of the action, would be prejudicial to us. Why could it not be held in a place like Mauritius, which for this purpose was neutral? But the point was never raised in court.

The case was destined to drag on for months longer at a crippling cost to all the accused. As it was, some of the days' attendances were no more than an hour or two long, which prompted the judge to say: 'One of my personal ambitions in this case is to have a full day in court!' As it was costing me R1000 a day I agreed with him wholeheartedly.

The Statue of Liberation erected by the René regime
on 5th June Avenue in Victoria

The town of Victoria

The Independence Day Parade, 5 June 1980

RPG 7 rocket-launchers, the newest and most formidable weapons on parade

BMR armoured car with 14.5 mm and 7.62 mm machine guns

A platoon of the Peoples Liberation Army

G.P.-S *Rekord Allem* DD 12

SOUTH AFRICAN DEFENCE FORCE
SUID-AFRIKAANSE WEERMAG

ISSUE VOUCHER UITGIFTEBEWYS		RECEIPT VOUCHER ONTVANGSBEWYS
Account Rekening	*Poster/Inskrywing*	Account Rekening ....
Station/Standplaas	*Checked/Nageguan*	Station/Standplaas ....
No............ Date Datum............		No............ Date Datum............

AMI.   Issuing Unit / Uitreikeenheid   Receiving Unit / Ontvangseenheid

No. and date of order/No. en datum van bestelling   Authority/Magtiging

Catalogue or part No. Katalogus- of onderdeelno.	NOMENCLATURE/BENAMING Stores section Naamlyshoof	Condition Toestand	Quantity Hoeveelheid	Rate Tarief	R	c
1A390	Rifles AK 47 Rumanian folding butt.	S	60			
1A285	Rifles AMD .7,62×39mm Bulgarian	S	15			
1A65	Launchers Rocket 40mm RPG 7	S	10			
1D235	Rifles AK 47 kits cleaning	S	60			
1D240	Rifles AK 47 Mags	S	240			
1D250	Rifles AK 47 Slings	S	60			
	Ammo:					
1Q231·02	Rnd 7,62×39mm. Ball.	A.	23800		17 Boxes	
12200·01	Grenade Hand RGDS. Offensive	A	20			
12203·01	Grenade Hand F1.HE Defensive	A	20			
1B101·01	Rocket 40mm Heat RPG7	A.	102		17 Boxes	
	Radios: 2 way w/Batteries and Slings.	S	15			

Signature of Issuing Officer
Handtekening van Uitreikoffisier

Signature of Receiving Officer
Handtekening van Ontvangsoffisier   M. Hoare

*The South African
Defence Force
delivery note –
'far in excess of
what I had
requested!'*

*The dummy holdall and false bottom,
with AK-47 packed in polystyrene. Note the
AOFB emblem*

The Fokker Friendship on the tarmac at Matsapa in Swaziland,
with our luggage ready for loading

The Air India Boeing 707 after landing at Louis Botha airport.
Note the 'task force' surrounding the plane

*The crew of the Air India Boeing 707 at Durban, 26 November 1981:
(left to right) Ricky Stannard (one of the author's men),
Navigating Officer Vasan, Captain Misra, Captain Saxena*

*Peter Duffy and Mike Hoare outside the Durban courthouse during
their trial. Phyllis Hoare is in the background.
(James Hutton, Natal Mercury).*

Peter Duffy
(The Sunday Tribune)

Tullio Moneta, star of The Lion's Share,
September 1985

The Topsail Schooner TULLIO MONETA
is typical of the schooners which
traded in the Mediterranean Sea
at the end of the sailing era. She is
about 95 ft on the water line and
25 ft beam. Her gross tonnage
might be 150.

The model took 2 months to build,
working alternate evenings. The
hull is meranti, the keelson, spars,
yards, etc in iroko. I apologise
for its crudity, but my cell, no.
44 in B Section, whilst charming in its monastic austerity,
lacks something in workshop
amenities.

Even so, it was made with love
and I would like to present it
to you with that sentiment to
mark our long friendship,
your never-failing courage, and
your fortitude in these unjust
and abominable conditions.

Solamen miseris, socios habuisse doloris

Mike Hoare
April '84   Col

*The topsail schooner made by the author
for Tullio Moneta, with scroll on its base*

*The birthday card sent to the author by Peter Duffy on 17 March 1983
while they were both still in Pretoria Central prison.
On the back was written: "25-11-81 No regrets!! P.D."*

*7 May 1985: the author and his wife
celebrate his release from prison*

CHAPTER 7

Sentenced to Prison

ON 14 APRIL 1982 the commission began its hearings in Victoria under a local judge. It got off to a bad start when it was discovered that there had been no written application to the court for the hearing to be held, but this was soon sorted out. Then Captain Saxena was ill and could not attend for a day or two. So they began with Loustou Lalanne.

He confirmed that he had been in the tower alone for a period of about fifteen minutes when Air India flight 224 began to call, and that it would have taken him less than a minute to answer them, but he failed to do so. Yes, he had seen the red pyrotechnic flares being fired at the plane as it was approaching the runway, and agreed that shortly after the aircraft landed heavy firing had started.

Asked about his meeting with me for the first time he said: 'Immediately I entered the room he [Colonel Hoare] informed me that the flight should not have landed and he then asked Patrick Elizabeth to telephone the Commissioner of Police and that I should speak to the Commissioner.'

> *Hannon:* And may I put it this way, that he [Colonel Hoare] was annoyed about it [the plane] landing. Do you agree with that?
> *L.L.:* Yes.
> *Hannon:* And that his attitude was that the plane should be refuelled as soon as possible and fly out. Could that be correct?
> *L.L.:* Yes.

Hannon: And that it was in order to facilitate the flight out by the Air India plane that Mr Hoare immediately after saying the plane should never have landed suggested negotiating with the authorities to cease fire and [gave] orders specifically to get the plane off the ground. Is that correct?
L.L.: Yes.
Hannon: At no stage were you informed by Saxena that a hijacking was taking place or that he was being forced to do anything. Isn't that so?
L.L.: That is correct.

On several occasions Hannon complained that it was not possible for him to conduct his cross-examination as thoroughly as he would have liked owing to the absence of instructions from the accused, who were of course absent, and that it was not possible for him to receive instructions arising out of matters contained in statements made by Saxena and Misra to the South African Police, as the defence had not been supplied with these statements.

It seemed to me then, and since, that the suppression of Saxena's and Misra's statements made to the police soon after landing in Durban was a miscarriage of justice. One can only conjecture as to what they might contain, but it certainly looks as though the authorities had something to hide. The law in South Africa is, however, that a statement made by a State witness to the police is a privileged document, and as such its contents need not be divulged in court if the prosecution so decides.

Saxena began by admitting that he only had sixteen tons of fuel on board when he landed and that with that small amount he would not have been able to fly anywhere. If I had been there, I would have been able to prompt Hannon to ask some very damaging questions in this connection. Hannon then caused a stir in the courtroom with the following exchange.

Hannon: And are you telling me seriously that in your statement to the South African Police you never mentioned that a hijacking had taken place?
Saxena: Yes. I have not.
Hannon: You have not mentioned it to the South African Police?
Saxena: As far as I remember I have not mentioned it.
Hannon: Well now a lot of things fall into place for me. I can understand how Mr Le Grange, the Minister of

Police said . . . because he must have been apprised
of your statement that didn't mention a hijacking . . .
that 'they ran around in the bush and shot out a few
windows', and I can also understand why the Attorney-
General of the Transvaal didn't prosecute on the hijacking charges. . . . Now, can you tell us in what statement
(of the four you made) you first mention that a hijacking
had taken place?
Saxena: The one I gave to the Company [Air India].
Hannon: Yes I can understand that. . . . Didn't you
actually in fact tell the company that a hijacking had
taken place because otherwise your position was completely untenable with your own company? Is that so?

Asked by Hannon why he had not told the police that he
had been hijacked, Saxena replied: 'There was an apprehension
among us that we might be handed over back to the hijackers
again.'

Hannon: Are you seriously suggesting that once you
had been removed from the hijacked aeroplane and
taken into custody by the Police, and made a statement
to the Police, and the hijackers had been removed
ostensibly in the custody of the Police . . . and I can tell
you they were held under the security regulations . . .
you thought that you might very well be released by the
Police, put on another aeroplane together with the
original hijackers and flown up into the wide blue yon-
der!
Saxena: Quite possible, sir.

But he was unable to answer the most intriguing question of all.
He had several opportunities of 'escaping' from us if he had wanted
to that night, or of saying the aeroplane was too badly damaged to
take off. Why didn't he?

Hannon: You could have said when you inspected the
flap on the port wing . . . you could have said to them
at that stage I am sorry the damage is too great I can't
fly. Correct?
Saxena: Yes, sir.
Hannon: You had an opportunity to escape from them
completely when you went to examine the runway with

your co-pilot; that would have left them high and dry?
The point I am trying to make is that you could have
left [them] and they would have been left high and dry
without a pilot and co-pilot, isn't that so?
Saxena: Yes, sir.

But Saxena stuck to his story that I had said: 'If you follow our
instructions, you will not be harmed. You try to double cross us we
will shoot one of you and blow up the aircraft.' Allow me to say for
the hundredth time this was absolute nonsense.

It became obvious during the hearing that Saxena's memory was
not very good; but, as he said by way of excuse, it all happened
some time ago. Four and a half months had passed in fact. But when
he denied ever seeing the British Airways doctor at Louis Botha
Airport, shortly after his arrival, there was an unexpected reaction.
The doctor in question, Dr Rathgeber, who had appeared earlier in
the Supreme Court as a State witness, having read Saxena's evidence
in the newspapers, immediately rang up Hannon in Mahé to tell him
that he, Dr Rathgeber, had no doubt in his mind that he had attended
to the whole crew including Saxena at Louis Botha Airport. Hannon
took the matter up the next day.

> *Hannon:* Do you remember Dr Rathgeber when you
> left Durban on the aeroplane?
> *Saxena:* No, sir.
> *Hannon:* He asked inter alia, did you require to stay on
> in Durban after your ordeal?
> *Saxena:* No, sir.
> *Hannon:* Somebody said 'what ordeal'. Then he said
> that you said the mercenaries were fine people and
> offered to buy drinks?
> *Saxena:* But, sir, I didn't meet him!

Justice James had ordered that the evidence of three people,
Lalanne, Saxena and Misra, was to be taken on commission, but for
some reason Misra was never called. We were anxious that Misra
should be heard because we had reason to believe that his evidence
would be very favourable to us and in some respects contradict
Saxena's. In the event he was not called by the prosecution even
though they had brought him all the way from Bombay for the
purpose. Why not?

When the court reconvened in Pietermaritzburg the 780-page
court record was read to us in a matter of two hours. Hannon was

confident that he had destroyed Saxena and we began to feel more confident. From a personal point of view I found Saxena's failure to tell the court why he did not abscond on his recce of the runway, when he had the chance to do so, inexplicable.

My evidence-in-chief began. It lasted four days and was memorable, to me, for the unbelievable venom with which the Attorney-General of Natal conducted his cross-examination. It was as though he bore some very special grudge against me in person. At one stage he saw fit to call me an unmitigated liar! I protested vehemently to Hannon, who said I must not take these things too literally; it was only court language! The gap between what I had always assumed was the way in which courts of law behaved and actual practice grew daily. But what really astounded me was the frequency with which the judge intervened with questions of his own so that I got the impression I was being prosecuted by two prosecutors! Looking at the court record now I find that the judge put over one-third of the questions that I was asked in my four days' grilling in the witness-box. I don't know whether that is normal or not, but it certainly came as a surprise to me. I had always supposed a judge was some sort of umpire in a trial, and kept aloof from the argument the better to assess it, but of course it is also logical to assume that he must ask questions when he is not clear on the situation. But when he said on one occasion that he found it hard to believe my version of an event before he had even heard all the evidence on that point I began to get worried.

It was Justice James's last case before retirement from a long and distinguished career. Mr Neville James was about seventy-five, I judged, bald except for some greying tufts of hair above his ears, with a broad forehead. His black-rimmed spectacles gave him a slight Pickwickian air. He was perhaps six feet tall with sloping shoulders, a little stooped and hump-backed. He took small shuffling steps on entering the court, but this may have been due to the restrictive nature of the long scarlet robe which he wore adorned with a wide cummerbund and black scarf. He had short stubby fingers and a gold signet ring on the small finger of his right hand. He had some strange mannerisms. Whenever he made a statement he would cover his mouth and chin with the palm of his right hand and then bow in the direction of the press gallery, on his left hand where a jury might have been, as if seeking approbation. We found this very disturbing, but it appeared to have no judicial significance. Tullio suggested this was what was called in the theatrical world a 'credit call'. His diction was perfect and his English flawless, enlivened occasionally by a sense of humour marred somewhat by biting sarcasm. The Afrikaners said his Afrikaans was fair but he preferred not to use it unless absolutely necessary.

The Attorney-General was no oil painting. He was short, stout, and of markedly porcine features. It was also his last case. Mr Rees had served the law well in a notable career, and it was thought that he might be elevated to the Bench shortly. He was infamous throughout Natal for his aggressive manner when prosecuting. I felt this to be so unfair that at one stage I protested to the judge about the way in which he was trying to bully me – for example, with constant repetition of questions – but I was overruled. At the end of the cross-examination I was exhausted and somewhat demoralised. But worse was to follow. I could see from the lack of interest which my advocate was showing that something was afoot. As soon as I had finished Hannon asked the court if he could be excused from the remainder of the trial on the grounds that there had been a conflict of interest between his clients! Exactly what Mr Slomowitz had warned me about.

Hannon then visited Johannesburg to consult with the Bar Council. On his return he informed the judge he had been instructed by them to withdraw from the case. The court was then cleared so that Hannon could tell us what had caused this action. He never explained the reasons for it to me personally and I remain to this day in ignorance of it. The judge did not think it was necessary to order a retrial. Should he have done so? A nice point which might exercise a legal mind somewhere.

My funds being exhausted I had no option now but to defend myself. Kurt Priefert and 'Blue' Kelly decided on the same course, but the remainder of the men, less the ten Recce boys who were still defended by their counsel, engaged a new advocate whom they would pay themselves. This gentleman then put each and every one of them in the box with the principal object, it seemed to me, of showing the court that I had bamboozled them into joining the operation. All thirty of them gave substantially the same evidence and bored the court to tears. It seemed endless.

But I did have the opportunity of cross-examining them individually. At the beginning I asked them questions which would show them in a good light as experienced soldiers obeying orders, which I hoped might distance them from me and absolve them to some extent of any blame. But when I came to cross-examine Nick Wilson there was also a chance to disprove a prosecution contention, namely that the passengers on the aircraft were in a state of near-hysteria because of our presence. This was nonsense. Most of the men had slept the entire time or become friendly with other passengers and chatted pleasantly. However, you might be interested in this interchange with the bold Lieutenant Wilson.

> You were a member of the Rhodesian Special Air Services for 3 years?
> Yes.
> You were trained in counter insurgency, demolition work, parachuting, freefall, etc., and had seen action against the enemy?
> Yes.
> With this extensive experience in combat would you say that our unit was in dire peril on the night of the 25th November?
> No. I would not.
> Have you been in worse circumstances in your career as a soldier?
> Yes, often.
> In your statement to the SAP at Sonderwater you say, concerning the attack on the barracks: 'By this time it was getting dark and it was decided to fall back to the airport and try again at first light.' Was that common knowledge among the men?
> Yes.
> Now I come to a most illuminating passage in your statement and one which I would recommend to any commander who might be suffering from illusions of grandeur. You are describing the situation prior to embarkation on the Air India plane. You say . . . 'Some of the Resistance movement and some of the guys refused to go. Colonel Hoare was one of them. We ignored him and put him on board anyway.' (Laughter.) With the baggage I presume. But would you say it was common knowledge among the men that I intended to remain behind?
> Yes.
> We heard from a prosecution witness that some of the passengers on the Air India Boeing were on the verge of hysteria when they disembarked at Louis Botha Airport. It was suggested that the hysteria was caused by the conditions of their flight from Mahé. Among the passengers was a pretty young girl who actually burst into tears on leaving the plane. It was suggested that her tears were tears of relief on her escape from a

ghastly situation. Am I correct in saying that this attractive young party was sitting next to you on the flight?
Yes. (Laughter.)
And that you took the opportunity of getting to know her and becoming friendly?
Yes.
On the basis that romance can, and very frequently does, blossom in the most unlikely circumstances, and that it is self-evident that you are an extremely handsome young man, is it not more probable that the tears the young lady was shedding were not in fact tears of relief at her escape from the dreaded mercenaries, but tears of sorrow, shed because of her parting from you and the anticipation of what might become of you?
I hope so. (Laughter.)

If we couldn't do anything else, at least we could have an occasional laugh!

Hannon's departure from the scene caused me no serious problems in the Supreme Court but left me with nobody to represent the men in Mahé. Dalgliesh then informed me that he had made contact, through a Glasgow newspaper, with a barrister in Britain who had offered his services to defend the Mahé men pro deo. This was a heart-warming piece of news. I had to pay his expenses out to South Africa so that he could consult with the solicitor representing the men, and those in the Seychelles, but apart from that there would be no charge. The trial of the six men in the Seychelles was set down for 20 June. The barrister was none other than the famous Nicholas Fairbairn, the Member of Parliament for Perthshire, a true blue Conservative and previously a member of Mrs Thatcher's Cabinet. His entry in Who's Who under 'Recreations' lists 'philogyny'.

I entertained Mr Fairbairn at La Popote, the Durban restaurant famous for its haute cuisine, owned and managed by the charming Victor Janssen, and thanked him sincerely for his generous offer and his humanity. Single-handed this brilliant man took on a daunting task in the face of a hostile administration in the Seychelles. As he said to me that night, no client of his had ever suffered the death penalty. I took comfort from that and, as it turned out once again, his record was to remain unblemished.

We had been over three months in this court of law and were all heartily sick of the proceedings. From time to time there had been leaks, unofficial of course, from the judge's chambers to the effect that 'the sheep will be treated lightly, the shepherds will be punished

severely'. It was more or less what Tullio and I expected. As Mr
Slomowitz had said, we would most certainly be sent to prison; it
was only a question of how long. The fact that the government,
through the agency of the SADF and the NIS, were involved in our
case was played down. Things seemed to be going so badly for me
I now had to give serious consideration to the calling of some of
these people to give evidence in my defence under a subpoena, in
particular Mr Jimmy Claasens and Brigadier Hamman. I asked the
judge for guidance on this point. He pointed out that these witnesses
might not be so helpful to my case as I imagined and inferred that
it might be better not to call them. I took his advice, much to the
disappointment of the other accused. Even so, before the case had
started, Hannon had urged me to call Gerard Hoarau and had served
a subpoena on him. I was saved from the embarrassment of putting
him in the box by the news that he had vanished from the country
overnight. Rightly or wrongly, I saw the hand of the NIS in this
somewhat questionable disappearance.

The prosecution brought their case to a close and it was now for
me to make my final defence. I had half-decided to say nothing, but
my friends reminded me that I was a fighter and if I was to go down
I must go down with all flags flying and drums beating. It was sound
advice. On 16 July 1982 I presented my case and took the precaution
of recording it myself when I discovered, to my surprise, that my
defence would not be included in the official court record. This is a
part of what I said:

> I wish to thank the Court for the consideration which it
> has shown me in the conduct of my case. I am a layman,
> m'lord, and I realise that from time to time my manner
> and ignorance of procedure may have been irksome to
> the Court. I think you will agree my manner owes more
> to Hollywood than to the Inns of Court. (Laughter.)
>
> I intend now to defend myself in the first instance
> against the attack made upon me by the Attorney-
> General, and in so doing I may use some homespun
> language. This is not intended in any way, m'lord, to
> give the Court offence.
> *Judge:* If that should occur I shall tell you at once.
> (Laughter.)
> Thank you, my lord. I begin m'lord with the attack on
> my credibility. I have sat here in this court for over 100
> days and suffered, day after day, insult, innuendo and
> slander . . . most of it undefended and without any right

125

of reply or refutation. These attacks culminated this Monday morning when the Attorney-General called me 'an unmitigated liar, a selective liar, smooth tongued and persuasive'.

Now it is quite obvious to me, m'lord, that the object of these allegations is character assassination, which I submit m'lord is quite out of place in a court of law. I take the strongest exceptions to these labels . . . it would be, I might say m'lord, a very brave man who would speak to me in those terms outside this court . . . a far braver man m'lord than the Attorney-General. I have never been slandered in my life, and I regret that I now have occasion to be slandered in this court. I presume my lord that the Attorney-General has the protection of the Court?

Judge: Yes, if what is said by the Attorney-General is in the course of his prosecution.

Thank you my lord. Even so, I find that these methods are entirely in line with the way in which the Attorney-General has conducted his case against me . . . overbearing, bullying and offensive; and quite unnecessarily so m'lord when compared with the conduct of the charming Mr Hendrik Klem and the delightful Mr Gideon Scheltema. (Laughter.) Therefore, my lord, the Attorney-General has only himself to blame if I answer him in the same coin.

Judge: Yes, but I must point out to you that you would only be justified in doing so where you answer specific points which the Attorney-General has made.

Thank you my lord. I was going to say that what is sauce for the goose is sauce for the Wild Geese. . . . (Laughter.) I was also going to mention that Shakespeare very nearly said 'Hell hath no fury like an Irishman slandered!' (Laughter.) However I take your point my lord and I now give you examples of those specific points. The Attorney-General has been trying to discredit my every utterance, has been trying to throw dust in the eyes of the Court. For example, when I say 'The government knew about this operation' he says I am a liar; but does not attempt to prove his point. Asked to name the members of the government who knew about this [operation] I name them, but only under severe pressure. I am then described as 'a names dropper'.

When I say that the army had provided the arms it is inferred by the Attorney-General that I forged the Delivery Note!

Judge: Now I don't think there was any mention by the Attorney-General . . . any intention on the part of the Attorney-General to do that. . . .

When I say the army has given us support I am discredited because I am a mercenary soldier and therefore not to be trusted. If I am annoyed, as stated by Lalanne in his independent evidence, that the Air India Boeing has landed against my orders then I am an actor, and I am acting . . . you cannot win! Everything I do is suspect, but no real evidence is advanced [by the A-G] to sustain his theory. I maintain m'lord that this is not good enough . . . these allegations should have been backed up with fact . . . he must actively prove these allegations that I am a liar, but he cannot. He merely shouts 'liar!' like a schoolboy losing an argument. He has hidden behind generalities to mask the paucity of the facts at his command.

Now my lord I want to deal with the second part of the allegation that I am smooth tongued and persuasive. Now here m'lord Mr Rees is trying to prove that I am insincere and shallow and unreliable; that I hoodwinked my men into believing half truths . . . and all this merely because I have a reasonable command of the English language!

To be smooth tongued and persuasive are apparently, according to Mr Rees, misdemeanours per se. I have no wish m'lord to compete with Mr Rees in offensive language – I doubt if such a thing were possible – but surely m'lord to be smooth tongued and persuasive does not brand one necessarily as being evil? There are of course differences in standards of speech between people, and this may sometimes give rise to an assumption of glibness between them. This is nowhere more true, m'lord, than when I examine the standards set by the Attorney-General himself. Now, what do we find? First of all he is inaudible! Fifty per cent my lord of everything that the Attorney-General has said in this court we have been unable to hear despite daily protest!

Judge: Now look here Colonel Hoare . . . when you

127

talk of fifty per cent I think perhaps that you are exaggerating.

It could be less m'lord, but there is no doubt about it, we have suffered abominably in trying to hear what the Attorney-General has said. Secondly, on examination of the standards he himself has set, my lord, what do I find? I find him to be . . . a graduate . . . a graduate member of the Marlon Brando School of Mumbling! (Laughter.) He is a graduate mumbler, my lord. (Renewed laughter.)

(Attorney-General rose at this point to protest.)

Judge: Now Colonel Hoare I am not going to allow any personal attacks upon the Attorney-General . . . he is a very senior member of the Court . . . I'm sorry but I think you have gone too far . . . I am not going to allow you to call him a graduate member of the Marlon Brando School of Mumbling . . . that is beyond the pale . . . I'm not allowing that.

Am I allowed to say m'lord that he mispronounces common English words?

Judge: That is irrelevant in this case. We all mispronounce some words, but we understand them, don't we?

I stand corrected my lord. Naturally, therefore, with this background it is understandable that he would find me, an average man of moderate fluency, glib, smooth tongued and persuasive. I reject therefore my lord the Attorney-General's insinuation that I am a cunning schemer, turning every situation to my advantage by base and questionable methods.

My lord, here endeth my response to Mr Rees's unwarranted attack on me. I might add m'lord that my family, my friends and myself have been hurt by his allegations which are untrue and totally unnecessary.

I now deal with a hotchpotch of facts. The first is Sonderwater. We were held there under Section 22, and nothing to do with the charge of hijacking. Statements were taken from us in order to help the authorities. At the risk of boring my lordship I would like to explain once more that General Zietsman said to me: 'Mike, get the boys together. I've got to find out what happened. Ask them to co-operate. If they do we will give them certain privileges.' At no time were we warned that these statements would be used in evidence against us. Now my lord to the layman this looks totally unfair and a fundamental breach of a human right.

I want now to refer (in this connection) to Judge Earl Warren, Chief Justice of the United States from 1953 to 1969, a shining light, m'lord, in the annals of world jurisprudence . . . albeit somewhat Liberal. Chief Justice Warren m'lord will go down in history as the man who championed the rights of criminals, and in particular their rights to three things. One, the right to free legal aid; two, the right of the accused to be warned that any statement that he may be asked to make could be used in evidence against him. And finally, and most important of all. . . .

Rees: My lord this is all very interesting and perhaps of very great interest to the world press but it has no bearing on the case.

Judge: Yes, yes, I understand your point Mr Rees, but Colonel Hoare is trying to prove that certain statements used by you were made without there being any warning.

Thank you m'lord. I would like to complete that sentence. . . . May I do so m'lord?

Judge: Yes.

Thank you m'lord. And most important of all he gave the right to convicted criminals to be released . . . convicted criminals to be released . . . if they were not told at the time of their arrest of this new privilege. Further, m'lord, I feel that we have been prejudiced severely by the practice of the prosecution in taking selections, extracts, from these very statements. It would seem to me m'lord, a layman, that it would have been fairer to put the whole statement into court. To us it seems they were trying to hide something.

I want now to comment on the evidence on commission. I submit that the entire evidence should be disallowed for the following reasons. One: it was not possible for me to be at the side of my counsel during cross examination. Two: why was the commission not held in a neutral place like Mauritius where the accused could have been present? Three: why was Misra not called as instructed by this court? I maintain m'lord that the prosecution knew very well that Misra would not corroborate Saxena's evidence. Lastly m'lord, please consider this hypothesis . . . the prosecution obtained the commission from your lordship on the basis that statements made by Saxena and Misra alleged they had been hijacked; that was the important evidence they wanted to lay before the court. The Attorney-General was in possession of these statements and could easily have put them into court to substantiate his claim. But in his evidence in Mahé, m'lord, Saxena stated he had not mentioned anything about a hijack in his statement to the SAP!

I submit my lord that this commission was absolutely vital to the prosecution's case against us. I suggest that in order to get this commission, which they had to have at all costs – this is only a hypothesis, m'lord, I don't mean to be offensive – I suggest they lied to you! To a layman, m'lord, the whole thing stinks.

Judge: Why do you say they lied?

Because they said Saxena and Misra stated they had been hijacked when they [the prosecution] knew all along their statements said nothing about a hijack.

Next point m'lord: I wish to stress that the agreement with Saxena was definitely not made within 20 to 30 minutes of his arrival. I ask the Court not to take an armchair view of the improbability of this agreement having been made. It may seem improbable to the Court in the cold light of this Court, but I ask you to consider the circumstances prevailing at that time:

It was pitch dark.

A heavy gun was firing at the plane at intervals of a few minutes.

There was the imminent danger of the plane blowing up and the incineration of 65 passengers by 46 tons of fuel.

There was the acrid smell of cordite in the terminal building.

There was the palpitating fear of mortal injury from slabs of broken glass or shrapnel.

The fear of death was in the air.

In these circumstances Saxena and I were working to a common purpose – to get the plane off the ground!

Finally, when I did succeed in getting permission for him to take off, and a ceasefire was arranged, gratitude was uppermost in his mind. That was the thinking of a brave and adventurous man. Then he offered to take us with him, saying to himself no doubt, 'I will deal with the consequences later.'

I must admit m'lord, that when this proposition was put to me at first I did not think he meant it. And in any event I was not interested in it at that moment. Why should I be? I was not looking for a way out. Saxena's offer in any event was in general terms, he could fly us to a destination five hours' flying time away. He did not know that we were a South African based group. Durban emerged as a destination during the subsequent discussion.

Saxena and Misra were present at this meeting. I submit m'lord that had they been under any duress or pressure they would have made it plain at this point. And at this point my lord I want to ask if any evidence has ever been led that I threatened Saxena or Misra? Did anybody ever see me threaten them?

And now I want to ask the Court if it believes the subsequent behaviour of Saxena was consistent with one who had made an agreement under duress. Why, for example, did he come to my seat immediately after take-off, in great spirits, and congratulate me for getting the plane off the ground? Then, would I as a man who had threatened Saxena make an order to the men NOT to take their arms on the plane? Finally in this connection I ask the Court to give due consideration to Mr Reid's evidence [a first-class passenger and State witness], in which he said he overheard me say: 'The Captain has kept his side of the bargain.'

Once on the plane my lord I never moved from my seat. How can it be said I interfered with the crew? As far as I was concerned Saxena and I had an agreement which had been made on the ground.

May I mention, my lord, a general point with regard to the use of the term 'mercenary'. The Attorney-General has used it as one of opprobrium, in common with the leftist press of recent years. His intention is to use the word as a slight on me and to influence the Court. It is also a slight on my men, which I take hard

. . . a slight on a brave and professional body of men, who, as I said, I am proud and privileged to have led. Perhaps I may remind the Court that had it not been for 3000 mercenary soldiers in the Congo in the years 1964 to 1966 Zaïre would be a Marxist regime today. I submit my lord there is nothing shameful in being a mercenary soldier. It is a question of how honourably one carries out one's duties. After all, it is well known that Swiss mercenaries have provided His Holiness the Pope with a bodyguard for over 500 years. And that there are 5000 Gurkha mercenary soldiers, perhaps the finest soldiers in the world, forming part of the British army which fought recently in the Falklands, and. . . .
Judge: Yes, yes, yes. We don't want to go into all that now.
I conclude my lord with the observation that I know I am not being tried for an attempted coup, or for my political beliefs, but I ask you to weigh my actions in the light of what I am now about to say.

I see South Africa, my lord, as the bastion of civilisation in an Africa subjected to a total communist onslaught. In the last twenty-two years I have watched, in many cases physically battled against, its inexorable encroachment into Africa. The catalogue of Russian conquest by default is formidable: Ethiopia, Congo Brazza, Senegal, Angola, Mozambique, Zimbabwe, Seychelles – until South Africa itself is threatened. The enemy is at the gates my lord. The hour of reckoning is at hand. I prophesy that South Africa will fall a prey to Marxist doctrine before the turn of the century unless South Africans of all races become actively engaged now in the fight against communism!

My lord, I see myself in the forefront of this fight for our very existence. I see my men as a noble band of patriots motivated by the same ideals. It is my sincerest wish that South Africa will recognise us as such.

On 27 July the judge handed down his judgement. He held, amongst other things, that in view of the fact that the external doors of the Air India Boeing had not been opened for the purpose of disembarkation when the plane landed (at Mahé) the plane was technically in flight during the whole of its stay there, and that when we boarded the plane prior to flying off we had performed an act on a plane in flight. He then spelt out in detail the provisions of the Act which treat virtually every unlawful interference with the smooth operation of civil aviation with the utmost seriousness, regardless of motive. Then he analysed the events of those two days meticulously; but in the end it all amounted to one thing: the judge believed Saxena and disbelieved me.

In his 13,000-word judgement he said, among other things:

> If the accused's conduct can be properly described as a hijack in the popular sense, [then] it was a most unusual one. It was not a planned hijack specifically embarked upon to escape from an oppressive regime, or to advance some political or sociological theory, or to exact some political or financial advantage by taking hostages. The accused's conduct in getting on to the plane and persuading the captain . . . to fly them to Durban was not part of a long term plan but arose as a result of the providential arrival of the Air India plane on a routine flight at a time when the accused were in a perilous situation of their own creation when their plan to take over the Seychelles by force of arms was in serious danger of collapse. During the flight they had no occasion to treat the members of the crew or the passengers impolitely or uncivilly. This was wholly unnecessary as long as their decision to fly to Durban was respected, and very little can be made out of the fact that the accused behaved well on the plane.
>
> The Court is left with an overwhelming impression that once Saxena fell under his control Hoare gradually put the pressure on him and by stages manoeuvred him into a position where he was obliged to fly them to Durban. The Court has no doubt that Saxena never voluntarily agreed to take the accused to Durban, that there was no firm agreement on the lines stated by Hoare and that Saxena had no choice in the matter.
>
> Most of Colonel Hoare's evidence regarding the knowledge or involvement in his plans by various governments, government departments and individuals is unsupported and the Court has little or no belief in any unsupported statement made by him. Even on [Colonel Hoare's] own story he heard indirectly through Dolinchek that the Government had refused to be involved in the affair many months before it took place.

133

> It is clear that Colonel Hoare does not claim to have had any direct contact with Mr P. W. Botha and the cabinet and any allegation that he has made about their involvement in the affair is pure hearsay. (South African Law Reports, 1982–3, Vol. 3, State v. Hoare and others, p. 306)

This last paragraph came as a shock to me. I recalled clearly that the judge himself had advised me against calling any government witnesses when I had wanted to. However, he seemed to have absolved the government of all knowledge of the affair very satisfactorily, which is what most of us imagined the trial was all about.

The judge found that the State had been unable to establish the guilt of any of the accused on count 4, the possession of arms on the plane. But on counts 1, 2 and 3 I was guilty. Moneta and Doorewaard were guilty on 1 and 2, and Duffy was guilty on 1 and 3. Charlie Dukes, the American, was found not guilty and discharged immediately amid loud cheers from the public gallery. The remainder were found guilty under count 1. The judge would pass sentence on 28 July.

We were still on bail, of course, and I went down to Durban to consult with a barrister about the possibility of an appeal. He was very confident. He knew the judge well and felt sure he would grant leave to appeal. Not to worry; everything would turn out all right. In his opinion the case was shot through with irregularities, particularly in the hearing of the evidence on commission. We would win on appeal to the Appeal Court in Bloemfontein. All it would cost was money.

But meanwhile in the Seychelles the trial of the six men had at long last taken place. Their High Court had postponed its hearings on eleven different occasions in order not to reach any conclusions before our case in South Africa was disposed of. Mr Fairbairn conducted the case for the defence with his usual brilliance, hampered to some degree by the refusal of Dolinchek to be one of his clients. Dolinchek decided to conduct his own defence.

The main charge was treason, for which the penalty was death. Treason, however, by definition, is a crime which can only be committed by a subject against his own country; but in this case the law of the Seychelles had been altered previously by Mancham himself to include foreigners. On 8 July, Aubrey Brooks, Barney Carey, Roger England and Gerry Puren were sentenced to death. Dolinchek was given twenty years and Bob Sims ten. The Attorney-

General of the Seychelles, Mr Rasool, remarked that until Dolinchek began his own defence they had no case against him!

Before sentence was passed on us in the Supreme Court we were given a chance to plead in mitigation. Counsel for the men delivered an impassioned plea. I kept mine to one short sentence: I did my duty as I saw it; I brought my men back and I am proud of that.

The morning of 28 July saw me walking in my orchard as usual just after dawn. July is mid-winter in South Africa and first light an enchanting time of day. The birds, which know nothing of law courts, delight the ear. As I left my house for the last time to hear my doom the telephone rang. It was an estate agent from Howick with a heavy Afrikaans accent.

'Man, Colonel, I'm blerry glad to have caught you before you left. I've been figuring it out. You're going to go to gaol for a very long stretch, hey! Well, I just thought I'd tell you I can sell your house for you. Your wife's going to need the money you know. . . .'

'Yes, thank you . . . kind of you. By the way, how long have you been an estate agent?'

'Only just started, man. Why?'

'I thought you might have been a great success in the diplomatic corps!'

I called at the post office to fetch my mail. There was a letter from America. Of all the days it chose to arrive it couldn't have come on a better one. That letter kept me warm in gaol for many a month. It said:

> Dear Colonel,
> On the 25th November 1964, the day of the Stanleyville massacre, you and Colonel Raudstein of the American Army, and some of your men, rescued an American family who were living on the edge of the *cité* which was held by rebels. You put a small girl in the back of your truck and drove the family to safety.
> I am that little girl. I am now 23 and I have my own husband and my own children and I love them very dearly.
> Thank you for giving me my life.

The Supreme Court was abuzz with excitement and the public gallery overflowing, mostly with relatives of the accused. My wife and my two young sons who had taken the day off school were right there. I was sentenced to ten years' imprisonment on count 1 and five years on each of the other two, to run concurrently. Duffy,

Moneta and Doorewaard were given five years each, three others were given twenty months, one ten months, and the remainder six months. The public received the sentences in shocked silence followed by a murmur of disapproval. The general feeling was that the sentences were unnecessarily savage and that we were being sacrificed to mollify world opinion.

We sent a message to the judge asking if we could have leave to appeal as he had left the court so hurriedly the lawyers did not have a chance to address him. He said he would let us have a decision in seven days. We learned later that the judge had broken down in his room with emotion; this was, after all, his last case in a very long and distinguished career. Meanwhile the warrant officer from the South African Police, in an act of kindness, cleared the courtroom of the public and allowed relatives and friends to take leave of us for one hour.

It is probably true that one is never tried beyond one's capacity for endurance, but I have noticed that when I am very close to my limit my mind seems to be lightly anaesthetised in some peculiar way. Nothing seems to hurt or matter any more. The outward manifestation would probably be diagnosed as a state of shock. This happened to me now. It was the culminating stroke of many months of unbelievable anxiety, but in many ways there was a relief in knowing it was all over. I said good-bye to my family and took my place in the truck which drove us to Pietermaritzburg New Prison.

The following morning at dawn the men were taken off to Diep-kloof Prison to serve their sentences which, with one-third remission for good behaviour, would not be longer than four months. The rest of us waited for the outcome of our appeal. On 3 August 1982 we were told leave to appeal had been refused. At half-past five the following morning we were herded into a one-ton truck and driven at full speed to Pretoria Central Prison.

CHAPTER 8

Pretoria Central Prison

SEVEN HOURS LATER we crawled out of the back of the truck, cold and cramped. Our breath hung on the chilly air. So this was the infamous Pretoria Central Prison which everybody feared and nobody knew anything about. A rough stone wall sixteen feet high stretched for eighty yards, the length of the road frontage. An armed sentry overlooked the road at each end. In the middle of the wall was a Gothic arch enclosing two massive wooden doors studded with bolts. In one of them was a small well-worn door. Our guards knocked. A peephole flew open, the guard held up his identification and we were let in. We found ourselves in an iron-barred cage. A warder on the far side was summoned to unlock us, and we walked across a cobblestoned yard to the main gate of the prison proper.

We hurried inside, climbed two flights of stairs, and stood in front of an iron grille until let in by yet another warder. The huge gate clanged behind us. We were now on the edge of a highly polished square about fifty feet across. This was the hall. We watched pairs of prisoners drag 'donkeys', makeshift polishers weighted down with blocks of stone, from end to end in total silence. Others polished away on their hands and knees, dumb and morose. The pungent smell of the black polish on the bitumenised surface caught me in the back of the throat. That smell is prison *ou swaar*; it is compounded of fear, sweat and misery. Old lags say you never forget it; you die with it in your nostrils.

On three sides of the hall were triple-storey cell-blocks, each block called a section, marked A, B and C, and each barred with iron gates. The hall square was an island, a special place. Sixty feet above it the roof was domed and supported by massive iron girders like a Victorian railway station. The walls were in the common brick of eighty years ago, red and oversize. It was cold, stark and forbidding.

We crossed the square and were screamed at by a warder sitting in a hut built to one side of the entrance gate. We must not cross the square. We must walk round the sides. We had entered the realm of petty discipline, and woe betide anyone who transgressed. We were taken to the second floor of B section and given olive-green nylon trousers and open-necked shirts. The shoes were second- or third-hand, curled up at the toe and two sizes too big. The trousers were too small in the waist by three inches. 'They don't fit,' I said to the warder. 'They will,' he said laconically, and he was right, but then I did not know I was going to lose twenty-eight pounds in weight in the next seven weeks.

The prison had been built in 1908 by British Army Royal Engineers, and was planned to house 400 prisoners. Now there were over a thousand, and nothing had changed since 1908. Cells designed for one were frequently occupied by three men. One or three or five was the inflexible rule. Never two. We were in a section known as B2. This and section B1 on the floor below it were called 'Observation'. Down each side of the section there were twenty-five single cells, all identical, facing each other across an iron-floored passage fifteen feet wide. In the middle of one side were four open showers, and opposite on the other were three lavatory cubicles without doors, and a sluice into which lavatory buckets could be emptied. A warder sat in a small office by the iron barred gate leading out of the section. Looking up we could see the catwalks leading round section B3 above us. Those were the punishment cells.

We were lucky to be allotted a cell each. Mine was twelve feet long by seven feet wide. It had two doors, the inner an iron grille covered with steel mesh, the outer solid iron. A small peephole was let into the outer one. Opposite the doors was a barred window high up near the ceiling. In one corner a stone shelf held a metal basin and a plastic one-litre water-bottle. Under the shelf was a steel lavatory bucket with lid. A steel-framed bed, coir mattress, three blankets, a pillow, two sheets and a towel completed the furnishings. A rickety wooden cupboard with its doors hanging off was nailed to the wall next to the bed. The floor was of highly polished wooden blocks, the warmest touch about the place. The walls were painted with a high-gloss cream enamel, cold and institutional.

As soon as we were settled in we were taken for registration and our private possessions, watches, rings, clothes, and so on, placed in small white bags and entered in a book against the day of our release. Many convicts, realising that their clothes will be mouldy and possibly moth-eaten by that time, sell them before they come in. This prison was for long-termers; anybody who had a two-year sentence or more automatically came here, or to Pollsmoor Prison in the Cape. There were only two other prisons for the 5000 White prisoners in South Africa and they were at Sonderwater and Kroonstad, but everybody came to Pretoria Central first for observation. Headquarters for the Prisons Department was in Pretoria.

We were given a card on which was written our name, religion, sentence and number. Mine said 1496/82; sentenced to ten years under the Civil Aviation Act; date of sentence 28 July 1982; date of release 29 March 1989. That was ten years less one-third remission for good conduct. If you were a second-timer, you only got a quarter of your time remitted. The card, or ticket as it was called, had to be carried at all times. Not to have it was an offence punishable by a day in the Bom, the punishment cells. If you were sent to the Bom, you lost your meals automatically so that twenty-four hours in the Bom was referred to as 'three meals'. You were allowed to take your Bible and a plastic bottle of water with you; nothing else. You lay on a mat. Both cell doors were locked.

A man in the cell next to mine who had done a previous stretch said that observation was the worst part of one's sentence. If we could get through that, he said, the rest was a piece of cake. It was usual to spend about three months in observation, unless of course you had been in before, when it was shorter. One in four prisoners came back for another stretch within a year.

We were separated from each other, but there was some comfort in coming here as a group. We were too exhausted by the long ride in the back of the truck and the strangeness of our new surroundings to feel like talking. We were all pretty downcast. Pete Doorewaard asked me if I thought the NIS would do something for us. 'Give them a chance,' I said. 'They know we're professionals. They know we'll keep our mouths shut. After a few days when the dust has settled they'll probably move us quietly to another prison. There must be plenty of farm prisons where we can be treated differently. We're not rapists and murderers. They know that. Have faith in them. Just give them a bit of time.' I really believed that loyalty would have its reward; I was certain of it. But an hour later I began to wonder. A brigadier from Security, in civilian clothes, visited the cells, apparently to see how we were settling in. Duffy asked him if anybody would be coming to see us, officially. Nobody will come to see you, he said, now or ever.

At four o'clock we were ordered to stand to our cell doors while

139

a head-count was carried out. When the numbers were found to be right we were locked in with a great clanging of iron doors. It was knocking-off time for the warders and the only time they seemed to show any animation. When the outer door closed on me I realised for the first time what it meant to be confined in a small space. A wave of something like claustrophobia struck me; I felt as though I was going to suffocate, as though there was not enough air in the cell. I climbed up on the cupboard to see if I could look out of the window. I felt better when I could see men moving around in a yard below me. But an awful wave of hopelessness overwhelmed me. It was just like the beginning of term at boarding school. I felt again that ache of misery and loneliness which boys call homesickness. I slept little and was glad when the public address system blared out the next morning it was time to get up. The announcer said it was twenty to five. It was still dark outside.

We stood to our cell doors at six o'clock and when the numbers were right we were unlocked. We stood in line holding our lavatory pots in both hands and shuffled forward slowly awaiting our turn to empty them. The stench was nauseating. Half an hour later we paraded again for breakfast. At no time was talking permitted.

The breakfast queue jerked forward a few feet at a time, down the iron stairs and past the iron grille which led out on to the polished hall. I could see now it was some sort of nerve centre. The Head of the Prison stood in the middle of the floor. He was a major, and despite his high-sounding appointment was not in fact in charge of the prison. A more accurate description of his post would have been Administrative Officer. He controlled the day-to-day running of the prison, no more. In no way did he correspond to the idea most of us had of a governor of a prison. Governors do not exist in the South African Prisons Department. More senior officers, presumably with the authority of former governors, were tucked away in offices somewhere in Pretoria and were seldom if ever seen by prisoners. In my opinion this gap in the visible chain of command led to a loss of contact by senior officers with the events of day-to-day prison life. When I got to know some of the senior officers I could feel that this disturbed them not at all; they were only too glad to distance themselves from the sordid routine, the convicts, the complaints and the misery. The Head of Prison, the Major, bore the brunt.

It soon became obvious that this particular Major, the Head of Prison, was rather unbalanced. Every morning at six o'clock he was, in theory, available to any prisoner who wished to present a complaint. The Prisons Act laid this down. But many prisoners discovered it did not always pay to take advantage of this piece of benevolent legislation. The Major was apparently a man of many moods. Some days he could be heard screaming and ranting and raving in Afrikaans from one end of the building to the other. On others he was pleasant and compliant. The job was too much for him, I assumed. Hardly surprising, I thought. How would I like to be in charge of a thousand of these pretty babies? But at the same time he held our destinies in his hands.

Breakfast consisted of a cup of coffee and a plate of mealie-pap, a sort of ground mealie porridge. The cup and the plate were made of steel. Duffy and I drank the coffee. It was lukewarm and full of grounds. I would not have given the mealie-pap to a dog of which I was fond. The same went for all the meals I ever tried to eat in this infernal place. It is little wonder we all lost weight alarmingly. The so-called mess-hall was in fact just the passageway between the two rows of cells in B1, the section below us. Owing to the overcrowding we were unable to get a seat at a table and had to eat standing up. I complained about this. Nobody in authority seemed to be able to deal properly with legitimate complaints. Some of them could not have cared less. It soon became a waste of time to complain. 'Stiff!' they would say, the Afrikaans for 'Your bad luck, mate!'

For the first time I learned that the Prisons Department was completely separate from the South African Police. They were a law unto themselves. I had heard that phrase before in Sonderwater and now I was to discover how true it was. The responsibility of the police ended the moment they had delivered a convicted prisoner to the prison door and obtained a receipt for his body. At that point the Prisons Department took over. No criticism of the Prisons Department was permitted by the press, or anyone else, and it was an offence punishable by law to print any comment whatsoever about the conditions in prisons in South Africa or the way they were run. Only one book has ever been written about Pretoria Central, or any South African prison for that matter, and that was published in 1948, twenty-five years after the author, the famous Herman Charles Bosman, had served four years in this very place for murder. The book, *Cold Stone Jug*, is as true today as the day he wrote it but it contains very little actual criticism of the Prisons Department. This restriction on publicity gives the authorities power to do whatever they wish, free from all criticism. In law they are answerable only to the Minister of Justice. It may be that the conditions under which common criminals are held is not of any great interest to the public at large, apart from a few humanitarians. If your sister or your daughter has been raped, you want only to know that the criminal is receiving condign punishment, disclosed to the public or undisclosed, and nobody cares very much about that. But there is another class of prisoner in South Africa whose treatment is a matter of great concern to the whole world. I refer to political prisoners, and I have something to say about them and their treatment later on. But as far as the public are concerned prison conditions in South Africa are a closed book, and likely to remain so.

A bigger surprise was to discover that despite being organised on a military basis the Prisons Department was not in fact a paramilitary formation, nor a reserve force available to assist the South African Defence Force in time of trouble. This was not the impression they gave, or tried to give. Ranks began with warders, sergeants, warrant officers, and continued with lieutenants, captains, majors, colonels, brigadiers, all the way up to lieutenant-general. Why? Surely this must be the only prison service in the world which finds it necessary to organise itself on military lines. What is the object? Apparently it had not always been so. Twenty-five years ago it had been a wholly civilian establishment with warders, chief warders and governors, as in Europe and America, all dressed as one would expect in civilian clothes. Was the change made with some sort of aggressive intention towards the Blacks who make up 95 per cent of the prison population at any one time? Was the military stance intended to intimidate them in some peculiar way? Improbable as that sounded, it seemed to me to be the only reasonable explanation. None of the staff members I spoke to could enlighten me. My own view was that a change back to the good old days was long overdue. Perhaps civilian clothes would make the rank and file a little more humane in their treatment of the criminals in their care. A military uniform and automatic rifle, to my mind, put a spurious emphasis on the basic purpose of the service; a prison warder is the custodian of a human being, he is not a military man.

What made this military posture slightly ludicrous was that the staff were very plainly the most un-military types you could meet. The profile of a typical South African prison warder is the distended belly with trouser belt straining below it. But, overlooking the beer belly as being an occupational hazard, what made military rank and organisation somewhat incongruous was the knowledge that very many of the recruits between seventeen and nineteen years old had volunteered for the prison service deliberately to avoid conscription into the Army.

I soon discovered that what seemed to be the minimum require-ments for the prison service on entry were a standard 6 education and an aggressive nature with a predisposition towards bullying. I generalise, of course, but I was in a position over the next three years to observe successive intakes at six-month intervals as and when they came fresh from their training at the Prisons College. Some of the brighter ones took one look at the ancient and sordid set-up, the all-pervading misery, the way of life with no humour or dignity and opted out. The better-educated ones who were left soon disappeared into a rarefied region known as Head Office. That left the prison manned largely by illiterate louts whose one and only saving grace was that they could speak Afrikaans, and had the divine right of white skin. Had they not, they would have been unemployable.

The older, established staff, most of whom had ten or more years' service, were for the most part extremely efficient sadists, never losing a chance to scream or shout unnecessarily at a man for any reason from failing to have a button done up or for walking too slowly in line. The exceptional few who transcended bullying were soon transferred to other prisons. It was as though Pretoria Central had some sort of reputation for cruelty to maintain. Convicts were obliged to call warders 'sir', or 'meneer'. Except of course Duffy, who called them all 'manure' with schoolboy glee. Some of the chief warders, known as adjutants, had very long service. One wholly obnoxious character named Oom Paul must have been there for more than forty years. He could remember the days when warders carried wooden truncheons and used them freely on prisoners, as indeed they do to this day in the Black prisons, in one of which I was destined to serve some of my time. This particular chief warder never lost an opportunity to chivvy me along for the slightest reason. 'You're not a colonel here, you know' was a favourite remark amongst these gentlemen. He was forever chasing and bullying the convicts from pillar to post, quite unnecessarily, usually shouting the words 'Kom, kom, kom!' at the top of his voice. The words wake me from a deep sleep to this day. I got the impression Oom Paul's mother must have been frightened by a sheepdog. Some of the old lags who quite liked him said the last time he was known to smile was in 1953 when he apprehended two men in the same bed facing the same way.

But even in the twenty months I spent in Pretoria Central I could discern the hand of enlightenment and change. Men of education, mostly majors and above, began to appear on the scene. Some had degrees in criminology and were long on brainpower; others, regrettably, whilst highly educated, were short on humanity, and never really understood men, let alone criminals. Not an easy task at the best of times. Someone at the top was trying to rid the service of the old order. I wish them luck. In its way a reflection of the struggle which is affecting Afrikanerdom today in the political sphere.

The following day we were paraded for a medical examination. We were weighed, measured and asked if we had any complaints. Fifteen seconds later the District Surgeon, a very busy man, signed a form stating: 'I have carefully examined this prisoner and in my opinion his health and state of mind condition [sic] is as follows. . . .' The English used was quaint but in line with the extraordinary document issued to every convict on arrival which purported to explain the daily routine in prison. There were over a hundred grammatical errors in the first four pages. I suggested in a helpful spirit that I might be allowed to correct the English, but this was regarded as a frivolous suggestion.

In the afternoon we were visited by Colonel Harding, the officer in charge of the maximum-security block known as Beverly Hills, a new and ultra-modern wing of the prison at the back of us which housed maximum-security prisoners, Black and White, and where executions by hanging took place most Thursday mornings. The gates were electrically operated, powerful searchlights shone twenty-four hours a day and armed guards patrolled the walls. Colonel Harding was young, highly intelligent and helpful. He outlined the way in which we should try to behave towards the warders, gave us the official viewpoint on the purpose of observation and promised to speed up the process as much as he could. He explained the routine whilst we were here. We were entitled to one thirty-minute visit each month. We could write and receive one letter a month, which must not contain more than 500 words. All letters in and out would be censored. We could put in an order for R15 worth of toiletries and cigarettes each month, if we had the money, but could buy no sweets or groceries. Finally he cautioned us against developing bad habits by contact with our fellow-prisoners.

Colonel Harding was exceptional in a number of ways. For a start he was an English-speaker. This was exceptional because the prison staff were almost all Afrikaners. The Prisons Department was no different from the Defence Force in this respect; they were both predominantly Afrikaner and the chances of making your way to the top as an English-speaker in either service were generally regarded as zero. An all-English name is bad news and leads many English-speakers to add an Afrikaans name gratuitously for effect; hence Du Toit Brown and Marais Jones, for example. To have risen to the rank of colonel, therefore, he must have had some remarkable talent. The prisoners incidentally were 96 per cent Afrikaans-speaking, about 3 per cent English-speaking, and the rest foreigners,

Germans and Portuguese mostly. At a later stage I longed to hear English properly spoken and loathed what passed for that language amongst the convicts. The slang, which I shall not burden you with, was abominable. Things got to a pretty pass when I would deliberately seek Tullio's company in order to hear him speak English with a pure unsullied accent. His training as an actor gave him that, thank heavens. And whilst I am talking this way you may like to know that the average age of the inmates was twenty-three. Many of the younger ones were here on drug-abuse charges, either for using drugs themselves, which did not carry a very heavy sentence, or for pushing drugs, which did. The need for the drugs led them in the majority of cases to burgle chemists' shops, to muggings, armed robbery and so on, which ended in sentences seldom of less than six or seven years.

The theory behind observation, as explained to us by Colonel Harding, sounded reasonable. A new convict must spend up to three months in this part of the prison, entirely segregated from the rest of the gaol, in order to acclimatise himself to prison life, the routine and the regulations. He would be available at all times for interviews by social workers, psychologists and others who would try to help him adjust and perhaps solve some of the personal and family problems which he had left on the outside. That was the official view. Nothing was ever said about rehabilitation. But having experienced it myself I know the theory was so much poppycock. The principal object behind observation was unquestionably to break a man's spirit, nothing else. He must become institutionalised as quickly as possible. Discipline in observation was harsh, and the food ration on a lower scale than for other prisoners. This, it was calculated, would lower a man's resistance and make him more tractable. 'We tame lions,' the bully bouncing type of warder liked to say. And when a man finally emerged from observation there was no fight left in him. That was the theory anyway. But they had overlooked one thing: the unconquerable spirit of man.

I remember seeing a young Greek boy of nineteen who was serving a twelve-year sentence for armed robbery emerge from thirty days' solitary confinement in the Bom, half-starved and on the point of collapse. When he reached the yard where we had gathered he held his head up high, and a defiant look in his eyes said: 'Bugger you, Jack; it will take more than that to kill me.' As Cassius said:

Nor stony tower, nor walls of beaten brass,
Nor airless dungeon, nor strong links of iron,
Can be retentive to the strength of spirit.

But in the long run they usually wore you down.

In observation a man did no work, a privilege which we soon came to appreciate. In theory, as allowed for under the Prisons Act, we were supposed to be taken out into an exercise yard once every day for one hour. For over three weeks we never stirred outside the section gates. I complained, and eventually something was done. The answer I was given then and thereafter for any infringement by the authorities of their own rules was always the same: we are understaffed – which was true.

Whilst in observation a man was said to be processed – like a can of meat, I supposed. He had to undergo four different examinations – from the social workers, the psychologists, the officer in charge of education, and the religious worker. I am sure the system meant well but broke down in practice through unqualified or uninterested staff, with of course honourable exceptions.

First of all he must be interviewed by a social worker. She – they were all women – would go carefully into his background, investigate his home life and the conditions under which his family were now living, and so forth. She would then contact the social workers in the man's home town to check up on what he told them. Sometimes he was lying. This involved further interviews and further delay. At times a man would stay in observation for six months or longer because of the problems he had caused by lying. The Social Welfare section was usually conscientious and attracted intelligent girls, some of them with university degrees in sociology. But they were hamstrung from the start. The disciplinary side of the department rarely acted on their recommendations, and many of them left after a few months frustrated beyond words. The convicts, convinced that the social workers could do nothing for them, soon lost interest in meeting them, and as this was not compulsory once a man had left observation contact was lost. As this was in many cases a man's only window on the outside world, his lifeline to family and relatives in many cases, it was nothing short of tragic. I am certain that given the necessary encouragement and muscle this very progressive department of prison life could render a much needed and vital service. But while the old brigade are still in power this is not likely to happen. Their attitude remains as before: Let the bastards suffer.

The psychologists were not nearly so successful or so well qualified. The general standard of those calling themselves psychologists was abysmally low. Furthermore they invariably acted like sheets of blotting paper, soaking up whatever a man volunteered to tell them. Seldom did they make any helpful suggestions, or discuss anything so basic as, for example, the results of a man's intelligence test. This remained a close secret.

We spent the morning playing cards and whiling away the time. I sent an urgent appeal to a lawyer in Durban to visit us in gaol. We were allowed a legal visit, as it is called, because our case was deemed to be still alive – alive, that is, from a prison point of view. Once a man's case has been settled in court he is not entitled to see a lawyer. Could we petition the Judge President to allow us to appeal to the Court of Appeal in Bloemfontein, even though this had been disallowed by Justice James? Yes, we could, but it would cost a lot of money. Did we have a chance? Yes, he thought we stood a very good chance. It would cost R6500, of which I would pay R5000. The others would share the balance of the costs. The lawyer's bill for visiting me in prison, including the R175 air fare from Durban, was R800. This incredible fee put paid to any further visits. He said he would put me in touch with a Pretoria lawyer. Everything now depended on the Judge President. Meanwhile we prayed for success.

A week later the series of interviews began. These would culminate in a combined progress report which would be laid before a prison board comprising the head of each department and the Head of Prison. If we were found fit, we would pass out of observation and be graded as B-group prisoners. It was therefore a matter of some importance to get a good report from each section.

My social worker was a pretty girl named Lieutenant Le Grange. She was well qualified, efficient and a good listener. She disposed of the formalities in a very short space of time, after which we discussed the Johannesburg stock market. I advised her to put some money which she had inherited into a fishing share named Kaap Kunene. As this trebled in price in the next two years she regarded me thereafter as her private investment-broker. I enjoyed every visit I paid to this attractive young lady over the next year or so, not so much because of the official business transacted, which was minimal, but because she was kind, sympathetic and helpful; and one of the very few sane and sensible people in a prison world which seemed to be staffed by screaming psychopaths intent on reducing every one of the inmates to cringing obedience.

But, if my visits to the social worker were pleasant, those to the psychologist were a disaster. Five of us were seated in a warrant officer's room. This was to be a form of group therapy. He would begin, he said, by remarking on some characteristic evident in one of us, which he would then invite the remainder to criticise in any way we chose. No holds barred. Nobody must take offence, you understand that, don't you? Barbaric notion, I thought, but at least it was something new. He decided to begin with me.

'Now, you,' he said, 'Hoare. You're sixty-two. Right? You've got a ten-year sentence? Right. So you'll be seventy-two when you get out. If you get out. But it's more than probable that you'll die here in Pretoria Central. Right? Would you like to start by giving us your views on that?'

I said, No, I bloody well wouldn't, and he could stick his group therapy up his arse as far as I was concerned. I got up and walked out uttering an ancient Irish oath which would have turned Brian Boru a rich magenta.

That was the start and finish of my examination by a pseudo-psychologist. I am convinced that the majority of them were charlatans and only used the prison service to advance their training. We were certainly guinea-pigs, and from the rapidity with which these people moved on to other and better-paid jobs I assumed they found us a good stepping-stone.

Next, the Education Officer. He turned out to be a singularly uninterested party whose main aim in life was to conduct his interviews with maximum speed and minimum assistance to the prisoners. I asked about studying for a degree with the external branch of the University of South Africa. Yes, that was possible, but it was expensive and no special privileges were granted to those who opted for the course. Ten days were allowed for revision immediately prior to the exam, but apart from that a prisoner had to study in his own time. Yes, there was a concession. He could have the light on in his cell for an extra hour. No, no financial assistance; the prisoner must pay for the course himself. But surely this doesn't interest you at your age, he asked. I told him I had read in the papers that prisoners qualified in all manner of degrees whilst in gaol, regardless of their age. No, no, I had it all wrong. Only certain prisoners. I was confusing my status as a criminal with that of a political prisoner. Politicals, as they were called, were in a privileged position. They were not obliged to do any day work as we were. We hard-labour prisoners had to work eight hours a day, but they could spend all day studying for degrees if they wished. Now, you, as a criminal and a hard-labour—

'Yes, yes. I get you. Don't rub it in.'

There was a pause. The simple idiom had floored him.

'OK, then,' I said, 'how about Afrikaans? Perhaps I can enrol for a course and learn the language.' At least I would get something out of my time in prison, if it went on long enough.

'Sorry,' he said, 'that's not possible.'

'You joke. Why not?'

'No facilities exist.'

It was the first of the hundred times I was to hear that infuriating remark, the refuge of all small-minded bureaucrats when faced by a situation which calls for a little innovative thinking. And work.

'Now,' he continued, 'don't let's waste any more time. As you have been sentenced to ten years we are obliged to train you in some trade to fit you for life on your release.'

'If I live that long,' I said. It passed over his head.

'What would you like to qualify as?' he asked.

I got him to read out a long list of trades. When he came to cabinet-maker I stopped him. That was just the thing for me. I am a bit of a home craftsman myself; I love woodwork and the feel of wood and the smell of sawdust.

'Right, then, once you have been given your B group you will start work as a learner in the carpentry shop. Sign here.'

He really believed that what he was saying was true. Unfortunately, so did I. But it was all a sick joke as I shall tell you shortly.

Very few men in this prison subscribed for correspondence courses with the University of South Africa, and of these none was for the normal BA or BSc degrees. Perhaps it was the expense involved or perhaps they agreed with Herman Charles Bosman that prison was after all the finest educational establishment there was, and what need was there of any other? As he said:

> If they couldn't learn from being locked up in a prison, the grandest and most imposing and most ancient school that there is in the world, how could they hope to acquire any knowledge from an orthodox educational institution that could teach you only as far as BA, and could confer on you no higher degree than a doctorate?

How, indeed? But, then, I have never regarded a university degree as the beginning and ending of all learning. Neither would I recommend a stretch in gaol, the College of Knowledge, the University of Life as the prisoners call it, as being its superior or even its equivalent. I sometimes think a three-year voyage round the world in a small yacht is the finest education in life a young man can have, particularly in the sphere of human relationships, which is the real basis of life, isn't it?

The religious worker asked me if I believed in God. Did I know who Jesus Christ was? Why did He come among us? He ticked off the questions from a long list which would have shaken an atheist to the roots of his disbelief. If there are times when religion is very much the in thing, this was plainly one of them. The official view was that religion was a good thing. Its absence indicated abnormality. Fortunately, none of my answers disturbed him. He regarded me as a middle-of-the-roader, not completely lost but on the other hand no competition for Billy Graham. However, if I wished to attend a religious service, I could choose one from the list he handed me. There were Anglican, Roman Catholic, Seventh Day Adventists, Jehovah's Witnesses, Dutch Reformed Church, and other services held once a week, some on Sundays, not forgetting the Jews on their Sabbath. I could also have a religious interview once a week if I put my name down for it. Any questions? Next! I made way for another sinner.

Every evening at six o'clock the public address system burst into raucous life and made me miserable. The infernal contraption was immediately outside my cell door and practically deafened me. The bane of my existence was the pop music which they played each evening for about an hour. It is a truism that nothing separates the generations like music. As the music was intended for an average age of twenty-three I could hardly expect it to appeal to me. But it was not the quality of the music which disturbed me so much as the volume of the sound, which was all-pervading. A bare cell is to some extent like a sound-box, noise is multiplied until it becomes unbearable. A year later I became friendly with a prisoner who was serving a sentence for murdering a youth who had, it was said, goaded him into this extreme action by the incessant noise of his hi-fi turned up at full blast, causing him sleepless nights and continual frustration until something snapped in his mind and he went berserk and killed him. I suggest to some academic who is looking for a suitable thesis for his doctorate that the tyranny of noise masquerading as music might make a rewarding study. Can it produce criminal tendencies? In my case, yes. I certainly felt like strangling the perpetrator.

The thought that I had said good-bye to Mozart, Beethoven and Brahms and the classical composers that I had loved since I was a boy affected me more than the hurt of separation from old friends or my comfortable existence in the Old Vicarage. Good music has been, I am most grateful to say, an integral part of my life. For me it is a spiritual food. In prison there is no substitute. From time to time I tried to comfort myself by humming, for instance, the haunting slow movement of Mendelssohn's violin concerto to myself in the privacy of my cell; but after a while it was beyond me, although I suppose a real musician could go through it in this way from start to finish. It made me realise that the incidence of hardship in prison falls unevenly, and depends to a large degree on one's background. To have been lucky enough to experience some of life's cultural joys merely added to one's misery in gaol. If I had never known them, I would never have missed them. I learned there in Pretoria Central that the tangible good things of life are easy to live without; the abstract ones impossible.

The purpose of the public address system was not primarily entertainment. Each evening a list of appointments for the following day was read out. This included those who must report sick, were being transferred to other prisons, hospitalisation, and so on. In its way it was like an in-house magazine. In addition there were messages to the lucky men who were due for release the next day. These often raised a smile. I liked the sentimental one from the old lag to his 'lightie' – usually the 'female' half of a homosexual relationship – please play 'Have I Told You Lately That I Love You?' Later on in my time I was able to appreciate the sheer unsullied poetry of these valedictory messages. True, they had a certain sameness about them but they came from the heart, kindred spirits clutching hands through the bars, as it were. My outright favourite was this one: 'Well, *mei bra*, now that the time has come to say good-bye, please take a little advice from your old *maat*. Keep out of this hell hole, my pal. This place is not for you. Cheerio and God go with you, and stay in the fast lane!' On one occasion my curiosity was too much for me. Why was this hell hole no place for *mei bra*? Answer: he had just finished eight years for armed robbery, GBH and rape. The proverbial full house. Well, of course, one could understand why prison was no place for him.

But this particular evening in September 1982 we heard some good news over the air. We would have a legal visit at 1000 hours the next day! A lawyer was coming to see us. But who?

Mr Ernst Penzhorne was a lawyer in practice in Pretoria. He was young, clean-cut and highly intelligent. He came quickly to the point. He wished to offer us his services for nothing. He thought we might have misheard him. He repeated the offer and said he would give it to us in writing. The hard-headed Tullio asked him what his motive was. He replied that he had followed our case from the start and felt that we had got a raw deal from certain people and he would try to do whatever he could to help us. We accepted with gratitude. Henceforward Ernst Penzhorne acted for us expertly, tirelessly and with a considerable degree of success. He had given himself a Herculean labour. He visited the Minister of Justice, the Commissioner for Prisons and all the prison authorities in turn. He hoped we would be successful with our appeal to the Judge President but thought it might be wise to start making alternative plans in case we failed. Just when it was needed most, Ernst Penzhorne restored my faith in the fundamental goodness of human nature.

At this stage my main request was that he should try to get us moved to another prison. I accepted that there was no way round it, we would have to serve our time; but I objected to being placed in the same category as rapists, murderers and child-molesters. He said he would do what he could but he must point out that the law made no distinction between sentenced prisoners. I reminded him that the South African government, as represented by the NIS, had no part in the crimes of the other inmates; *in our case they could be regarded as accessories before the fact.* He was not hitherto aware of the evidence leading to this crucial distinction, but now that he was he would use it to our best advantage. Meanwhile he would speak to the Head of Prison and try to get us moved out of observation as fast as possible. I cannot speak too highly of this fine man. At no time did he give us any false hopes, but he tried always to buoy us up with his conviction that decency and fair play, and perhaps even a sense of loyalty, must prevail amongst those who ordered our destiny. He never gave up. It was a lucky day for me when Ernst Penzhorne came into my life, unbidden and unpaid. God bless him.

The day for my first visit arrived. The visiting-room was a converted passage ten feet wide and thirty feet long. Down the middle a solid partition had been erected, the visitors on one side, the prisoners on the other. Twelve places were marked out. We stood looking at each other through a thick pane of glass twenty inches square. On either side of the glass was a narrow wire-mesh screen through which one was expected to shout. It was barely possible to talk and see one's visitor at the same time. To make matters worse there was no partition between prisoners on our side or visitors on theirs. The bedlam was unnerving, and the scenes of distress amongst the visitors added to the confusion. A warder timed the visit to the minute. Phyllis was determined to look cheerful and full of hope. She shouted. The Durban lawyer had said there was every chance of our appeal being allowed. If so, we would get bail. A friend said he would put up the money. I must not worry; everything was OK at home. Yes, she had sold my car (that year's Rover 2600) for R10,000. Pat Cannon, an old friend and Pietermaritzburg's leading auctioneer, had sold it free of charge. The kids were well. They missed me. She had given my bulldog away. Yes, yes, a good home. Sorry, but she just couldn't manage him. People had been wonderful. Why was I so thin? Was I cold at night? Could she bring me a duvet?

Then it was my turn. How was she managing? You know, I mean financially. She looked down. Please don't worry, her church had been wonderful. I hardly had time to tell her she looked beautiful and the visit was over. She had motored 350 miles for a thirty-minute visit. And now 350 miles back home.

The conditions of the visit were a downright disgrace, unfair and unnecessarily brutal to both visitors and prisoners. I complained. They thought I was mad. The visiting-room had been like that for more years than they could remember and who the hell was I to try to change things? 'You're not a colonel here, you know. . . .' That rubbish all over again. This was prison, man, not the bloody Carlton Hotel, couldn't I get that into my thick head?

Many men suffered agonies from the aftermath of a visit. I am happy to say that every visit I received left me happier than before, revitalised me and made me more determined to stick it out. But I was lucky. Many the tragedy I saw and heard played out in that wretched visiting-room. Men would come away from that abominable little window knowing they would never see their wife or family again; their lives were in tatters; they had agreed, sometimes amicably, that the best thing was divorce, perhaps that would be fairest to the children, the shame of a father in gaol was too much for them to live with, and so on. Poor devils, my heart went out to them.

But life was not all negative. There was time to think and time to read. The tranquillity of a prison cell can be a solace to a bruised mind. The last nine months since Mahé had been a mental torture for me. Here in prison one was beyond the reach of lawyers, the press, adverse criticism, the whole machinery of life which tries to grind you down, especially when you fail. There was a certain unexpected peace about the place, and for that I was thankful. But a good night's sleep, that sleep that 'knits up the ravell'd sleave of care . . . the balm of hurt minds', evaded me.

We were entitled to pay one visit to the library in order to make up a book-list. After that the library was out of bounds. The books, if available, would be given to us at the rate of one a week. Newspapers were prohibited until one became an A-group prisoner. I cannot say that worried me but I missed following the stock market. The library was run by a superior-type prisoner who was serving ten years for fraud. He was assisted by two men, both former policemen. The library was a plum job. As I was the author of two published books I suggested modestly they might think I was suitably qualified for the job. But not so. I was not an Afrikaner, and I was not a former policeman, both essential qualifications. I soon learned that

153

certain people got certain jobs. There was no doubt that the prison service looked after the ex-police types as though they were errant cousins. But it was a treat getting a book to read. The more popular ones had suffered at the hands of prison editors with the usual gloss of underlinings, exclamation marks and witty comment, but one even learned to overlook this form of vandalism. I yearned for my own books. The one I wanted more than any other was a dictionary. The need for it grew day by day. I sent in a written request to be allowed one.

Six weeks passed before I received a refusal. I asked to see the Head of Prison. He arranged for me to meet the officer in charge of prison education, a full colonel, on her next visit. Meanwhile in answer to my question he could tell me why dictionaries were not allowed to prisoners. They would look up words which the warders did not understand and in this way they could talk to each other in a form of code. *Mirabile dictu!* In due course I saw the colonel. She was a charming individual, a Doctor of Philosophy, and a keen student of human beings, in which category she did not exclude prisoners. I put my case to her with persuasion. It was turned down. But I had resolved to ask at this high level for something else, something which would enable me to keep my mind bright, clean and slightly oiled, if only to stop it from petrifying.

'Colonel,' I said, 'may I have one of those books of crossword puzzles which the *Sunday Times* and the London *Daily Telegraph* publish from time to time? I have done those all my life and they are just what I need to keep my mind sharp and active.'

She considered the request for a moment or two.

'Sorry,' she said, 'quite impossible. It cannot be done.'

'But why ever not?' I asked.

'Well, you see, my dear Colonel Hoare, once we allow you to have the *Sunday Times* or the *Daily Telegraph* crossword puzzles all the other prisoners will want them!'

I have no doubt that answer must have delighted the shade of the illustrious Adrian Bell, but for me it was just another absurdity of prison regulations.

Seven weeks had passed since our arrival in observation. We came before the prison board, were regarded as group-B prisoners and moved into A section. Now we could work. Now we could receive twenty visits a year and thirty letters in and out. And, if we behaved ourselves, in another six or seven months we could be recommended for promotion to A group with all its dizzy privileges, too breathtaking to contemplate. Peter Duffy and I moved across to our new cells in A section, exactly opposite each other and only four feet apart. Tullio was on the floor above and Pete Doorewaard below. That evening the Afrikaans news announced that our appeal to the Judge President had failed. We would not be home for Christmas after all.

There was nothing for it; we must soldier on and hope that somehow, somewhere, someone was working quietly trying to get us moved from here. I refused to believe that my loyal attitude to the South African government throughout the trial and since would be ignored. I was certain they would send someone to see me, if only to say 'Thank you, Mike, we appreciate it; but no way can we release you yet. You understand, don't you? You're a professional. Sorry, but you'll have to serve a year or two, but when the dust settles a bit we will let you go. Meanwhile we are going to send you and your friends to a prison farm where you will be treated differently.'

That was not an unreasonable expectation. I tried to anticipate what their difficulties might be. Obviously they could do nothing for us while the men in Mahé were being held. Once the men were off the island things would be easier for them. Brigadier Hamman had told me way back in February that high-level negotiations were going on behind the scenes with regard to their release, negotiations which involved a very large sum of money. I never had the slightest qualms about their safety. I fully expected them to be released very soon. As things turned out everything had been arranged for their release right then, in September of that year, but the South African press got hold of the story and blew it. René had no alternative but to move the men to a distant island and wait a few months longer. But at no time did I really believe they were in any danger of being hanged according to their sentence.

Work began. Pete Doorewaard was in demand as a professional draughtsman, his normal occupation. He disappeared into an office where he worked every day of his sentence and gained a splendid reputation for discipline and ability. We very seldom met after that. Tullio was also to start in the carpentry shop, but as he hated working with his hands he was not very sanguine about his future as a maker of furniture. No training was stipulated for him as he had a mere five-year sentence and in those circumstances the authorities did not feel it incumbent on them to train him. Pity, the outcome might have been entertaining. But Tullio had no need for concern. The nearest he ever got to making a piece of furniture was having a strip of sandpaper in his hands for eight hours every day, sanding down odd pieces of wood. Hard labour was intended to be both hard and menial. If it was not always the former, every effort was made to ensure it was the latter. There was no such thing as working as a clerk. That was too sedentary, and in any case it did a warder out of a job. The fact that I was a chartered accountant interested them not at all.

Peter Duffy was busy carving a panel of iroko, an African hardwood, into the design of a bunch of proteas. The panel would form part of a grandfather clock which his bench was mass-producing. The warders would buy the wood, the prisoners would supply the labour gratis, and on delivery the finished product would, in most cases, be immediately sold by the warders for a fat profit. Various items of furniture suffered the same fate. Good luck to them. The chief warder in charge of the workshop interviewed me. He led me to a bench where a man was making window sashes. He gave me a piece of sandpaper and a block of wood and told me to start sandpapering.

'Excuse me, Chief,' I said, 'but I'm a ten-year man. I'm supposed to be trained as a cabinet-maker.'

'Well, who do you think is going to train you?'

I said I did not know, but, with respect, sir, that was not really my concern. The chief wasn't a bad chap and I could see he had gone through this mildly embarrassing explanation many times before. The inescapable fact was that there simply was nobody capable of training a man as a cabinet-maker. 'The facilities did not exist.'

'No problem,' I said. 'Train me as a carpenter, then.'

But this was no solution, either, amenable though my attitude was.

'Look,' he said, 'you've been given the wrong impression. There is no formal training, no formal instruction given here in any trade. The best you can do is to work on the same bench as a journeyman, if you can find one, and ask him to teach you out of the goodness of his heart. Some of them will, some won't. You may have to bribe one a bit.'

'OK. How many qualified tradesmen have you got working here today?'

'Two,' he said, 'and they have already got their friends working with them. I tell you what, I'll put you in the stores.'

I spent a day in the stores, which involved five minutes' work issuing and receiving the tools. I asked if I could join Duffy. The chief was glad to get rid of me. Peter turned out to be an ace. He had won a prize for carving when he was at Gordonstoun. He said he never thought he would see the day when his time at public school would stand him in such good stead; for there is no doubt about it, boarding school is the finest training a man can have for prison. Not that it was much comfort to us.

But Peter's heart was not in it. He was something of a chef, loved good food and hankered after a post in the kitchen, which, he thought, would lead him eventually to the officers' mess, called in Afrikaans the *menasie*. That was the summit of all ambition. A white suit, a chef's hat and plenty of grub. And he got them all, and lost them, in the fullness of time.

Neither of us was enamoured of the degrading ritual which took place four times each day on our way to and from our work-place. I refer to the 'skit' or search. The work squads, or 'spans' as they called them, would line up in a solid phalanx about ten or twelve men deep. On a signal the front row would advance to a line of warders who would begin the search. The prisoner must have the linings of his pockets pulled out, his ticket in one hand and handkerchief in the other, and raise both arms above his head. The warder would pass his hands firmly over the man's body. The man would then take off his shoes and socks one at a time and raise them to eye level so that the warder could see inside them. The prisoner would then take down his trousers and pull down his underpants displaying his genitals, but more particularly the strategic space below them, to the bored gaze of the warder. If modesty demanded, one was permitted to cover one's private parts with the other hand. Simultaneously one was required to open one's mouth wide and stick out one's tongue as far as it would go. All highly entertaining and elevating. And in case you had any ideas about smuggling dagga in any of the cavities of the body you could see bowls of water and plastic gloves ready and waiting for whatever probe might be required. Normally, however – and this was done at fairly regular intervals – a group of suspects would be marched off to the prison hospital to undergo a thorough anal search. Charming place, Pretoria Central. Never a dull moment.

Dagga (cannabis indica, Indian hemp, marijuana) was the root of all trouble in prison. A very large number of prisoners could not live without it. They smoked it outside and they had to have it inside. This involved the smuggling in of money, which of course was strictly forbidden, and the purchase of the weed either through warders or by contact with outsiders whom one might meet in the course of one's duties. But in the building group with which I worked for a year the tradesmen warders saw things differently from the disciplinary staff inside the prison. Certain old lags simply could not work unless they had their morning *sol*, and provided they were discreet about it nothing was said and the work got done. With the Blacks it was a way of life and when it was denied them, as on one occasion when I was in a Black prison, it caused a riot.

Saturday mornings we were allowed to walk about in what was called the cement yard, an area sixty yards by twenty, being in fact the space between two cell-blocks. The sun never reached this area. Shallow gutters ran down each side of the yard, part of which was marked out for volleyball. Men sat in the gutters and played cards, or chess or draughts, or just sat. A group of dedicated body-builders ran their own club in one corner, raising and lowering enormous weights. Tullio joined them later on and kept his magnificent physique in good shape despite the appalling food. One part of the yard had clothes lines and two baths for the laundry, which every man was expected to do for himself, of course.

Nearby there was another space, slightly bigger, perhaps seventy yards by forty. This was known as the football field, but as there was not a blade of grass on it a more accurate description would have been the mud patch. Even so the convicts played many a spirited game of soccer on this pitch and even ran some sort of league and a knock-out competition on Saturday mornings. An armed sentry watched from the wall which enclosed it.

This was the only time one mixed socially, as it were, with the rest of the convicts. At first I was intrigued by their stories and their schemes for bigger and better crimes. Some of them were remarkably ingenious, especially those involving the manipulation of credit cards, a form of crime which was experiencing something of a vogue at this time. Credit card companies have my sympathy! The exercise yard was fertile ground for the germination of criminal tendencies, the younger convicts avid to learn from the older ones. I liked to talk to the old lags, especially those 'doing a coat', the term given to convicts who had the indeterminate sentence, nine to twelve years. The 'coat' was a hangover from the days when a man would wear a blue coat to indicate he was serving an indeterminate sentence. They knew all about 'pushing time', a most descriptive phrase. The common wisdom among these chaps was that the only way to serve a long sentence was to forget the outside, to realise that one's life, whether one liked it or not, was here in prison. The here and now was all that mattered. Live your life one day at a time, they said. Fill your belly if you could and sleep away the weekends. Don't struggle; it won't make the slightest difference. The only things the screws could not do was to put you in the family way, or stop the passage of time. 'Come what come may, Time and the hour run through the roughest day.' I found this acceptance of their fate, self-inflicted though it was, indescribably sad. The struggle had gone out of their lives and with it their manhood in many cases. Some of them who had been there for more than eight or nine years could not contemplate life outside prison; many didn't want to, the prospect was too frightening for them. When they finally left they would have eight rand in their pocket and nowhere to go except, thank God, the Salvation Army. How well that wonderful organisation is named.

In the twenty months I spent in Pretoria Central I only made three real friends, two white and one black. One of them, Tom, was thirty-five, well built, raven-haired, and with that flawless complexion which goes with northern peoples. He was a child of the Glasgow slums – the Gorbals to be exact – and had joined his first street-gang at the age of fourteen where he learned to use the knife, the razor and the chain in attack and defence. Strong drink made him violent. His loyalties and dislikes were extreme. If he liked you, he would die for you. In short a typical Celt. He was within months of finishing a four-year sentence for murdering his wife, who had played him false. He had used a knife but, as the short sentence implied, there were extenuating circumstances.

None of that was exceptional, I suppose. What lifted him out of the rut was his doctrine for survival in gaol. In the quiet of his single cell on a Sunday morning when I was supposed to be attending a church service he taught me lessons which I imagine he would be astonished to know Jesus Christ taught two thousand years ago. In gaol, he would say, there is only one thing you can do to improve your inner self, your real self, and that is to help others, deserving or otherwise. He did it by becoming King Rat, setting up a complex network of barter, smuggling, buying and selling through a loyal gang, unique in itself, until he had amassed an amazing pile of groceries, cigarettes, toiletries, which he gave away to those who had nothing and needed help. He said he did it because he was selfish. It made him feel good and decent. He never accepted anything in return; that would have ruined it, he said. Incredibly he had built it all up from nothing. He came in without a cent and he never had an order. His doctrine was: 'Find someone that needs help and help him till it hurts. And see what it does for you.' Other times he would say: 'The only thing you can get out of gaol is the knowledge that you did your time like a man.' They deported him to Britain at the end of his time.

Today as I write this I wonder how that extraordinary man is getting on. Our favourite daydream was that one day we would spend an evening together at a famous dog-track in London, back eight winners and get stocious on the proceeds. Maybe we will. If you want anything enough, it usually happens. See you, Tom, old buddy!

CHAPTER 9

Durance Vile

A GIANT AFRIKANER stopped me in the yard one day. His face was vaguely familiar. 'Couquilhatville, 1965, Colonel,' he said. 'You court-martialled me. Don't you remember?' Yes, I did. We shook hands. His right hand had no fingers, only a thumb. 'What happened, Van?' I asked. 'Oh, that. Sonderwater in '79. I got the hell in with them one day and put my hand under the guillotine. Lost four fingers. They thought it was an accident and gave me four rands compensation. One rand a finger.' The years hadn't done much for him.

I wondered what drove him to do it, but he went on quickly: 'Do me a favour, will you? You go to the Roman Catholic services, don't you? Get me a rosary if you can.' Conversion, I mused to myself; lightning strikes in strange places. I said I'd ask Father Armstrong, but before Sunday came there was an announcement that only bona-fide Catholics were to be allowed rosaries and these were to be worn around the neck and on no account to be broken up in any way. Curiouser and curiouser. The explanation was not long in coming.

After work one day we were told to stand to our cell doors for a 'short arm inspection'. The expression was new to Peter Duffy, who had never served in the armed forces of the Crown.

'They wish to examine your wedding tackle,' I explained. 'Nothing to it, old son. When the Head of Prison and his mates come round just take down your trousers and flash it. Wait a moment for it to astound them and then put it away modestly.'

'Bugger that for a lark,' he said. 'That's my private property. They'll have to ask me nicely first.'

He said he was going to play hard to get. But Duffy was taken aback with the effrontery of this demand. What the hell was it all about anyway? Surely that was something for the prison doctor if they suspected VD or whatever. I concurred.

We stood to our cell doors and determined we would not submit to this barbaric inspection. We looked like a couple of self-righteous virgins defending our honour. Our neighbours, on the other hand, stood there completely unabashed, displayed their genitals in all their glory, naked and unashamed, and in some cases with a totally unwarranted pride. When the Major came opposite Duffy and me he found us fully dressed. He raised an eyebrow in enquiry. 'We refuse,' we said. The Major, who was no monkey and knew how far he could go, walked on. I got hold of one of his underlings and asked him what the inspection was in aid of. 'Rosary Club,' he said by way of explanation, which satisfied our neighbours but left Duffy and me as nonplussed as before.

But it soon transpired that certain gentlemen had been taking the beads from rosaries, making tiny incisions in the foreskin of their penis and inserting the beads therein. Presumably this erotic surgery gave them a sexual thrill. The mace-like effect was certainly arresting, one could concede that, but did nothing to enhance the appearance of one of nature's lesser masterpieces!

Regrettably, if that is the right word, the incisions by razor blade had led to inflammation and all sorts of dangerous complications. Quite rightly the Major intended to stamp it out. The morality of this extraordinary behaviour was not called in question; it was on medical grounds alone that the inspection had been ordered.

'Takes all sorts to make a world, don't it?' I said piously to the gentlemanly chap in the cell next door.

'Frankly,' he said, 'I couldn't care less. My name is Ginsberg.'

The small rains had arrived, and during the night water from a leaking gutter splashed through the broken window in my cell and drenched my bed. In the morning I felt bad. I joined the queue for pills in the yard at reveille. I was given two large green bombs guaranteed to cure all ailments from bots to pneumonia. A warder stood by to see I actually took the pills and did not smuggle them back to my cell, grind them down and smoke them. I protested mildly that I never took anything stronger than Disprin, but swallowed them with misgivings and a glass of water.

An hour later there was a parade. Our hair was being checked for the regulation shortness. I felt dizzy and fainted, but before I hit the deck Peter caught one arm and Matt O'Hara, a friend I had just made, the other. Matt, who was an old hand, got the maximum mileage out of the drama. He called out urgently for a stretcher, and he and Duffy carted me off to the hospital where Matt put me to bed after telling the lieutenant in charge that he was sure I was on the point of death. And there I stayed for ten days. The lieutenant, whose name was Cook, was efficient, humane, highly intelligent, and sympathetic in genuine cases. He ruled the thirty or so patients in his three wards with a rod of iron, knew every trick in the book and wasted no time in sending a man to hospital in Pretoria if he was seriously ill. Both here and in Pietermaritzburg later, I found the prison medical services to be beyond reproach. A little austere at times, but that was understandable in the circumstances.

While I was there Duffy left the carpentry shop and became a cook in the men's cookhouse. Part one of his master plan had materialised. When they saw what a sparkler he was he felt sure they would move him to the *menasie*. Meanwhile, as he was the only qualified cook there he tried teaching the other ten, all novices, how to go about it. He was very discouraged. The equipment was antiquated and most of it unserviceable. His first job every morning was to cut the ends off a large number of loaves where they had been gnawed by rats during the night. But, as he pointed out, basically there is no such thing as bad food, only bad cooking, and that was the situation here. Given decent utensils and some qualified cooks he could turn out reasonable meals. He was pretty sure the full weight of rations was not finding its way into the kitchen. The warder in charge didn't help, either. He had to be fed steak sandwiches all morning to keep him sweet.

As the cooks had to get up in the middle of the night to cook breakfast they were housed in a special wing called the Married Quarters. The name harked back to the days when the cooks were notoriously homosexual, said Peter, and he didn't think they were much better today. One young lad was selling his sexual services for a 'cutty', Peter complained to me one day. A cutty was four slices of brown bread, a man's ration for one day, and incidentally the only thing that was worth eating in the so-called balanced diet. 'And if that isn't bad enough,' he said, 'the perverted little bastard knows full well the usual rate is eight slices!' A great joker, my old friend Peter Duffy. His sense of humour transcended the sordid misery of durance vile. His spirit was unconquerable. I never saw him down for more than two minutes the whole time we shared in prison.

When my ten days were up Lieutenant Cook suggested that I might like a hospital job as a 'tea boy'. This involved keeping the hospital kitchen clean, making tea and serving it to the hospital staff, and serving meals to the patients. I accepted with gratitude. This unique experience brought me into contact with every type of man in the prison. Following on Tom's golden rule I adopted an old lag who was very sick indeed. He was in his late fifties, a cheerful little Charlie who was employed as the hospital handyman. He was busy, as they say, on his third coat. His whole life had been spent in and out of prison. He was due for release in March but he knew he'd be back. He had no point of contact with the world outside, which for him was a shadowy place of work, wages, rent and, thank God, pubs. He was an orphan without a single relative.

'But why do you keep coming back, Jimmy?' It puzzled my little bourgeois mind.

'Booze. I'm a confirmed alcoholic,' he said, as though stating some sort of qualification, knowing it would end all discussion. But what was the connection between drinking and his sudden illness?

'Retty,' he said, prison slang for retribution. 'Thirty years drinking cheap wine, meths, gavine, shimmyaan, you name it. It's caught up with me. Cookie tells me my spine has crumbled. Here, Mike. . . .' There was a bewildered little-boy look in his eyes. 'I've got no feeling in my legs. That's not right, is it?' They took him away in the night after giving him a shot of morphine.

Another convict I came to like was a Jew named Bacus. There were about fifteen orthodox Jews in the prison at this time and they attended a Sabbath prayer-meeting every Saturday conducted by a rabbi who had been visiting the prison for over forty years. He had forgotten more about prisoners than the authorities would ever know. Bacus was on the hospital staff as a *schoonmaker*, a cleaner, just as I was, and was the most popular man in the place – but only twice a year. On these two occasions the very rich and generous Jewish community on the Witswatersrand gave every Jewish prisoner a special gift of food, traditional delicacies such as gefilter fish, matzos, pickled herrings and so on, which was intended to tide them over the fasts which they celebrated at that time. The rabbi would interview the faithful three weeks before the fast began. Inexplicably, at these times the Jewish population of the prison, which had been lying dormant, so to speak, awoke and proclaimed its Jewishness with Old Testament fervour; instead of fifteen orthodox lads there were now 135! The rabbi, who had seen it all before, examined each aspirant for a parcel in turn.

'And what is your name, my son?'

'Du Plessis. André du Plessis. But my mother's name was Bloom. Rebecca Bloom.'

'How nice. And you are one of our faith, I believe?'

'Yes, yes. I qualify for the parcel, don't I?'

'If you are a Jew, yes. But how comes it that I have never seen you before? Where do you hide yourself on the Sabbath?'

'Well, you see, Rabbi, man, they treats me very rough here. Knowing I am a Jew they sends me out to work every Saturday morning just to spite me. They know that upsets me. That way I miss my religion.'

'I see. My sympathies. By the way, what was your name at your bar mitzvah?'

'My what . . .?'

'Nice try, lad. Next!' And another hopeful Hebrew entered the lists. Very few new boys made it all the way to the chopped chicken livers.

Father Armstrong conducted Mass in what had been the gallows room before it was moved to Beverly Hills. He had been an army chaplain in his time, and that manner was just right for this environment. He was a no-nonsense priest, very learned, with a light sense of humour. Matt O'Hara (seven years for fraud) and Greg Phillipson (twelve years for murdering his wife) were his altar boys. About twenty of us, mostly foreigners, sat on benches facing him. The altar was only a collapsible table, but when the holy Father began to preach he transported us in spirit to the glory of St Patrick's Cathedral. He cautioned us against self-pity, a destructive force, and reminded us of the day when Jesus Christ was crucified and abandoned by all who followed Him save only his Mother and a reformed prostitute. That put my little trouble in its right perspective. Another time he told us, with an uncharacteristic show of emotion, of the heart-rending bravery of the Blacks, mostly ANC terrorists, whom he accompanied and tried to comfort on their last brief walk to the gallows. Probably my only happy memory of Pretoria Central is of this busy little priest with the corrugated brow, bulbous nose and laughing eyes.

Unexpectedly, in December I was summoned to the Head of Prison. He had given two men special permission to see me. They were Messrs Klem and Scheltema, the assistant prosecutors at my trial. They came in pursuance of a remark, not an instruction, made by Justice James. The judge had said at some time during the course of the trial that perhaps the Attorney-General's department should make some enquiries concerning possible government involvement in our case. I remembered it at the time, but it was rather vague. But now, I assumed, they had been instructed to follow this up. They began by reading out formally the section of an Act which dealt with the treatment of witnesses who were prepared to give evidence on behalf of the prosecution. Would I turn State's Evidence? is what they meant. But against whom? They didn't say.

I told them to watch out, they were treading on eggs. If they opened up this can, they might find it contained worms. I suggested they should proceed very circumspectly indeed as some very highly placed people in the government and the Defence Force were involved in my case and interference at this stage might not be wise. Wasn't the position that the government were accessories before the fact? Wasn't it trite law that if you gave a man a gun and he committed murder with it you were just as guilty in the eyes of the law as he was? This gave them pause. Furthermore, was it not possible that their enquiries at this stage might harm their careers? It was probably coincidental but this prospect seemed to cause a sudden diminution in their interest, followed by a great clicking of document-cases. But if they really wanted me to co-operate with them after they had thought that over, then I suggested they should contact my lawyer Mr Penzhorne, who would advise me in the matter. They took down his name and address and promised to phone him. They never did. I never saw them again. Wiser counsels must have prevailed, as they say in legal circles.

On my way back to the hospital through the hall I became aware of an atmosphere of excitement among the disciplinary staff. A birching was in progress. The A frame, a solid timber construction in the shape of the letter A, about ten feet high, had been laid on the ground in a secluded yard near the reception office. A young prisoner lay on the frame, which was raised slightly at the sharp end of the A. He was naked apart from a thin wet cotton cloth covering his buttocks. His arms and legs, which were spreadeagled, were clamped to the frame. The prison authorities and the District Surgeon were in attendance. The doctor sounded the man's heart. OK. Lay on, MacDuff! A hefty warder raised a four-foot cane about half an inch thick above his head and brought it down on the cloth with all his might, grunting as he did so. The youngster bit his lip and grimaced with pain. The doctor adjusted the cloth and sounded the man's heart again. Proceed. The third stroke drew blood. Deep purple-red weals scarred his bottom, beads of blood welled up along them. After ten strokes the prisoner signalled them to stop. He would serve out the rest of his time. One stroke was the equivalent of one week's imprisonment. The competition among the Boere (the warders) for the sadistic privilege of administering the punishment was keen.

I often wondered about that choice. I imagine he regretted not sticking it out, but who knows? I thought a lot about alternative forms of punishment whilst I was in Pretoria Central. I suggested to the Defence Force, via Mr Penzhorne, that they should recruit a penal battalion from some of the young men in South African gaols who were rotting away, learning bad habits and being totally unproductive. Surely service in a penal unit would have been of some benefit, both to them and to the country? A number of other countries had this system. But nothing came of it. Dame Agatha Christie held the view that criminals sentenced to very long sentences would welcome a chance to volunteer as guinea-pigs in dangerous medical experiments in exchange for a substantial reduction in their time. I canvassed opinion on this one among the long-termers. On the whole I would say she was right.

Every few months the prison would be visited by a group of magistrates. The whole time I was there I never saw or heard of a judge visiting the prison. The routine was always the same. The select group would be closely shepherded by a senior prison officer, who would make certain they did not come into contact with a single convict, by accident or otherwise. Care was taken to see that the prisoners were well out of the way, or safely locked up. The establishment, or such parts of it as the prison authorities thought they should see, was quickly inspected and the representatives of the courts whisked away to the *menasie* for pre-lunch drinks and entertainment. This gallop round the prison was known by the prisoners as the 'Gilbey's Gin and Tonic States'. It was nothing short of a farce. But when the inspection of the prison was carried out by the Red Cross that was very different, skin and fur began to fly. Full colonels and brigadiers dashed about looking worried; potted plants and similar decorations made a sudden and incongruous appearance. After the inspection everything went back to normal.

But the interest of the Red Cross was primarily in the political prisoners, common criminals did not normally fall within their purview. For a political prisoner the visits by the Red Cross were a momentous occasion; they held out a lifeline to the world beyond. And the Red Cross carried out a proper examination. The diet laid down for the politicals, which was of a much higher standard than ours, was carefully examined and their living conditions severely monitored. Political prisoners had an opportunity to voice any complaints they might have, and action was taken quickly to redress legitimate complaints. Certainly there was a great gulf between politicals and criminals, and that, in my humble opinion, is how it ought to be. It is true that they were not given hard labour and could spend their time reading or studying as they wished, but apart from that and the fact that their general conditions and their food were better than ours their privileges and visits were substantially the same. Television, which would have been a boon, was not one of the amenities in Pretoria Central, for politicals or criminals alike. A movie, paid for by the prisoners, was shown once a week in such abominable conditions as to make it virtually unwatchable. The choice of film was predictable. D. H. Lawrence would have been gratified at the reception Lady Chatterley received *chez nous*.

If I have given you the impression that South African prisons as represented by Pretoria Central are sixty to seventy years behind the times, I am satisfied. Not only in their establishments, which are woefully outdated, but also in their thinking, they lag behind the remainder of the world in penal reform. On a few occasions I asked about the possible introduction of the system in force in America where a majority of prisoners serve one-sixth of their sentence before release on parole, and are then carefully supervised and counselled by a corps of highly intelligent, well-paid, caring men and women. These social workers succeed in very many cases in keeping the released convicts out of gaol, and help in reshaping their lives. To a very real extent they help to rebuild a part of the nation. Financially it is a worthwhile proposition. In South African terms it costs, at an informed guess, ten rand to keep one man in prison for one day. Probably more. If a counsellor can keep only three ex-prisoners from returning to gaol, he is well on the way to saving the State the cost of his own salary!

The months went by. Phyllis visited me regularly, and her half-hour visits kept me alive. The three letters a month became a vital link with the outside. She was selling my books and the 5 Commando badge in America to people who had seen her advertisement in *Soldier of Fortune* magazine. Not to worry, she was managing. I thanked God on many occasions for a brave girl and loyal wife.

Inexorably the past slid away and the present began to take over, much as I hated the thought. Prison was my life, just as the old lags had said, and I had better get on with it. Christmas Day 1982 passed almost unnoticed. A multi-denominational Christmas service was held in the hall and droned on in both languages, interminably. Certain church organisations had donated some funds, and every man received a packet of sweets and a cold drink. It was a kind thought. We were well into the New Year when two things disturbed the monotony of my life.

A senior officer from Head Office interviewed the four of us. He was examining the possibilities of transferring us to a small prison, Eshowe in Zululand to be exact. He wanted our reaction to this suggestion and warned us that in Eshowe 'no facilities existed'. Regardless of what that might mean, Duffy and I agreed with alacrity that we would like to go, and the sooner the better. At long last they were moving behind the scenes. The mere thought of being closer to home and among English-speakers once more filled us with hope and excitement. Weeks passed, then months, and the mirage flickered and died. What finally killed it was the unexpected death of the Commissioner of Prisons, General Otto. He had a reputation for liberal treatment of prisoners and represented a new wave of thinking in the prison service. We assumed this had been his idea and now it would be forgotten. In the event the new Commissioner, General Willemse, was every bit as progressive, but it was the end of 1983 before he was firmly in the saddle.

The other event was a little more personal. Oom Jack sent for me. At noon, as Senior Warder, he dealt with official mail affecting prisoners. 'You've been fired, Mike,' he said. As it was unheard of to be addressed by my Christian name I assumed there was some bad news in the letter. There was. The Institute of Chartered Accountants in England and Wales had removed my name from their register. Qualifying in 1948 had been the proudest moment of my otherwise undistinguished career. It was a blow. On the other hand, I wouldn't have to pay the annual subscription, would I?

The days were getting drabber and longer. Peter had graduated to the *menasie* and I saw him no more. I missed his cheerful mug. If I saw Tullio and Peter Doorewaard once a month, it was only by accident. And in the hospital I was witnessing ugly scenes.

In his book *One Day in the Life of Ivan Denisovich* the great Solzhenitsyn speaks of the inhumane treatment of prisoners by one another. In that Siberian prison-camp, he says, one's fellow-prisoners were sometimes worse than the warders. It was exactly the same here. In *The Devil's Disciple* Bernard Shaw says: 'It is man's indifference to man which is so devastating in its effect.' From my personal experience I endorse that sentiment and confirm that it can become one of the principal horrors of imprisonment. This may illustrate the point.

I was serving the midday meal in the kitchen one day with another prisoner whom we will call Jaapie. He had just finished five years of an eight-year sentence for pimping, his third offence. A young well-built patient came in and asked for a spoon. The kitchen was strictly out of bounds to him, so to that extent he was in the wrong, but hardly enough to warrant the flow of foul language directed at him by Jaapie. An altercation followed. A warder appeared. Unwisely he raised a hand to the boy, who just happened to be a

heavyweight boxer. A short jab to the solar plexus and the warder
was out cold on the floor at his feet. Jaapie raised the alarm. Here
was a chance to get in good with the Boere. From nowhere, like a
pack of hyenas, fellow-prisoners converged on the spot, over-
powered the boxer, flung him to the ground and put in the boot.
More warders appeared, who joined in the fun. I could see nothing
but a forest of boots kicking the life out of the boy. After a while
his inert body was handcuffed and removed to solitary confinement.
What was it all about? He came in for a spoon, now look at him.

Many prisoners found life unbearable and attempted suicide;
sometimes the rate was as high as one a week. This was a crime in
itself, punishable by solitary confinement. The authorities regarded
it as no more than a ruse to gain sympathy. The only means available
was a razor blade. They know that the possibility of actually killing
oneself in this way is small, but what man knows that? God knows
what mental torture a man must have endured before taking that
hideous step. On several occasions I saw a man brought in on a
stretcher covered by a blanket drenched in blood. Usually he was
white as a sheet and unconscious. A warrant officer nursing warder,
a pronounced sadist, would tip him off the stretcher to the ground.
Later he would be examined and cleaned up. It was never regarded
as an emergency.

The mere slashing of the wrists or, in some cases, of a main artery
is not, apparently, sufficient in itself to kill a man. This astonished
me. I was told that the only way it could be done with a razor blade
was to cut the main artery in the throat, and even then it would take
a considerable time before death. Some of these unfortunate men
recovered within hours, their problems and the hopelessness of their
lives increased.

But one day a young boy of nineteen did manage to commit
suicide. He had been placed in chains and in solitary confinement
for swearing at a warder. I knew the warder well; he was the typical
shouting martinet. The boy's parents and girlfriend had travelled a
great distance to visit him, but as no man is allowed a visit if he is
in the Bom they left again without seeing him. It must have been
the final straw that broke him. The boy twisted the chains round his
neck and then round a bar in the grille and strangled himself. He
was discovered at unlock the next morning. The press never publish
these matters, it goes without saying. I doubt if they even know
about them.

Six Blacks were to be hanged that Thursday morning at dawn.
Since lights out the previous evening we had heard singing coming
from the hundred or so Blacks in Beverly Hills. There were hymns

and traditional prison songs like 'Down in the Valley', haunting, plaintive and never-ending. They went on steadily right through the night to keep up the courage of the doomed men. 'Abide with me; fast falls the eventide. . . .' I could not sleep and stood looking through the bars towards the prison a bare hundred yards away until the first rays of dawn broke red across the hill behind it. Their families waited at the gate. The whole of our prison was quietly astir and full of an indefinable expectation. Dawn broke. The singing rose to a mighty crescendo and stopped suddenly with a triumphant 'Hallelujah!' In my mind I heard the awful clang of six trapdoors dropping simultaneously. A shiver ran through me. The horror of judicial murder was a physical reality which had taken place the other side of that wall. The law, an impersonal thing, had killed six men. An Act of Parliament, the will of the people, had demanded it. The reality of it ran through our cells with the shock of an electric current. A brooding silence settled on us. We whispered. No warder shouted. We were kept locked up for an extra hour before everything returned slowly to normal.

Outside the prison walls there would be a small knot of faithful relatives, weeping, keening, waiting for the moment when they could ask permission to go in and carry away the bodies of their loved ones. They carried blankets for the purpose. Later that day a black-edged notice would be posted on the prison gate proclaiming that justice had been done. In terms of such and such an Act prisoner X had been hanged by the neck until he was dead. In the horror of that moment the world had forgotten his crime, whatever it may have been.

I began to think it was time I asked for a change of scene. Matt O'Hara, whom I saw on Sundays at Mass, said he could pull strings for me to join the building group, even though it was unusual for permission to be granted to a man who had not completed two years of his time.

So in due course I returned to B section and awaited a summons to appear before an industrial board. This imposing title was given to a brigadier and two full colonels who deliberated on my application to join the building group. I was told that if they agreed to it they would like me to know that I would be denying some deserving youngster (sic) the chance to be trained as a tradesman. However, if I was really keen, I could go as a handyman plumber and await my chance to be trained as an artisan. Once again these well-meaning gentlemen really believed that such an organisation existed. Need I tell you that the training programme, or absence of it, was exactly the same as for the so-called cabinet-makers. It simply did not exist.

Of the eighty-one Whites assigned to the building group during the year I worked there not one man went for a trade test in any single trade. One man was teaching himself to be a bricklayer and another was learning to be a plumber, in the same way – picking it up for himself, as it were – but as for actual instruction by a qualified artisan there was none. Lest there be any doubt on this point let me explain what I consider to be proper instruction. It is where a fully qualified artisan instructs a learner in his trade on site, and sometimes in the classroom, teaching him exactly how to perform the many and varied requirements of the trade, and supervises him in actual practice.

Four or five of the 230 Blacks who worked in the building group had been before this industrial board and found fit for training as artisans. They were supposed to receive proper instruction in a trade and go for trade tests. They never received any. They also tried to teach themselves. I knew only of two Blacks who went for a trade test the whole time I was there.

Let me finish with this subject by describing an event out of chronological order. A year later I had the opportunity of discussing this matter with the prison chaplain at Pietermaritzburg New Prison. The Reverend Kruger, a hard-working and compassionate priest – 'One day in prison is one day too much' was his favourite saying – was sure I was wrongly informed. He sent for the data. He showed it to me. It stated clearly that so many thousand prisoners, black and white, were being trained to work as plumbers, bricklayers, carpenters, and so on, throughout the prison service. The lie was in the tyranny of words. It was a question of semantics. Certainly it could be held that a man who installed a geyser or a lavatory pan was being trained *to work as* a plumber, or that a man who spent his day sanding down a block of wood was being trained *to work as* a carpenter, but there was all the difference in the world between 'working as' anything and being trained to become an artisan in that trade. There was the rub. To qualify in a trade it was self-evident that there must be a proper training by qualified instructors who would also supervise practice. Such an organisation, like the famous facilities, did not exist.

Before I lay down my pen on this subject, on which you can see I feel strongly, I must enter a small caveat. Everything I have said refers to Pretoria Central Prison where I had personal practical experience of the situation, and to no other. If proper training exists in other gaols, I shall be the first to congratulate the authorities. The gravamen of my argument is not that proper training does not exist – that is an incontestable fact – it is that the prison service pretends that it does.

While I have my small artillery out let me talk a little about the doctrine of rehabilitation. The Prisons Act 1959 says at Section 2 (2)(b): 'The functions of the Prisons Department shall be . . . as far as practicable, to apply such treatment to convicted prisoners as may lead to their *reformation and rehabilitation* [my italics] and to train them in habits of industry and labour.' Further on at Section 20 (c) it refers again to 'training of selected prisoners with a view to their classification and training . . .'.

If one could say that in the training of artisans the Prisons Department was guilty of hoodwinking the public, this was certainly not the case with regard to rehabilitation. There was none, and they made no bones about it. General Otto is on record to this effect on many occasions. He may have regretted it, but it was a fact of prison policy. We prisoners were under no illusions whatsoever on this point, either; the purpose of imprisonment was, from first to last, punishment for crimes committed and nothing else. And while that remains the *raison d'être* of the South African prison service I see no hope for the future of the 105,000 White, Black, Coloured and Indian prisoners presently serving out their sentences in the 240 prisons all over the country.

Let me make a constructive suggestion. Pay prison labour for work done. I do not suggest that this should be at even half the going rate outside, but perhaps at some rate which would help a prisoner make a new start in life when he finally leaves prison. As things are, no prisoner is paid anything in the way of wages for his labour, yet bigger and better prisons are being built each year with free prison labour at a fraction of the cost of a normal contract price. Yes, you are right, a man may receive a gratuity for his labour out of the goodness of the Head of Prison's heart. This is in his gift and is seldom in excess of one or two rand per month, to begin with. This may increase for qualified men in certain trades until they rise in the fullness of time to a maximum of sixteen rand per month. While this is better than nothing, it is a far cry from the nest egg I envisage, and in no way caters for the vast majority of prisoners who enter and leave prison unqualified in any trade. The average gratuity paid to those men who qualified for it in Pretoria Central was four rand per month, by my estimate. A pitiful sum. Of this they could spend half each month.

Tullio was granted one rand per month gratification for his sand-papering efforts. He stood before the august assembly of senior officers who had seen fit to reward him in this way.

'Any questions?' they asked.

'Yes,' said Tullio. 'With respect, gentlemen, is it taxable?'

They had the grace to laugh.

After we had been in prison for nine months we were regraded as A-group prisoners. We were now entitled to buy groceries and toiletries up to a total of R25 per month. More important, we were now allowed thirty contact visits per year. For me this was the most valuable privilege of all. The contact visit was conducted in the open under the supervision of a warder who was within earshot. One could sit next to one's visitor on a bench or on the grass and hold his or her hand as the mood took one. Phyllis now informed me that both opposition political parties were anxious to visit me in gaol, but they needed my written approval. After discussion we decided against this. I still hoped for decent treatment by the government; to let my case become a political football did not seem wise. But time was passing, and Penzhorne gave us no hope. He thought that once the men were off Mahé the government might be able to do something, but in the meantime we must not rock the boat.

My first day with the building group was a disaster. Matt O'Hara, who was in charge of the scaffolding section and had his own group of Blacks under him, showed me the ropes. I was assigned to the plumbers' squad. There were ten Whites and fifteen Blacks. I worked with the Blacks and you may say my education in prison began to a very large degree on that day. My job was to assist a Xhosa operate a pipe-threading machine called a Rigid. It was made in Toledo, Ohio. How can I ever forget it? I polished the plate for over a year. The Xhosa's name was James. He was patient and intelligent, and we got on well from the start. Black people have an inborn respect for their elders, it is part of their tribal culture; they are naturally good-mannered and, above all, they are compassionate. The Blacks in the squad treated me in this way, and as the days went by and as we shared the common lot this grew into a genuine affection.

There was distressingly little work to do, other than sweeping the workshop floor continually, so that I was glad when the siren went at a quarter to four. We assembled as a group to be walked back to the prison. A young warder of nineteen or twenty was in charge. While we waited for another span to join us the warder addressed us. He had never seen me before. He spoke in Afrikaans in a loud voice.

'You . . . old man . . . what are you in for?'

Matt, who spoke fluent Afrikaans, nudged me.

'Don't answer him. He'll try to make a fool of you. Just show him your card.' I held up my card. The warder ignored it. He loved playing to the gallery.

'Don't be shy. I know what you're in for. You —— your kaffir girl. Is that right?'

All the hyenas laughed obligingly. Matt told me what he said. He was fuming with rage.

'No,' he continued, mining the rich vein, 'I must be wrong. I know what it was. You —— your dog!' Another burst of laughter, but Matt broke ranks and said something in his ear which made him look at me closely and lose much of his bravado. A word to the Head of Prison and the buffoon would have been fired on the spot, I supposed. But I ignored it. It was prison after all; not that the realisation made me any happier, but it seemed to excuse his behaviour. That night in the quiet of my cell I realised I had indeed 'struck the very base-string of humility'.

As the days went by James and I and Shoeshine and Maurice and Jacob and Zungu and Timothy the wise, and all the other Blacks I worked with, talked about life, Africa, politics, education, religion and the future. We became friends. If they educated me in the humanities, I educated them in the ways of the world. What was this referendum? Would it make any difference to them? What did I think of apartheid? Was it really necessary? If they did away with apartheid, asked Maurice, an irrepressible joker, would he be white the next day?

I often told Matt that only now after living in Africa for more than thirty years was I really beginning to find them. If there was a meeting of minds, the reason was clear as crystal. In prison I was being treated exactly as Blacks are treated outside it! We were all equal, Black and White. I learned in prison what it is like to be totally ignored by Whites as though I did not exist, to be spoken to as though I was a species which had no feelings. The Blacks taught me to bear no resentment; to be, as James said, 'as humble as a dove'.

Matt never went through that metamorphosis. His was an old Cape family, rich and respected. Blacks were his people, they were in his care, his attitude was paternal. When Christmas came he ran extravagant risks to smuggle packets of cigarettes to 'his boys' as a present which they would expect from him and he would be happy to give. It was how his class behaved; it was part of the South African tradition. He spoke their various languages as well as they did. Why this remarkably talented young man had ended up here was a mystery to me. It was my very good fortune that he did, and I looked no further than that.

I had not been there long when I sensed that my new Black friends were having some difficulty in knowing how to address me – largely on account of the age difference, I presumed. I said they must call me Mike, of course, but they were not happy with that. On my side I ruled out 'boss' and 'sir', both of which were absurd in this context. The African has a genius for nicknames, and I really expected them to honour me with one, but in the end they settled for a combination of 'Mike' and 'sir' and called me 'Sirmike', all one word. This seemed to please them, and for my part I was delighted with the prison knighthood!

Some months passed and I graduated to helping James install handbasins, lavatory pans, urinals and geysers. In the process I got to know all about him. He was a most independent individual, ran a prison football team, 'the Gunners' (very distant cousins of Arsenal, he told me!), and loved good music. One day we had just finished running the lead into the pan connector joint and were resting. I was telling him about the infernal pop music we suffered each evening and the din of the public address system.

'I suppose you have the same thing, James?' I asked.

'Why, no,' he said. 'We don't. How could we? You know there are forty-eight of us in a communal cell and we all speak different languages – Zulu, Xhosa, Venda, Sotho, and so on. You know how it is. No, that wouldn't work. Instead they allow us to have individual radio sets. But of course they must be FM only, and we have to play them very softly.'

'Lucky devils,' I said. 'I'd give anything to have my own radio. By the way, James, what sort of set have you got?'

'I haven't got a set.'

'How do you mean?'

'Well, I haven't got one. That's all.'

'But why not?'

He mumbled something about money.

'How long have you been here, James?' I asked.

'Eight years.'

'And to go?'

'Maybe three, four years . . . with good behaviour.'

'And do you get visits from your family?'

'No.'

'Why not?'

'Too far for them to come. It costs too much from the Transkei.'

'And don't you put in an order each month?'

'No. Hold on now, Sirmike,' he said. 'Don't go feeling sorry for me. I manage all right. I take in washing, that sort of thing. We Blacks, you know, we help each other. Please, don't worry about me.'

But I did. The next visit I had from Phyllis I asked her to buy an FM radio and take it around to the Black prison and make sure it was given to James. She did. In due course it filtered through to him. Heavens, he was so happy. What a difference it had made to his life; he prattled on and on about it.

'Well, that's great, James,' I said. 'I'm glad it's made you happy. Would you like to do something to make me happy?'

'Of course. For you, Sirmike, anything.' He meant it.

'Well, James, listen. Read up the twenty-third Psalm in the Bible, learn it and recite it nicely for me.'

'Is that all? But I know it already. You know, when we were piccanins there was a preacher used to come to our chapel sometimes. He taught us. Easy.'

'OK, then. Give it to me.'

He struck a pose, concentrated and began slowly.

'De Lawd ees ma Shep-ed . . . I shall not want . . . He maketh me to lie down in green pastures . . . He leadeth me. . . .' He petered out. 'Gets a bit hard there,' he said. 'But I know it, Sirmike, just give me a few days.'

Two or three weeks passed. I prodded him.

'Hey, James, De Lawd ees ma shep-ed. . . . What happened?'

'I'm working on it. Won't be long now.'

Another three weeks went by and I asked him again. He gave me the same answer, so I assumed he had forgotten all about it and as I didn't want to badger him I dropped it.

Every day at a quarter to twelve the Blacks would gather round the Rigid machine, take off their overalls and wait for the siren which announced it was time for the midday meal. This day four of them approached me with their arms around one another looking for all the world like a barbershop quartet. Which is what they were. James beckoned to me.

'Sirmike, over here. Come. Listen to this. You're going to like it.'

He took up a piece of half-inch copper pipe, unthreaded, and gave them the down beat. They began to sing. In a golden moment the whole workshop was filled with a glorious sound. I listened spellbound. Great God! It was the twenty-third Psalm sung as a madrigal, each successive phrase climbing on the back of the previous one and floating out serenely through the bars.

I looked at the quartet. On the left was that huge Zulu with the beautiful baritone; next to him was that little villain from Soweto with the reedy tenor; and then that grave Shona from Harare with the deep bass voice. And over all the imperturbable James conducting, *con brio*. The lovely sound, their magnificent effort, the harsh and cruel surroundings of the prison were too much for me. To hide my emotion I turned away from them. They stopped singing. I felt a gentle hand on my shoulder.

'Sirmike, don't you like it?'

'Yes, James, yes. I do, I do. I . . . I hear better like this. Please, don't stop. Please, begin again at the beginning.'

Which they did; and when they got to the last verse and sang 'And I will dwell in the house of the Lord for ever . . .' the siren went, and they stopped. And then the most wonderful thing that ever happened to me in prison took place. Seeing the tears in my eyes they all came forward spontaneously, took me by the hands and embraced me!

I complained about the lack of something to do. I was offered an alternative job sandpapering walls, which I rejected. So to occupy myself I began to learn lines of poetry by heart. I found a complete Shakespeare and learned a number of the great soliloquies: 'To be or not to be', of course, 'Oh, that this too too solid flesh would melt', and very many others from *Hamlet* and *Henry V*. To my surprise I had no difficulty memorising long speeches sixty and seventy lines long. This was extraordinary for me because at school I had never been able to memorise anything very easily. Wanting to do it made all the difference, I suppose, and the fact that my mind was empty must also have made it easier. It helped me in a number of ways. Standing in those interminably long queues day after day, always silent, I practised my lines. I discovered a strange comfort in contrasting the sordid surroundings with the imagery of lines like 'daffodils, That come before the swallow dares, and take / The winds of March with beauty'. It lifted me out of prison. In it but not of it. So every day I tried to learn something. In this way I felt I was beating the system, and it gave me a lift.

Eventually this learning of lines got me into serious trouble. I had found an old volume of Marlowe's complete works in the library and was studying *Dr Faustus*. Early one morning in my cell I came across those magnificent lines describing Helen of Troy.

Was this the face that launch'd a thousand ships?
And burnt the topless towers of Illium?
Sweet Helen, make me immortal with a kiss.

and goes on for another ten superb lines to end with the incomparable:

177

O, thou art fairer than the evening air,
Clad in the beauty of a thousand stars,
Brighter art thou than flaming Jupiter,
When he appear'd to hapless Semele,
More lovely than the monarch of the sky
In wanton Arethusa's azur'd arms,
And none but thou shalt be my paramour.

I determined that this would be my learning for the day, jumped out of bed and hastily scribbled the lines on to a sheet of paper – completely forgetting the prohibition against this sort of thing. It was strictly forbidden to write anything other than the allotted three letters per month. Diaries, notebooks, anything of that sort were not allowed. So a few minutes after unlock I hurried down to the yard to join the building group, who were busy lining up for the morning search before being marched off to the site. The offending lines slept secretly in my shirt.

It was my bad luck to come opposite a large-size disciplinary warder, a loud-mouthed bully greatly to be avoided. He ran his hands over me expertly and extracted the piece of paper from my shirt pocket.

'Oh, yes! Oh, yes! What have we here?'

'Poetry, sir.'

He read some of it out, painfully.

'You write this rubbish?'

'No, sir. As a matter of fact those lines were written nearly four hundred years ago.'

He held the paper up to the light and scrutinised it.

'You don't fool me, *ou kerel*, these lines was written in the last half-hour!'

Well, of course that made my day. The warder had always suspected I was a bit of a nut; now he was sure of it. But his rejoinder kept me happy for weeks. Still does.

Matt and I always spent the lunch-break together. We used to carry our steel plates out into the builders' yard and sit on the ground, usually next to a latrine for the Blacks, an odoriferous twelve-seater. This day the meal was the usual soggy mess of congealed pork fat sloshed on top of stamped mealies. We gave ours away to two eager grubbies, the name for men who would eat anything.

'Eat that and die,' said Matt. 'Come on, Colonel, let's get some sleep.'

I always followed Matt submissively. He was a strong personality, hard and independent and, I suspected, wayward. Although he was twenty years my junior, with him I always felt like the new boy at school befriended by a sixth-former. We found a piece of shuttering and lay on it, side by side. 'Here you are,' he said, 'Japanese pillow.' I put the block of wood under my neck; it was surprisingly comfortable.

Matt had the reputation amongst the inmates of being a holy Joe, probably because he attended Mass regularly and was, as I said, an altar boy. He was a practising Christian. The genuine article. This day we discussed the possibility of asking God for a sign. The sign I needed was one which would indicate that the men on Mahé would be released very soon, unharmed. Basically it was a selfish wish, I realised that, but for me it was crucial. Until their release nobody would be able to do anything for the four of us here in Pretoria Central. That was my thinking. Matt said we must pray. If we had faith, a sign would be sent to us. All we had to do was pray. 'When two or more are gathered together . . .,' he explained; it was all there in the Gospel. I felt that perhaps two sinners like us might not be enough for the special thing we were going to ask God for; so to make up a quorum, as it were, we co-opted an old lag who always seemed pretty devout despite the fact that he was serving a coat for armed robbery and heaven knows what else. So in the full glare of the concrete yard and under the gaze of a puzzled warder and a slightly amused gang of convicts Matt led the three of us in a small prayer. But it had to be offered with due humility in the kneeling position. It was really a one-liner, the 'short prayer that pierceth heaven' as they say: 'Please, God, send us a sign that the men on the island will be released very soon, unharmed. Amen.'

Later that afternoon Matt and I climbed up the scaffolding to the third floor and looked over Pretoria. Below us were the yard, the concrete-mixers and two huge gates leading out on to Potgieter Street. A Black warder opened and shut them whenever there was a delivery of sand or stone, which was not very often. But now a delivery was imminent. The gates swung open and as we watched an enormous red pantechnicon stopped immediately outside in the road, blocking the gates. On its side it had a sign in huge white letters two feet high. It read: 'Everything's OK!' (The slogan of OK Bazaars, South Africa.) Matt and I looked at each other absolutely astounded. Matt crossed himself quickly and said: 'Thank you, Lord.'

The next day the men were released from Mahé and flew back to South Africa.

We hoped that the government would be able to release us now. The men on Mahé, who had been condemned to death, had been pardoned and set free. This display of leniency should give them some scope in our case. But nothing happened. Month followed month, and as Christmas 1983 approached I decided to write to the Commissioner for Prisons and ask for a personal interview, a right stipulated in the Prisons Act. The authorities were horrified at the effrontery of the suggestion. The best they would allow me was to write to the Commissioner, subject to their veto. My fifth draft was passed. All I asked for was a transfer to a prison nearer to my home so that my wife, who was not well, would be spared the 1300-kilometre drive for our thirty-minute visit every three weeks. I referred to an interview the Prisons Department had given to *Rapport*, an Afrikaans Sunday newspaper, in which they stated that every effort was made to place prisoners as near to their homes as was possible. This statement had raised a gasp of disbelief in the communal cells of Pretoria Central, but I persevered.

I was now back in B section. Peter had run foul of the warder in the *menasie* and been fired. Always outspoken on the question of food and behaviour at table, he had overstepped the mark one day and told the Boere that only barbarians ate like they did, putting sugar on vegetables, cooking meat until it looked like shoe leather, heaping their plates up like children at a party, and so on. He returned to the men's cookhouse and then to the hospital as store-man. In this capacity he was able to lay his hands on small things like cotton and pieces of wood and glue, which I needed in the building of a model ship, my hobby in better times. It took me two months to make a model brigantine for Peter, about six inches long to a scale of 1:300, and a topsail schooner for Tullio, using only a penknife blade. This gave me hours of quiet entertainment and, though the finished product was necessarily crude, overcoming the problems was half the fun of it.

As a special concession, and as an experiment, the Head of Prison allowed the cell doors in B section to be left open on alternate nights. This meant we could mix more freely one with another if we wished it. As we were all A-group prisoners it was assumed that we would behave ourselves. Of course this licence opened the door in every sense to homosexuality, but very little of that took place to my knowledge. I used to talk very freely with one chap about these things, and he openly admitted that he was a sodomist. He was under thirty and had the lusty sexual appetite of the average young man; for him sodomy was a sexual outlet. It was as simple as that; it was uncomplicated by any of the aesthetic considerations of homosexuality, such as love or a common sensitivity. For him it was the satisfaction of a brute desire only. Yes, he agreed that to some extent he was an animal. But wasn't this one of the classic moments in a man's life when he could permit himself the relief which masturbation was thought to bring? I asked. He said it was too impersonal (strange use of that word) and too passive for him. Prison was certainly an education in life. Where else would I ever learn these things? But, then, again, would I want to in the normal course of events?

Sublimation of sexual desire is more easily discussed than experienced. I often thought of the degeneration of a man who had served with me in the Congo. He was in his early thirties when he received a fourteen-year sentence for some sexual offence – rape, I believe. He was heavily oversexed. During his time in Pretoria Central he suffered agonies of frustration in this all-male environment. As an outlet he practised sodomy. He disgusted himself in so doing. Religion was suggested to him as a way out of the mess. He embraced it with enthusiasm, looking desperately for sublimation. But his sexual desires did not abate. If anything, they grew. An intense self-hate overtook him. He loathed himself. In a religious fervour he decided to punish himself for his wicked practices. Early one morning they found him in his cell, naked and covered in blood, his legs wide apart. He had castrated himself with a razor blade.

At the end of December 1982 an event took place in Barberton Prison in the eastern Transvaal which rocked the South African public and caused considerable speculation concerning the treatment of Black and Coloured prisoners. On a day when temperatures were in excess of 100 degrees Fahrenheit eight White and four Black prison warders had forced a gang of Black and Coloured prisoners to push wheelbarrows loaded with stone up an incline for several hours. Thirty-four of them were assaulted with batons and three of them died from heat exhaustion. Now in September 1983 four of the White and two of the Black warders had been found guilty on charges of assault with intent, but not guilty on the three charges of murder. The White warders were given sentences ranging from one to eight years in gaol.

The whole of Pretoria Central buzzed with anticipation. It was an inviolable rule that all sentenced prisoners serving a term in excess of two years must undergo a period in observation in Pretoria Central. Would the prison authorities treat these four warders differently? I was particularly interested in this case, not only in comparing their sentences with mine, but also because I had been told *ad nauseam* that the Prisons Department could not make a special case for me as all prisoners must be treated alike and I was no different. Now we would see.

No prizes are offered for guessing the outcome. The ex-warders arrived at six-thirty one evening and were placed in cells in C section where they would have no contact with any other prisoners. They were taken out at four-thirty the following morning before the general unlock and sent to Witbank, a town a few miles from Barberton. There was to be no period of observation for them. They were to be treated differently. The assumption is that they are serving their time in a local gaol near their homes and families. But nobody knows for sure, least of all the press. For an organisation that bends over backwards to ensure that all prisoners are treated alike this was an extraordinary departure from the norm by the Prisons Department.

In February 1984 I was given the good news. The Commissioner had acceded to my request. Duffy and I would be transferred to Natal. Not only Natal, but Pietermaritzburg, a bare ten miles from my home! A likely date was the middle of April. That was joy enow. I hastened to tell Tullio. He was delighted for my sake. When I came to say good-bye to him a few weeks later I took with me the knowledge that here was a man who lived with a steady superiority over life; prison and this degrading experience had not touched him.

It was St Patrick's Day and my birthday. The famous Nat King Cole and I were born on the same day of the same year, but that was where my claim to fame began and ended! This year my birthday fell on a Saturday, which meant Phyllis could visit me. We sat on a bench and I held her hand.

'Well, my love,' she said, 'how are you . . . I mean . . . today?'

'Oh, that,' I said. 'Not too bad. To tell you the truth, I don't mind getting old' (which was a dreadful lie!) 'but you know what really bugs me? I'm getting so bloody ugly.'

'But, my darling,' she cried, 'you've always been ugly!'

I don't know what I was expecting, but it certainly wasn't that!

But before we leave Pretoria Central let me tell you one last story about the building group. I hope I have made it clear to you that the disciplinary warders who work within the prison and the building group warders who work outside it are two very different species. The latter are gentlemen by comparison. Their job is to supervise the building of prisons, alterations to establishments, and so on. For the most part they are humane and understanding, more concerned with labour and production than with making a man's life miserable. They never seemed to find it necessary to scream and shout.

So I was not altogether surprised when the warder in charge of the tiling section invited me to his office one day for a cup of tea. There must be a good reason for the invitation, I figured. There was. As I enjoyed the strangeness of a chair and the pleasure of a proper cup to drink out of, the warder, who was your typical family man, explained his problem. It appeared that his fourteen-year-old son was not doing well in his study of the English language and in fact could hardly make himself understood in it. And now, to make matters worse, there was a special examination which he had to pass or else. He laid a pink form on the table. The main stumbling-block was this damned English Composition: 'You come home from school unexpectedly and you find two black men are burgling your house. What do you do? Write 300 words. . . .'

'Well, now, Mike, you're a bit of a writer, they tell me. Just you sit here and take your time and let me have that composition by lunchtime, hey? Philemon will bring you tea whenever you want it. OK?'

'Very much OK,' I replied.

Paper, pencils, tea, peace and quiet, and four hours in which to write 300 words. Better than being at home! I finished the composition in half an hour, polished it up for another half-hour and drank five cups of tea. I thought it was pretty exciting stuff, full of heroic action and youthful imagination. I shoved in the odd grammatical error to make it look like an authentic fourteen-year-old effort and included a couple of passages where 'then we had lunch' and 'then we had tea' appeared in reasonable context. The warder was delighted with it, but didn't bother to read it. At this point I began to miss my wife. She always reads my work and tells me everything I write is wonderful; 'the greatest thing since Shakespeare' is her usual comment. I never have any difficulty believing her. So the aftermath of this little event came as a mild surprise to me.

After a week the same warder sent for me and gave me the composition back. Written across the top in a severe schoolma'amish hand was the inscription: 'Four out of ten. Not your best. Can do better.'

CHAPTER 10

Pietermaritzburg New Prison

———

IT WAS JUST AFTER nine in the morning. Duffy and I stood outside the gates of Pretoria Central together for the first time in twenty months. A five-ton truck manned by three armed warders waited for us. The back of the truck had been converted into a Black Maria, a small compartment in front just behind the driver's cab for White prisoners, the larger back part for Blacks. We got in, delighted to be leaving this hell hole at long last. Apart from Matt we were unable to say good-bye to anyone. It was a most impersonal departure, but we were elated.

The warders were taking no chances. We were both put into leg irons and handcuffed to one another. We sat on a narrow bench and peered out of a small slit in front of us to see the countryside roll by, which was a sheer delight. We were to make a tour of other prisons in the area, picking up and dropping other prisoners. At Diepkloof we picked up a White prisoner. He was about thirty, tall and handsome, and wanted for murdering a bank manager in Zululand.

About three hours out of Johannesburg on the road to Natal we heard a clank of chains and saw our new friend stand up and stretch, chainless! Nothing to it, he said. Look, I'll show you. He took a bootlace from his shoe, threaded it through the lock of the handcuffs and pulled hard. The handcuffs sprang apart. We tried it. It worked! Duffy and I felt rather proud of ourselves, like old lags exercising our art. After we had attended to the leg irons we were relatively free to lie down on the floor or take it in turns on the narrow bench.

Some hours later we pulled into a petrol station. Our friend sounded us out. He had a plan; it couldn't fail. As soon as the metal door was unlocked from the outside he would jump out, overpower the warder and seize his pistol. The warder was a gross jolly type full of smiles and goodwill to all men, and thoroughly unfit. Then he would order the three warders into the cage we now occupied and we could drive ourselves to freedom. OK? You game? Not OK, we said, without even giving it a thought. Quite feasible, of course, but we had too much to lose. Duffy expected to be released any day now; he had completed one-third of his sentence and we knew of murderers and others who had got out on that basis, so it was not a proposition for him. For a man facing a murder charge, of course, it must have looked different. Thanks, but leave us out, *ou maat*. Just an idea, he said, accepting our decision with good grace, and then replaced our manacles against the moment when we would be let out for a breather.

We were in the best of spirits. The sheer novelty of a simple thing like a ride in a thoroughly uncomfortable Black Maria, viewing the countryside with difficulty, half-remembering places we knew of old, kept us happy and full of expectation. At Ladysmith Prison we were allowed to go to the lavatory, in tandem, still chained to each other. In our former life that might have caused us a twinge of embarrassment, but not now. And at two-thirty the next morning, stiff and exhausted, we pulled up outside the corrugated-iron entrance to Pietermaritzburg New Prison, the gaol we had left so chirpily twenty months before.

A captain met us. He escorted us along wide corridors and up flights of steps which had been built since we were here last. We struggled with our paper carrier-bags containing the balance of that month's grocery order. 'Here,' said the captain, in perfect English, 'let me give you a hand with that. You must be damned tired. Have you had anything to eat today?' Duffy and I exchanged glances. It was unbelievable. We were home again.

We had a cell each, complete with handbasin and lavatory and rendered concrete floor. Cold but comfortable. The next day we learned that there were twenty-five White prisoners on the floor below, all serving less than two years. Elsewhere there were over a thousand Black, Coloured and Indian prisoners, many of them serving ten or more years. The Head of Prison was Major van Rensburg, a sportsman in every sense of the word and well known as a marathon-runner. He was strict but fair. He sent Peter to the *menasie* as a cook and me to the petrol pumps as a petrol jockey. After three days I had a visit, and Phyllis brought me an FM radio. The rules permitted this as 'no facilities existed' for a public address

185

system, thank heavens. The warders in this prison never found it necessary to scream and shout at the prisoners but still managed to get the work done. If it is possible to say I was happy in prison, then I was happy here.

Two weeks later I had a surprise visit from Peter at my place of work. He was dressed in civilian clothes and had come to say good-bye! An hour earlier they had told him he could go. I was going to miss him. He had been with me every step of the way and, as I told him then, he had been a son, a brother and a friend to me. No man could wish for a more loyal companion. Before we parted I reminded him of the day he brought a copy of *Paradise Lost* to my cell in Pretoria Central and told me it contained the secret of how we should do our time. The passage read:

> Farewell, happy fields
> Where joy forever dwells! Hail, horrors, hail,
> Infernal world, and thou, profoundest Hell,
> Receive thy new possessor: one who brings
> A mind not to be changed by place or time.
> The mind is its own place, and in itself
> Can make a Heaven of Hell, a Hell of Heaven.

Well, if we hadn't succeeded in making a heaven out of that hell, we certainly turned it into a tolerable hell. And for that I am eternally grateful to Peter Duffy.

The Major came to say good-bye and asked him if he was thankful to be going. The Major was notably short on small-talk but Duffy took him literally. I am, of course, he replied, but I cannot forget that the South African government saw fit to let me serve twenty-one months in gaol only for trying to help them save face in the eyes of the world! I was mortified to see him go. He seemed to take a little of the sunshine and the laughter with him.

The visits were carefully monitored in this prison. I had mentioned casually to my wife that I thought I might be having problems with a hiatus hernia. This chance remark was overheard by the lieutenant sitting in on the visit and resulted in my examination by the prison doctor. He arranged for me to visit a specialist in Pietermaritzburg. Oom Piet, the senior chief warder and a fine man, took me in a VW Combi. Prison rules were that I should be in leg irons and handcuffed. I could see that he was torn between obeying the rules and the embarrassment he thought I would suffer when I had to walk the hundred yards or so from the vehicle to the consulting-rooms, not to mention the remarks which might be made by other patients waiting their turn to see the doctor. He didn't really know how to tackle this one.

Oom Piet had a tender heart, not the best equipment for a prison officer. I stood on the pavement and told him not to worry, it didn't upset me, and began to take the small shuffling steps, the only ones the leg irons permitted, up the slope. My moleskin Voortrekker jacket and corduroy pants completed the picture of the old lag coming for a check-up! Poor Piet, he suffered agonies, but we laughed it off. Incidentally, the eminent surgeon diagnosed my complaint accurately, assisted by a subsequent gastroscopy, and prescribed, amongst other things, a special diet of Marie biscuits and fresh milk. I had landed, once more, with my bum in the butter! But, better still, a year later I was completely free of whatever trouble had assailed me. If it wasn't a volcano-type stomach ulcer that caused the original trouble, then it should have been.

The Major thought I could be released after serving a third of my time. This was the minimum sentence which a model prisoner could serve, and I was regarded as a model prisoner. Perhaps a lawyer could help. And at this precise moment another stroke of good fortune befell me. Out of nowhere a highly respected lawyer, and senior councillor of the city of Pietermaritzburg, Mr Leslie Simon, obtained a legal visit and placed himself at my disposal without payment. Mr Simon was known to me and to thousands of others in South Africa as a man who had worked wonders for blind people of all colours. He now brought me hope and the knowledge that my case would not be forgotten at a high level. But for the moment 28 November next year, 1985, was the worst case he would accept and he intended to improve on that if that was the last thing he did.

The months went by. As there was no library in this prison the Major allowed me to have a book brought in from the public library. In this way I read my way through all of E. K. Chambers's works on Shakespeare, and everything I could find on Christopher Marlowe. With those books, and the radio, life returned to a tolerable level. It was now only a question of sitting it out. After some months news reached me that the Minister of Justice might be able to do something for me at the same time as clemency was shown to certain political prisoners. But that came and went. Then it was thought that an amnesty would be declared when the Prime Minister assumed office as State President. Nothing happened. I began to fear the worst.

One day I was asked if I would take a visit from a lay preacher who had obtained permission from Pretoria to minister to me if I was agreeable. I was of course. I had known Alistair Gilson as one of the leading Christians in the Hilton community where I lived. It was he who had made sure my wife and family were not suffering unduly while I was in gaol. It was a great moment in my life when I met this fresh-faced, young-looking man on terms of quiet intimacy here in prison. He came whenever he could, which was usually once every two weeks, and we discussed the Word and the world outside. It was a moving experience for me to come into contact regularly with such an ardent Christian. If ever a man lived his Christianity, it was he. In my study of leadership and man management (of soldiers) I had learned that personal example was the bedrock on which a real leader's other attributes were built. And here I was seeing it in practice, and being influenced and taught and comforted by a Christian who was leading with all the immense power his innate goodness gave him.

Some time later I discovered that this remarkable man was the chairman of a multimillion-rand public company with its head-quarters in Pietermaritzburg and branches all over South Africa. I shuddered to think what the time he spent with me so selflessly must be worth, but he shrugged it off without a thought.

I appreciated deeply what Alistair Gilson was doing for me and began to think that perhaps his actions bore the seed of a great idea. The concept of 'prison visitors' is well established in Britain but is quite unknown in South Africa. Under this system approved visitors, usually people of some social standing but not necessarily wealthy or famous or celebrated, although many such exist, are permitted to visit prisons and talk to individual convicts, with the approval of the governor, on any subject which may be of interest to both parties. In this way a convict who has perhaps lost touch completely with the outside world may be made to feel that he is still of value and that somebody out there cares. Prison visitors help re-establish that confidence which is the first casualty when a man enters prison. Some visitors have been able to assist in actual rehabilitation once the convict has left prison, the time when their sentence really begins.

With something like this in mind I asked if I might be permitted to talk to the Reverend Kruger, the prison chaplain. I put the bare bones of an idea to him. It boiled down to this: prisoners should be encouraged to attend religious service so that their chaplain would get to know them personally. When satisfied that a man would benefit from such a contact the chaplain would introduce him to a prison visitor. Ideally this might develop into an acquaintance, or even a friendship, where the prison visitor 'adopted' the prisoner and assumed some sort of unofficial responsibility for his future welfare. Optimistic perhaps, but such wonderful people do exist. Of course they would be horribly disillusioned sometimes, but for the sake of the many who would benefit it would be a worthwhile effort. But the responsibility for vetting the inmate, so to speak, before he was deemed ready for introduction to the prison visitor must rest with his priest. This sifting process would form a vital part of the process. In this way some sort of mission to prisons could be started, a wonderful Christian prospect. As St Mark said: 'They that are whole have no need of the physician, but they that are sick.'

But the physicians are few and far between. In the whole time I was in prison, and of course abnormally sensitive to these things, I never once heard, on the radio or elsewhere, of a prayer being offered for those behind bars. The sick, the needy, the oppressed, those in danger, yes. But a prayer for a prisoner, never.

In twenty months I only saw one man embrace Christianity whole-heartedly with a view to his own salvation. He was a German who had murdered his wife. But in spite of this I formed the conviction during the time I was in Pretoria Central that the only form of rehabilitation which stood the slightest chance of success was through the Word. But it would need a massive effort on the part of the religious workers and the total encouragement and support of the prison authorities. Bible study, in the first place, in my view, is the avenue most likely to lead to success. The vast majority of prisoners are from the underprivileged strata of society in South Africa, and even the most elementary knowledge of the scriptures had been denied them. Of all possible rehabilitation programmes this one would be the most practical, the cheapest to implement, and the one most acceptable to the individual prisoner. It goes without saying that no programme will succeed without the co-operation of the convict himself. Very very few would deliberately set their faces against an attempt of this sort to help them.

I was transferred to the nursery at my own request. The beauty of the rose garden and the depredations of aphids filled my days. Life was not so bad after all. I worked with a gang of ten Blacks and another White prisoner named O'Reilly who had seen a bit of time in gaol, poor devil. An old-time warder was in charge of our span and entertained us with stories of the old days when hangings were still carried out in Pietermaritzburg gaol.

Towards Christmas, my third in prison, rumours of an amnesty began to circulate. Amnesties are usually declared every five years in the South African prison system. The next one was not due until 1986, but the rumours persisted. It was Boxing Day and I was busy transplanting an azalea when a shadow fell across me. It was the

brigadier in charge of the whole prison complex. 'We have recommended you for release on 24 January 1985,' he said, with a
smile. 'In terms of an amnesty men of your age who have completed
a quarter of their time may be released. Do you agree with that
date?' Fantastic news! My pulse raced. I figured the date out swiftly.
No, it was wrong. I came in on the twenty-ninth of the month so I
must go out on the twenty-eighth not the twenty-fourth. But the
month was right. I said so. The brigadier said he would check on it
and left me to my azalea, which flowered suddenly in my hands.

The amnesty had been declared by the State President as a special
concession to mark his accession. In all, eighty-one prisoners would
benefit from it. Two Black men in this prison were released the same
day, but the Major was worried that too much was being made of it
in the press. He hoped that it would not backfire on me for some
reason. I could not see why it should and worked out that I had a
bare twenty-eight days to go! But the left-wing press commented
that the amnesty had been arranged specially for my release. I feared
that the Prisons Department, ever sensitive to this sort of criticism,
would overreact in an effort to show this was not so.

Meanwhile prison routine ground on. We had to parade every
morning at six-thirty in the prison yard when we would form up in
squads to be detailed off for work. The process usually took about
twenty minutes. The thousand or so Blacks were obliged to squat
on their haunches as they waited in the heat of the strengthening
sun. They reminded me of that Zulu impi which concealed itself in
a donga just out of sight of the British army at Isandhlwana in 1879,
silent, powerful and ominous. A Black trustee called out the names
of men needed for certain jobs. He had a marvellous voice, rich and
resonant, and he made it bounce off the walls of the exercise yard.
'Listen to the voice of Tembu!' he would shout, flourishing his list
and calling out the names twice for emphasis: Mkize, Abednigo . . .
Mkize, Abednigo . . . Jabulani, James . . . Jabulani, James. . . . It
was his great moment and he made a major production of it. It
always gave me pleasure to hear him. Such are the small details of
prison life.

But on the third day of January 1985 the usually docile scene
took on a frightening aspect. The first and second days of January
were holidays, but only in the sense that the work squads remained
in the prison and did not go out to work. On New Year's Day
the authorities had conducted a meticulous search for dagga and
confiscated great piles of it from the Blacks. Unrest had broken out
and truncheons had been used freely to subdue the troublesome. If
a warder was about to use his baton, he would blow his whistle and

every warder within earshot would run to his assistance at once, laying about him indiscriminately. In many cases the Black warders were more ruthless than the Whites.

O'Reilly and I were the only Whites on parade that day. All around us the impi squatted. But O'Reilly was uneasy. He didn't like the look of things: there were too many Boere present, they all had truncheons, and some of them were armed. This was not normal. He spoke out of the side of his mouth: 'Mike, the Blacks are going to rush the Boere. I can just feel it. When they do fall flat on your face. I'll fall on top of you. For God's sake don't get up; you'll get trampled to death.' Five seconds later the impi rose with a roar which filled the air with thunder and made for the entrance gates in two huge groups. I fell flat, O'Reilly on top of me. We covered our heads as whistles blew and boots thundered past. I smelt the stale sweet smell of sweat and fear as they went by. We stood up. In one corner a Black mob was surging back and forth, warders pinned against the wall. Truncheons were flaying and bodies were dropping thick and fast. More warders appeared and began to chase a group of Blacks around the yard.

O'Reilly and I watched spellbound. It was like a three-ring circus; we didn't know where to look first. After a few minutes the warders gained the upper hand, but one small Coloured man with tattoos all over his face and shoulders was cornered. Seven warders advanced on him, truncheons raised. The Coloured man flicked out a home-made knife and invited them to come on. Whatever else he was, he was a game little bastard. A lieutenant pushed the other warders aside and walked up to him threateningly. With two quick flicks of his wrist the Coloured slashed a knife wound on each side of the officer's face. He dropped, his face covered in blood. But sheer weight of numbers told. The Coloured was felled by the truncheons and then systematically booted until within an ace of losing his life. His ribs were stove in and his lungs punctured. He was taken to the local hospital and was lucky to survive. Seven weeks later he returned to prison and was put in a cell near me. He was still only able to crawl around on his hands and knees. The lieutenant he had wounded visited him. He only said three words: 'Suffer, you bastard!'

But it was not dagga after all that was at the root of the trouble. This was a typical episode in gang warfare. In this gaol there were two main gangs, deadly rivals. One gang, 'the twenty-sixers', were made up of sodomists; the other gang, 'the twenty-eights', were murderers and armed robbers. This gang was commanded by a 'general', a desperado whose slightest word was law. Even the warders were terrified of him. To maintain one's position in the gang as a 'general' one had to commit a murder every six months, or so it was said. This morning's entertainment had been caused by both gangs acting independently. The twenty-sixers were evening up the score with an interloper who had seduced the affections of a 'lightie', a proceeding apparently outside their constitution and not to be tolerated. The other fracas was the obligatory attempt at murder in prolongation of the general's term of office. For this purpose he had used a spoon-handle ground down to a point in the prison workshops. Lovely chaps.

O'Reilly and I discussed the affair at our first break. I said I was disgusted at the way the warders had used their batons on the Blacks, as though enjoying the exercise. O'Reilly's attitude was more pragmatic and born of greater prison experience. 'Scum,' he said. 'Brute force is the only thing they understand. Let them loose for five minutes and you and I would be the first to go!'

As 28 January 1985 drew near excitement mounted at home and exciting plans were made for my return. Peter Duffy appeared in the local press in chef's hat, white jacket and choker basting a goose (tame) for my coming-out party. The Major didn't like all this publicity. Far too much was being made of it, he warned. But I was powerless to stop it. I was all packed up to go on the morning of 28 January. Nothing happened. The Major said he was sorry but no warrant had arrived for my release; I must just be patient. The days dragged by, nobody knew anything, but I continued to hope for immediate release. Some bureaucratic lash-up, I imagined; but there was no question about it, I qualified for the amnesty and this had been confirmed by the Prisons Department public relations office in a statement to the press. What had gone wrong then?

On the morning of 4 February, exactly one week after I had been supposed to go, I reported to the nursery as usual. About midday two warders arrived suddenly. Drop everything and come with us, they said. With a light heart I said good-bye to O'Reilly. This was it, release at last, but the warders were in a grim mood, and not talking. I was taken to my cell on the third floor and locked in, both doors being shut. What's this all about? I asked. They didn't know. Orders from Pretoria. An hour later I was taken out and told to report to a social worker for an interview. It was a farce. Would I run the library they were thinking of installing? I said No, I'm about to be released. On my return to my cell the whole thing had been stripped. An officer and two warders had gone through it with a fine-tooth comb; everything which I had accumulated surplus to prison regulations, books, papers, notes for a speech I was to make at a press conference, a couple of aspirins I had smuggled in, my radio, everything had gone! But what were they looking for and why the search?

The duty warder, Gerry Swanepoel, a decent and humane man, said he knew nothing about it. Had I smuggled a letter out? That was the only explanation he could think of. But why would I do anything so stupid? Damn it, I was supposed to be released seven days ago! He said he was sorry but his orders were that I was to be stripped of all privileges and to be placed in solitary confinement. I asked to see the Major. He came the next day. He said they had received these instructions from Pretoria and they had to obey them. Be patient; I would be told in due course. I never was. To this day I do not know what prompted Pretoria to take that extraordinary action.

But my fortnightly visit was not denied me. Phyllis was distressed. She had made enquiries at Prison Headquarters in Pretoria but they could tell her nothing other than that my case was being considered. But an influential journalist friend of ours had terrible news. He asked Phyllis not to break it to me: he had heard at the highest-possible level that the President himself had issued the order cancelling the amnesty for me. I was to remain in gaol for a very long time yet, possibly another three years! The President was reputed to be furious with me. I was supposed to have written a defamatory letter to President Mobutu about him, threatening all sorts of disclosures when I left gaol! The very idea was too ridiculous for me to take seriously, but I knew – in fact it was common knowledge – that the President had a violent temper and this type of action was not beyond the bounds of probability. I wondered whether some evil person had laid false information or deliberately blackened my name in high circles, or forged such a letter. Obviously certain people in the government were going to be nervous, understandably so, when I emerged from gaol. What was I likely to tell the press? I could appreciate that it might be in the interests of certain people to keep me in gaol for a considerable time longer, but why didn't they come and see me then? My actions from start to finish had indicated a loyalty to the South African government. Surely this was the moment for somebody to come and discuss the future with me. But nobody came.

Weeks passed and I never left the cell. To add to my misery the night warders left my lights on all night from time to time by accident. My spirits began to sink and my health to deteriorate. The poison of persistent introspection is lethal. Probably the worst thing a normally healthy man can do is spend hours and hours churning things over in his mind. Why were they doing this to me? If they had some case against me, why did they not bring some charge? Was this the way to treat a man who had been loyal and decent according to his lights? The Major didn't know. He was just carrying out orders, but he would make certain the lights were turned off at night.

Every day for hours I recited the two thousand lines of Shakespeare and Marlowe I knew and loved so well. It brought some relief, but the effort was wearing me down. I discovered a way of putting my mind in neutral, as it were, by thinking on some bland but pleasant thought which would require no further concentration, like watching scenery from a railway carriage. If I thought hard enough, I could actually see the bow wave on my old 36-foot cutter *Colin Archer*, charging through the water, throwing up the spray and drenching the foredeck. It worked. For a short while my mind was at rest, the relief was tangible. But once more sleep became impossible and I asked the Major if I might see a psychiatrist. Was it possible to damage one's mind permanently by solitary confinement, or undergo a permanent personality change? I would ask him that.

During this harrowing time of total solitude I often thought about those famous Yogis in India who allow themselves to be buried alive for days at a time in order to test the power their minds have over their bodies. If they remain perfectly calm, they live; if they give way to panic, they die. I tried in my small way to emulate their self-control and in the end I think I succeeded. But the root of survival lies in the end in a man's sheer determination to see it through and the knowledge that nothing lasts for ever. One must hold that thought. I often said to myself, like that famous Scottish king: 'They have tied me to a stake. I cannot fly, But bear-like I must fight the course.' I still had something in reserve. Thank God for that.

Despite his official and very correct stance I could see that the psychiatrist was not happy with the situation. He made sweeping recommendations. Two weeks passed and he saw me again. None of them found favour with the authorities. Now he was angry. In his way he banged the desk so that in a short while something was done. The Major said I would be allowed to make a model ship. I really believe this saved my sanity and I thank that far-seeing doctor for his perseverance. I spent eight hours a day on its construction and dedicated it from the very first chip to my two dearest American friends, Don and Elaine, whose letters and practical support during the whole of my time in prison had done so much to keep me hopeful.

Inevitably I grew bitter at this harsh and unfair treatment. I had been told I was due for release on 28 January and here I was several weeks later in solitary confinement and nobody could tell me why. I recalled James Joyce's brilliant invective and wished I could have sent it to the people who were treating me in this inhumane manner.

> O Vague Something behind everything . . . Give me for Christ's sake a pen and ink-bottle and some peace of mind, and then, by the crucified Jaysus, if I don't sharpen that little pen and dip it into fermented ink and write tiny little sentences about the people who betrayed me, send me to hell.

With the passage of time I hope I have lived down those baser instincts, but they existed then and I must acknowledge them.

Ninety days had passed since I had been put into solitary confinement. All the little milestones which a prisoner marks with hope had come and gone, days which he works out for himself must be the logical one on which he will be released. April 28th, three months after I was supposed to be released under the amnesty, was the last obvious one. But it passed unheeded. On 5 May I had a visit. I told my wife that I had decided to stage a hunger strike beginning on 11 May. She must alert the press. Repercussions would be instant and far-reaching. The prison authorities would be forced to give a reason for treating me in this manner. She begged me not to do it; it would damage my health and could be dangerous. Instead, she said, Alistair Gilson and his Christian group would begin a fast for my release that very evening. Would I agree? I said Yes, she must give them my love and my thanks. I pondered on the effects which this incalculable power might have on my life in the next few days.

The next day, 6 May, they sent for me at eleven o'clock. The brigadier and two senior officers said they had some good news for me. I was to be released that afternoon at three o'clock! They would take me to my home by car. No, my wife was not to be informed. A press release would be made at exactly 3 p.m. I spent the hours between in some sort of trance. I gave away all my belongings and waited for the hour.

At half-past two one of my friends, an old lag from the floor below, came to say good-bye to me. He had persuaded the warder to let him come, which must have taken some doing.

'Well, *ou maat*,' he said, 'your time has come at last. I'm going to miss you. But here's a little present for you.'

He took a small packet from under his brown jersey and passed it through the bars. It was wrapped in newspaper.

'Hell, man, Kleinkie, that's kind of you,' I said, touched. 'But what is it?'

'Open it and see.'

I undid the packet on my bed. To my amazement it was a small Bible. But not just an ordinary prison Bible. No, sir, this was an exquisitely made leather-bound job, with gold-edged pages, an index down one side, and the words HOLY BIBLE embossed on the cover in gold. A regular little masterpiece.

'Jeepers, Kleinkie,' I said, 'I don't know how to thank you. I'll treasure it, I promise you. . . .'

'Look in the cover,' he said proudly. 'I've written in it.'

One or two pages were missing in the front of the Bible but that was nothing. On the inside of the cover he had written in a tortured hand: 'To Mike. A staunch Ou. Go well, *mei bra.* Kleinkie.'

It is a wonderfully warm and rewarding feeling to be thought well of by one's mates and in prison life it is no different. I was really moved. But a small thing was puzzling me.

'But where did you get it, Kleinkie?' I asked.

He looked furtively up and down the passage and answered: 'I stole it!'

The Major helped me with my paper carrier-bag from the prison gate to a waiting car. There was something symbolic about that but it escaped me until later. We said good-bye and I thanked him for everything. He answered briefly he was only doing his duty. The ten miles to my home looked strange to me; so much had changed in the 1014 days since I had seen it last. The gates to the Old Vicarage were open and we stopped in the driveway. I asked the captain to sound the horn. A window shot up and my eighteen-year-old son Simon looked out. He couldn't believe his eyes.

'Mum,' he shouted, 'it's Dad!'

As I ran into the hallway I heard my wife say in utter astonishment: 'Dear God! He's escaped!'

Index

Aba, 8–10, 43
Act 62, *see* South Africa
Affretair, 43
Afghanistan: Russia invades, 7,
   25
African National Congress, *see*
   South Africa
Air India, 42; flight 224,
   82–100, 103, 104, 114, 117,
   119, 123, 127, 132
Aldabra, *see* Seychelles
Algeria: influence in Seychelles,
   6, 7, 21; loan, 7
ANC, *see* South Africa: African
   National Congress
Ancient Order of Frothblowers,
   Ye, 59–61, 67, 71–2
Anglican Church, 6, 35
Angola, 35, 50, 64; Cubans in,
   35; MPLA, 35; Russian
   influence in, 132
Armstrong, Fr, 160, 164
Atlantic Ocean, 64
Australia: exiles in, 2, 19, 28,
   34, 38, 41

Bacus, 163
Bagamoyo, 105
Baker, Sir Herbert, 48
Barberton Prison, 181–2
Barnard, Professor Neil, 48
Berbera, 13
Bérenger, Paul, 6, 92
Biafra, 23–4, 43–4
Bloemfontein, 97, 134, 147
Bombay, 83, 86, 91, 96, 120
Bosman, Herman Charles:
   Cold Stone Jug, 141, 149
BOSS, *see* South Africa:
   National Intelligence Service
Botes, Desmond, 65
Botha, P. W.: supports
   operation, 48, 49, 134;
   becomes President, 187, 190;
   angry with MH, 193
Boulder, Colo., 110
Braamfontein, 67
Britain, *see* United Kingdom
British Airways, 17, 61, 105, 120
British Indian Ocean
   Territories, 12, 13

Brooks, Aubrey: advance party, 64; on Mahé, 74; wounded, 78, 95, 106; arrested, 106; death sentence, 134; released, 179
Bryanston, 61–2
Buganda, ex-King of, 36–7
Bukavu, 16
Bureau of State Security (BOSS), see South Africa: National Intelligence Service
Burton, Richard, 19
Buthelezi, Chief, 26

Cambodia, 7
Camille, Eddie: MH first meets, 20–1; MH works with, 20–1, 23, 31, 33, 37–8, 46, 47, 105, 107; and South African support, 22, 24; and Mancham, 27–8, 70, 72; in Durban, 40
Cannon, Pat, 152
Cape of Good Hope, 12, 64
Cape Town, 23, 34, 47, 49, 50, 63
Carey, Barney: recruited, 45; advance party, 65; on Mahé, 74; attack on barracks, 76–8; remains behind, 93, 94, 95; arrested, 106; sentenced to death, 134; released, 179
Carter, Jimmy, 33
Chad: Libya invaded, 7, 33; France intervenes, 33
Chagos archipelago, 12
Chambers, E. K., 187
Chang-Him, Bishop, 6
Cherry, Brian, 55
Christie, Agatha, 166
Civil Aviation Offences Act No. 10, see South Africa
Claasens, J. Y., 47–51, 105, 125

Coetivy, see Seychelles
Cold Stone Jug (Bosman), 141
Colin Archer, 55, 194
Colvin, Ian, 36–7
Commonwealth, 107; Prime Ministers' Conference (1977), 4
communism: Africa, 7–11, 132; Indian Ocean, 11, 13–14, 21, 22, 64
Comoros Is., 73, 79, 92
Congo: rebellion (1964–6), 2, 7–10, 16, 20, 37, 45, 54, 62, 69, 108, 132, 135, 160, 181; Russian influence, 132
Congo Mercenary (Hoare), 3
Cook, Lt, 162–3
Couquilhatville, 160
Cuba, 19; influence in Seychelles, 6, 7, 13, 21, 57

Dahlak archipelago, 13
Dahomey, 42
Daily Telegraph, 36, 60, 154
Dalgliesh, Ken: recruited, 63; advance party, 64; on Mahé, 74, 86, 97; arrest, 100; on bail, 104, 124
Dar es Salaam, 106
De Beer, Vic, 62
De Wet, Dr: recruited, 63; death of Fritz, 75–6; defends airport, 78, 87, 93
Denard, Bob, 18, 69
Desroches, see Seychelles
Devil's Disciple, The (Shaw), 168
Diego Garcia, 12, 13, 14, 22
Diego Suarez, 13
Diepkloof Prison, 136, 184
D'Offay, Gonzague: first approaches MH, 2–3; MH

working with, 14–15, 19, 24, 40

Dolinchek, Martin: names, 25; NIS, 25–6, 98, 133; an embarrassment, 51, 65–6, 74; firing range, 52–3; arrested, 106; imprisoned, 134–5; released, 179

Donaldson, Martin, *see* Dolinchek, Martin

Doorewaard, Pete, 62; recruited, 61; on Mahé, 79, 91, 92, 94; arrested, 100; defence, 109; imprisoned, 134, 136, 139, 155, 168

Dr Faustus (Marlowe), 177–8

Drakensberg, the, 69

Du Plessis, Brig., 103, 104

Duffy, Peter, 45; recruited, 66; finds pilot, 67; rendezvous at Ermelo, 71–2; on Mahé, 82, 85, 90; flight to Durban, 95–8; arrest, 100; on bail, 104; sentenced, 134, 135–6; Pretoria Central Prison, 154, 156–7, 160–1, 162, 168, 180; Pietermaritzburg New Prison, 182, 184–5; released, 186, 192

Dukes, Charlie: advance party, 65; on Mahé, 74; wounded, 78, 80, 95, 98; arrested, 100; acquitted, 134

Durban: mercenaries in, 6, 60, 64, 66, 67–8, 108; Elangeni Hotel, 10, 47; Royal Hotel, 40; Riviera Hotel, 45, 63; Point Road, 46; Louis Botha Airport, 97–100, 105, 114, 120, 123, 131, 133; Wentworth Hospital, 98; C. R. Swart HQ, 108; La Popote, 124

Elizabeth, Patrick, 117

England, Roger: advance party, 65; on Mahé, 74; remains behind, 93, 95; arrested, 106; death sentence, 134; released, 179

Entebbe: Israeli raid, 3

Ermelo: Holiday Inn, 68, 69, 70, 71–3

Eshowe Prison, 167–8

Ethiopia, 132

Fairbairn, Nicholas, 124, 134

Falkland Is., 132

Farquhar, *see* Seychelles

Ferrari, Maxime, 4

Financial Times, 74

5 Commando, 110, 167

Forsell, Sven, 63, 90

France: and coup, 2; aid to Seychelles, 4, 7, 18, 22, 31, 72; defends Chad, 33; Foreign Legion, 33

FRELIMO, *see* Mozambique

French Cameroons, 59

Frichot, Robert, 28, 31, 32–3, 33–4, 41

Fripp, Sir Alfred, 60

Fritz, Johan: recruited, 62–3; killed, 75–6, 94

Gandhi, Indira, 6, 35

General Mining Corporation, 63

Germany, 31, 33, 35

Gilson, Alistair, 187–8, 195

Glacis, 18

Goatley, Charles: on Mahé, 82–4; flight to Durban, 96; arrest, 100; on bail, 104

Gordonstoun, 156

Gowon, Gen., 24

Green Berets, 62

Grey Scouts, 64
Guinea-Bissau, 43
Gurkhas, 132

Hamlet, 177
Hamman, Brig. Danie: MH in
    contact with, 26, 49–51, 52,
    53, 54, 61; rival operation,
    34; and South African
    involvement, 95, 103, 125
Hannon, Mike, 107–8, 111,
    117–22, 125
Harare, 82, 86. *See also*
    Salisbury
Harding, Col., 144
Harris, Richard, 19
Hendrikse, Paddy, 79
Henry V, 177
Hilton, 57, 103, 104, 151, 188
Hoarau, Gerard: MH works
    with, 18, 38–40, 63, 69, 93,
    107; arrested, 21; and
    Kenyan support, 32–3, 66,
    70; and Mancham, 41; Vice-
    President designate, 41; NIS
    connections, 47, 49, 57, 59,
    125
HOARE, COL. MIKE
    Background: in Congo
    (1964–6), 2, 7–10, 16, 20, 37,
    45, 69, 108, 132, 135, 160,
    181; *Congo Mercenary*, 3;
    anti-communism, 3, 7–11;
    National Forum, 10; on
    future of South Africa,
    10–11; promotes *Wild Geese*,
    19–20; on arms dealers,
    23–4; in Nigeria (1967),
    23–4, 43; *Three Years with
    Sylvia*, 25; and Angola
    (1975), 35; meets ex-King of
    Buganda, 36–7; on
    mercenaries, 44–5, 62, 83,

131–2; sailing, 55, 56, 149,
    194; *Colin Archer*, 55, 194;
    crosswords, 74, 154
    Seychelles operation: first
    approached (1978), 1–3;
    question of finance, 2–3,
    14–15, 19, 22, 24, 25, 27,
    31–2, 33, 35, 36–58, 96; visits
    Mahé, 2, 14, 16–18, 23–31,
    40, 41–4; Mancham's
    indecision, 14, 20, 22, 24, 28,
    32, 41; initial plan, 19;
    training camp, 19, 48, 51, 54;
    South African backing, 22–3,
    25–6, 40; Dolinchek, 25–6,
    51, 52–3, 65–6; meets
    Mancham, 26–7; rival plan,
    33–4; treatment of deposed
    leaders, 34–5; revised plan,
    36–58; contract, 38–9, 45–6,
    62; transporting men and
    arms to Mahé, 42, 46–7, 50,
    51–8, 65, 68–9, 73, 104; link
    with Seychelles resistance,
    42, 84–5, 93; recruitment, 44,
    61–7; sells shares, 46; meets
    NIC, 47–9, 51; and SADF,
    49–51; Botha's support, 48,
    49, 134; establishes Mahé
    safe house, 54–5; 'Ancient
    Order of Frothblowers',
    59–61, 67, 71–2; gives initial
    briefing, 62; advance parties,
    64–5; final briefing, 67–8;
    martial music, 70; rendezvous
    at Ermelo, 71–2; flight from
    Manzini, 73; 'Sword of
    Damocles', 73; arrival on
    Mahé, 74; disaster at airport,
    75–6; attempts to seize
    barracks, 76–8; retreats to
    airport, 78; captures
    armoured car, 80–2; arrival

of Air India flight, 82–5; negotiates, 87–9; flight from Mahé, 94–8; protects South African interests, 95, 103, 110, 134, 152, 155, 164–5 *Trial and imprisonment:* arrest, 100; hijacking charge, 100, 105, 108–9, 113–14, 118–20, 132–4; Sonderwater Prison, 100; prison conditions, 102, 103, 137–59, 160–83, 184, 185–96; statement to police, 102–3, 128–9; home searched, 104; 'man-stealing', 104; on bail, 104, 108; concern for men on Mahé, 106–7, 107–8, 124, 134–5, 179–80; legal representation, 107, 109–11, 151; back in custody, 108; fresh charges, 108; sells 5 Commando patch, 110, 167; trial, 111–16, 117–34; indictment, 114; evidence taken on Mahé, 115–16, 117–20, 129; evidence-in-chief, 121; defends himself, 122–32; closing address, 125–32; judgement, 132–4; plea in mitigation, 135; sentence, 135; appeal denied, 136; Pretoria Central Prison, 136, 137–59, 160–83, 184, 189; 'observation', 137–54; petitions Judge President, 147, 155; prison training, 149, 156, 171–2; meets Ernst Penzhorne, 151; wife visits, 152–3, 167, 173, 180, 182, 185, 186, 193, 195; prison reading, 153–4, 177–8, 186, 187, 194, 195; hospital, 162–3; asked to turn State's Evidence, 165; suggests penal battalion, 166; struck off roll of chartered accountants, 168; joins building group, 170, 173; refuses opposition visits, 173; 'Sirmike', 175; 'a sign', 179; model ships, 180, 194; Pietermaritzburg New Prison, 182, 184, 185–96; English composition, 183; health problems, 186–7; nursery work, 189; possible amnesty, 187, 189–90, 193, 195; recommended for release (1985), 190, 192; cell stripped, 192–3; Botha's anger, 193; proposed hunger strike, 195; release, 195–6

Hoare, Phyllis, 52, 104, 105; brother's involvement, 55–6, 106–7; fund-raising, 110, 152; attends court, 135; visits MH in prison, 152–3, 167, 173, 180, 182, 185, 186, 193, 195; MH's release, 196

Hoare, Simon, 135, 196

Hodoul, Jacques, 4, 18

Holland, 5

Hong Kong, 17

Howick, 135

India, 16, 35, 115

Indian Ocean, 5, 57; superpower rivalry, 6–7, 11, 12, 13–14, 21, 22, 23, 64

Institute of Chartered Accountants, 168

International Red Cross, 166

Iran, 25

Isandhlwana, 190

Israel, 92; Entebbe raid, 3

'Jaapie', 168–9

Jacob, 174
Jakarta, 5
James, 173–7
James, Hon. Mr Justice,
    111–16, 117–34, 164
Janssen, Victor, 124
Java, 5
Johannesburg: mercenaries in,
    33, 60, 64, 67–8, 108; stock
    market, 46; Pritchard Street,
    110
Joubert, David, 32–3, 34
Joyce, James, 195
Julius Caesar, 145

Kampala, 37
Katanga, 16, 69
Kaunda, Dr Kenneth, 27
Kelly, 'Blue', 98, 109, 122
Kenny, Don, 79, 90, 93
Kenya, 11, 12–13; support for
    Mancham, 32–3, 39, 66–7,
    92–3
Kenyatta, Jomo, 27
Khashoggi, Adnan, 27–8
Kivu, Lake, 16
Kleinkie, 195–6
Klem, Hendrik, 126, 164–5
Knoetze, Brig. Martin, 26,
    49–51, 54
Kroonstad Prison, 139
Kruger, Rev., 171, 188

Ladysmith Prison, 185
Lalanne, Loustou: in dustbin,
    80, 83, 86; negotiations,
    87–8; evidence, 115, 117–18,
    120
Lawrence, D. H., 167
Le Grange, Louis, 104, 118–19
Le Grange, Lt, 147
Libreville, 43

Libya: influence in Seychelles,
    7, 21; invades Chad, 7, 33;
    loan, 7
Lisbon, 43
Lloyd, Euan, 19–20
London: Commonwealth Prime
    Ministers' Conference
    (1977), 4; exiles in, 14, 19, 20,
    25, 34, 36–7, 38, 41, 45, 105,
    159; MH in, 20, 26–7;
    Carlton Hotel, 60
Lubick, Anton, *see* Dolinchek,
    Martin
Lynn, G. G., 111

Mackay, L. L., 111
MacLaglan, Andrew, 19
Madagascar, 6, 13
Mahé, *see* Seychelles
Malloch, Jack, 43–4, 46
Mancham, James: President
    (1976), 5, 7, 12, 17;
    overthrown (1977), 1, 2, 3, 4,
    15, 21, 25, 36; indecision, 14,
    20, 22, 23, 24, 28, 32, 41; MH
    meets, 27; character, 27; and
    Khashoggi, 27–8; taped
    message, 70, 93; and Sultan
    of Oman, 92
Mann, Alan, 83
Manzini, 59, 72, 73
Marlowe, Christopher, 187,
    194; *Dr Faustus*, 177–8
Marxism, *see* communism
Maurice, 174
Mauritius, 6, 17, 67, 84, 92, 116,
    129
Milton, John: *Paradise Lost*,
    186
Misra, *co-pilot*: Mahé airport,
    82–100; statement, 105;
    evidence, 115, 117–34
Mobutu, Gen., 8, 16, 193

Mombasa, 11, 12–13
Moneta, Tullio: actor, 37, 145;
   visits Mahé with MH, 40,
   41–4; recruiting, 44, 61, 63;
   and Dolinchek, 51; trouble at
   airport, 75; capture of
   armoured car, 82; Air India
   flight, 85, 86–7; flight from
   Mahé, 94, 95–6; arrested,
   100; on bail, 104; trial, 112,
   125; judgement, 134, 136; in
   prison, 145, 154–5, 158,
   182
Moore, Roger, 19
Morne Seychellois, 16
Moroni, 73, 75
Mouton, Col., 99
Mozambique, 26, 62, 74;
   Russian influence, 13, 132;
   FRELIMO, 13
Mozambique Channel, 13, 57,
   73
MPLA, *see* Angola
Mugabe, Robert, 64

Naboomspruit, 46, 51
Nacala, 13
Nairobi, 32, 43, 66–7, 70, 72
NASA, 57
Natal Sugar Estates, 53
Natal Supreme Court, 111–16,
   117–34
National Forum, 10
National Intelligence Service,
   see South Africa
New York, 20
Nigeria, 23–4, 43–4
Nkomo, Joshua, 64
Nkrumah, Kwame, 27
Noddyn, Bob, 69–70, 88, 106
North Korea, 19, 24, 35, 57
Nyerere, Julius, 4, 12

OAU, *see* Organisation of
   African Unity
Obote, Milton, 36
O'Hara, Matt, 162, 164, 170,
   173–4, 178–9, 184
Ojukwu, Gen., 23, 43
Old Vicarage, 45, 69, 71
Oman, Sultan of, 92
*One Day in the Life of Ivan
   Denisovich* (Solzhenitsyn),
   168
Oom Jack, 168
Oom Piet, 186–7
Oosthuizen, P. C., 109
O'Reilly, 189, 191–2
Organisation of African Unity,
   4, 17, 21, 23, 25
Orientale, 8
Oshoek, 72, 75
Otto, Gen., 168, 172

Paradise Lost, 186
Paris, 72
Paul, Bishop, 6
Penzhorne, Ernst, 151–2, 165,
   166, 173
Persian Gulf, 7, 12, 13, 19, 22,
   25, 64
Philippines, 12
Phillipson, Greg, 164
Pietermaritzburg: College
   Road, 111; Natal Supreme
   Court, 111–16, 117–34
Pietermaritzburg New Prison,
   136, 162, 171, 185–96;
   hangings, 189; drugs, 190;
   unrest, 190–2
Platte Is., 23
Pollsmoor Prison, 139
Port Harcourt, 23, 43–4
Powell, Albert, 60
Pretoria: MH in, 22, 26, 47–51,
   57, 100, 104, 110; Jan Smuts

Pretoria – *cont.*
  Airport, 47, 68; Burgers Park
  Hotel, 48–51; Proes Street,
  49; Zansa building, 49;
  University, 62
Pretoria Central Prison, 136,
  137–59, 160–83, 184, 189;
  organisation, 137–8;
  'observation', 137–54; Bom,
  138, 145; routine, 139–40,
  143, 144, 160–1; food, 141;
  political prisoners, 142,
  166–7; staff, 142–3; 'Beverly
  Hills', 144, 164, 169–70;
  Social Welfare, 146, 147;
  psychologists, 146–7, 147–8;
  training and rehabilitation,
  148–9, 154, 156, 170–2;
  religion, 149–50, 160, 164;
  sex, 151, 160–1; reading
  matter, 153–4; drugs, 157;
  sport, 158; hospital, 162–3;
  hangings, 164, 169 – 70;
  flogging, 165–6; inspections,
  166; suicides, 169; wages, 172
Priefert, Kurt: recruited, 62;
  attack on barracks, 77–8;
  flight from Mahé, 90, 92, 94;
  arrested, 100; in prison, 102;
  trial, 122; sentence, 133–4
Prinsloo, Vernon, 76, 80, 82
Prisons Act, *see* South Africa
Puren, Frank, 17, 18, 79
Puren, Gerry: visits Mahé with
  MH, 16–18; indiscreet, 28,
  69; Ermelo rendezvous, 72,
  73; action at airport, 75;
  disappears, 79–80, 95;
  arrested, 106; death
  sentence, 134; released, 179

Rand Daily Mail, 11, 109
Range, SS, 46–7, 50, 53

Rapport, 180
Rasool, Mr, 134–5
Rathgeber, Dr, 105, 120
Ratsiraka, Didier, 6
Raudstein, Col., 135
Reagan, Ronald, 33
Red Sea, 13
Rees, Attorney-General,
  113–16, 117–34
Reid, Mr, 131
René, Albert: ousts Mancham
  (1977), 2, 20, 41; political
  beliefs, 4–5, 6; foreign policy,
  6, 17; Prime Minister (1976),
  12; Russian influence, 13;
  army loyal to, 18; corruption,
  21; Tanzanian influence, 22;
  and Khashoggi, 27;
  Independence Day speech,
  29–30; visit to France, 72–3;
  MH negotiates with, 87,
  88–9, 90, 93
Reunion, 97
Rhodesia, 42–3, 45, 46, 62, 64,
  76; SAS, 43, 45, 64, 123;
  army, 63–4, 68; bush war, 64;
  Grey Scouts, 64; ZANU, 64;
  ZAPU, 64. *See also*
  Zimbabwe
Rohwein, Peter, 62, 81, 94
Roman Catholic Church, 6, 35
Rothman, Mr, 47
Russia, *see* Union of Soviet
  Socialist Republics

Salisbury, 42–3. *See also*
  Harare
San Tomé, 43
Sans Souci, 87
SAS, *see* Special Air Services
Saxena, Capt.: Mahé airport,
  82–100, 103; statement, 105;
  evidence, 115, 117–34

Scheltema, Gideon, 126, 164–5
Schramme, Col. 'Mad Jack', 16
Selous Scouts, 64
Senegal, 132
Seychelles, Republic of
  Aldabra, 13, 17
  character, 4, 18, 20
  church in, 6, 35
  communications, 16, 17, 57–8
  Desroches, 17
  economy, 5–6, 7, 16, 17, 22,
    28; agriculture, 5; fishing, 5,
    7, 23, 28; nationalisation, 5;
    tourism, 5, 7, 12, 16, 17, 22,
    23, 28, 61; loans, 7
  employment, 5
  Farquhar, 17
  geography, 11–13, 16–17, 64
  Mahé: US tracking station, 7,
    57; airport, 13, 74–100, 105,
    114; geography, 16–17;
    banks, 39; Customs, 42, 56,
    59, 61, 67, 68–9, 70, 73, 74–5;
    barracks, 76–8, 81, 85, 89,
    90, 105
  military strength, 4, 18,
    28–31, 35; Tanzanian troops,
    4, 12, 18, 22, 76, 81–2, 83, 93,
    96, 105–6; People's
    Liberation Army, 18, 29
  political history: French
    colony, 2; coup (1977), 2,
    3–5; exiles, 2, 14, 22, 24;
    communism in, 2, 4, 6–7, 11,
    18, 20–1, 35, 64; Tanzania
    and, 4, 12, 18, 22, 76, 81–2,
    83, 93, 105; new government,
    4–5; independence (1976), 5,
    12; repression, 5, 21, 32;
    Russian influence, 6, 13–14,
    64, 132; indoctrination, 6,
    20–1, 35; foreign policy, 6–7,
    12; self-governing (1971), 12;
    Democratic Party, 12;
    People's United Party, 12;
    Cuba and, 13; resistance, 21,
    24, 61, 68–9, 75, 76, 82, 84–5,
    93, 123; France and, 22; claim
    for compensation, 104
  population, 12, 41; grands
    blancs, 5, 20
  strategic importance, 12–13,
    21, 64
Shah, Kiernan, 107
Shakespeare, William, 126, 187,
  194; Hamlet, 177; Henry V,
  177; Julius Caesar, 145
Shaw, G. B.: Devil's Disciple,
  168
Shimurera, Mrs, 74–100
Shoeshine, 174
Shongweni, 55
Simon, Leslie, 187
Sims, Bob: Mahé safe house,
  55–6; at airport, 74; arrested,
  106–7; imprisoned, 134;
  released, 179
Singapore, 12
6 Commando, 69
Slomowitz, Hymie, 110–11,
  122, 125
Smith, Ian, 43
Socotra, 13
Soldier of Fortune, 110, 167
Solzhenitsyn, Alexander: One
  Day in the Life of Ivan
  Denisovich, 168
Somalia, 13
Sonderwater Prison, 100,
  101–4, 108, 123, 139, 160
South Africa, Republic of:
  exiles in, 2; Defence Force,
  10–11, 26, 34, 44, 49–51, 52,
  61, 109, 110, 125, 144, 165,
  166; military strength, 11;
  support for coup, 21, 22–3,

South Africa – *cont.*
24, 25–6, 38, 40, 61, 73, 92,
97; National Intelligence
Service, 22, 25–6, 38, 40,
47–51, 57, 59, 65–6, 73, 98,
109, 125, 139, 152; National
Security Council, 23, 47;
Cabinet, 23, 47, 48, 49, 50,
134; Police, 25, 26, 65, 100,
102, 104–5, 118, 123, 130,
136, 141; Progressive Party,
26; Recce Commando, 44,
62, 73, 75, 83, 92, 95, 109,
122; Security Branch, 49, 97,
139; Parachute Regiment, 62;
Railways Police, 98–100; Air
Force, 98–100; Act 62, 101,
128; Prisons Department,
102, 137, 140–4, 172, 180,
181, 182, 190, 192, 193; Civil
Aviation Offences Act No.
10, 108, 113–14, 139; Air
Line Pilots' Association, 109;
Welfare Department, 110;
judicial system, 111–12;
Prisons Act, 140–1, 146, 172,
180; African National
Congress, 164; political
prisoners, 142, 166–7
South Africa, University of, 149
South African Airways, 17, 23
South African Defence Force,
see South Africa
South African Police, *see* South
Africa
South African Railways Police,
see South Africa
South Yemen, 13
Special Air Services, 43, 45, 62,
64, 123
Stafford, Eddie, 109
Standish-White, 76
Stanleyville, 108, 135

Sudan, 8
Sunday Times, 154
Swanepoel, Gerry, 193
Swaziland, 59, 68, 72, 73
Sydow, Jan, 90

Tanzania: troops in Seychelles,
4, 12, 18, 22, 76, 81–2, 83, 93,
96, 105–6
Temple, Herbert, 60
Thatcher, Margaret, 108, 124
Three Years with Sylvia
(Hoare), 25
Timothy, 174
Tom, 159, 163
Topaz, 22, 31, 87

Uganda, 8
Union of Soviet Socialist
Republics: and Seychelles, 4,
6–7, 13, 21, 132; invades
Afghanistan, 7, 25; influence
in Indian Ocean, 13–14; 26th
Soviet Communist Party
Congress (1981), 14; in
Africa, 132
United Kingdom: and coup, 2;
exiles in, 2; aid, 4, 7. *See also*
British Indian Ocean
Territories
United Nations, 7, 41, 54, 104
United States of America:
Indian Ocean bases, 6–7,
12–13, 22; Mahé tracking
station, 7, 57; and Seychelles
operation, 21, 22, 25;
hostages in Iran, 25; NASA,
57

Van den Bergh, Gen. Hendrik,
22
Van der Merwe, SM, 51–2

Van Rensburg, Maj., 185, 186, 187, 192, 193, 194
Van Wyk, Alec, 22–3, 48
Vasan, *navigator*, 105, 115
Verlaque, Bernard, 21, 32–3
Victoria, 12, 76, 81, 86, 117–20; police HQ, 4; Government House, 4; bombs in, 4; 5th June Avenue, 5; Russian embassy, 6, 13, 23, 66; Bus Company, 17; Reef Hotel, 17, 79; Liberation Road, 18; Duke of Edinburgh Way, 18; coup, 21; harbour, 22, 71; Chinese embassy, 23; Russian flats, 23; safe house, 40, 55; convents, 60, 67, 69; La Sirène, 69; looting in, 106
Vietnam, 44
Visser, Brig. J. S., 100

Warren, Earl, 129
Waterkloof, 100

Weekend Life, 6
Westhuizen, Gen., 51
Who's Who, 124
Wild Geese, The (film), 19–20
Willar, Simon, 68
Willemse, Gen., 168
Wilson, Lt Nick, 99, 122–4
Witbank, 182
Witwatersrand, 163

Zaïre, 132
Zambia, 26, 62
ZANU, 64
ZAPU, 64
Zietsman, Gen., 102–3, 104, 128–9
Zimbabwe, 62, 82; communism in, 62; Cabinet, 88–100; Russian influence, 132. *See also* Rhodesia
Zululand, 167–8, 184
Zulus, 190
Zungu, 174